Praise for Mia Magik

"Living the essence of her teachings, Mia is the voice
for Mother Nature. Very few people carry the kind of high
magik Mia does; it doesn't get any bigger. This book will
teach you how to dialogue with all life and master
the art of communicating with the universe."

— **Sah D'Simone**, author of *Spiritually Sassy*

"Mia has single-handedly brought the cool factor
back into witchcraft to reach an entire generation
with an important arcane art. She is a woman
whisperer with magic at her fingertips."

— **Regena "Mama Gena" Thomashauer**,
author of *Pussy: A Reclamation*

"Mia Magik is my #1 resource for all things magic.
Everyone's favorite witch on Instagram and
beyond, she is a fairy-tale queen come
to life. Her book is dearly needed."

— **Sahara Rose**, author of *Discover Your Dharma*

—·✫·—

IntuWitchin

LEARN *to* **SPEAK**
the **LANGUAGE** *of*
the **UNIVERSE** *and*
RECLAIM YOUR
INNER MAGIK

Mia Magik

HAY HOUSE, INC.
Carlsbad, California • New York City
London • Sydney • New Delhi

Copyright © 2024 by Mia Magik

Published in the United States by: Hay House, Inc.: www.hayhouse.com®
Published in Australia by: Hay House Australia Pty. Ltd.: www.hayhouse.com.au
Published in the United Kingdom by: Hay House UK, Ltd.: www.hayhouse.co.uk
Published in India by: Hay House Publishers India: www.hayhouse.co.in

Cover design: Barbara LeVan Fisher • *Interior design:* Bryn Starr Best

Cataloging-in-Publication Data is on file at the Library of Congress.

Tradepaper ISBN: 978-1-4019-7356-8
E-book ISBN: 978-1-4019-7357-5
Audiobook ISBN: 978-1-4019-7358-2

10 9 8 7 6 5 4 3 2 1
1st edition, January 2024

Printed in the United States of America

This product uses papers sourced from responsibly managed forests.
For more information, see www.hayhouse.com.

THIS BOOK *is a* PRAYER.

A PRAYER FOR AWAKENING HUMANITY

from the SLUMBER THAT HAS KEPT OUR

INFINITE *and* INNATE SPIRITUAL GIFTS LYING

DORMANT BENEATH *our* AWARENESS *for* TOO LONG.

MAY WE RECEIVE *the* PERMISSION *to* RECLAIM

OUR MAGIK. MAY WE HEAL OUR WOUNDS

and BECOME THE MOST POWERFUL

VERSIONS *of* WHO WE ARE

DESTINED *to* BE.

∗ · ∗ · ∗

*I give so much gratitude to the benevolent ancestors
Who came before us, allowing us to be here in this moment,
To receive this message and transmission together.
Thank you for all the people who had to exist for our life right now.
Thank you to the changing seasons,
To the tides and cycles of life.
Earth. Thank you to all the ways you,
The Goddess, show us Your love.
The Mother cares for us,
Tends to us, nourishes and nurtures us,
Allows us fire and rage and a safe space to be ourselves.
Thank you for the orgasms.
Thank you for the castles and forests and meadows,
for the oceans and the rivers.
Thank you to all the animals,
To Artemis
And all the names for Her majesty.*

*Thank you to every tree who became a page of this book.
Thank you for your sacrifice so we can experience these pages.
Thank you for the roots beneath our feet,
Who, when we remember to ground ourselves into, we grow.
We flourish and thrive.*

*Thank you, thank you, thank you
For allowing me to be the messenger of the Goddess,
To sing her songs and speak the voice of the Earth.
Thank you for the wild rivers within me,
All the courage it has taken to be this fucking weird.
Thank you for my destiny,
To all the people who are willing to listen to me
To let my shining glow help them find their way,
Be the lighthouse guiding them home,
Sparking the flame of their candle.*

*Thank you to my sacred holy redwood forests,
The lands of Yurok, Wiyot, Hupa,
The creeks, streams, and waterfalls,
Dragons and fairies, all elemental beings.
Thank you to the witches and witch hunters
For making us stand and rise up
To rebirth the world
With fierce grace and gratitude.*

*Thank you, Mother.
Thank you to every one of you for being here with me.
I love you. I am you. And we are the Earth.*

∗ · ∗ · ∗

Contents

Introduction

It is the inherent, Divine right of every being on Earth to experience their connection to the Universe. Reclaiming our power and worthiness gives us the confidence to ask for what we want and go after our dreams. What I call *IntuWitchin* is our inner voice and innate Universal connection counseling us to communicate with the Natural world, heal our souls, and take inspired action. When we're connected to the wellspring of wisdom in our unconscious mind, the meaning and significance behind every moment's intricate interwovenness is instantly illustrated and illuminated. Remembering we are a part of this web reminds us that life is more than just meaningful. It's magikal.

We sense the subtle whispers and soft voice of our Goddess-given guidance system, but we can't seem to hear them. We have been severed from our magik, our higher consciousness, and our super*natural* power—a severing rooted in survivalism. Since the advent of current civilization, human beings have sought to exert control over Nature, both to keep us "safe" and to profit from her bounty. Over the centuries, this has created near-total separation from our corresponding inner Nature. Studies show simply living in *proximity* to Natural environments like trees significantly increases our life span. We've learned to survive without Nature, but are we really *living*? What if the key to reconnecting to our infinite wisdom lies in the magik of enchanted forests from our fairy tales and the symbolic significance of the world around us?

Have you ever had one of those magik moments where who you are melted away and you were one with Nature? Maybe surrendering to a downpour, closing your eyes, letting bursting drops splash upon your face? Or gazing out over an endless expanse, elevated to a new state of awe and oneness? Yes, our lavish, luxurious lives are beautiful in their way, but *nothing* compares to the purest bliss arising from the utmost simplicity in your instinctual kinship with the Natural world.

When we distance ourselves from our reciprocal relationship with Nature, Her song grows faint, and we forget how to hear it. Though we share Her as our source, we've lost our link with life, trading wild woods and starry skies for concrete jungles and skyscrapers. Our mirror of Her creative capacity, Her abundance of fruits and flowers, and Her flowing rivers, was blown from the landscape of our minds like clouds in an afternoon sky. Major religions altered our worship of the Divine through Nature by enforcing their rules and protocols, convincing us to mistrust ourselves and our inner voice. You are all you'll ever need to communicate directly with God, Goddess, or Spirit (or whatever you call the Universal force animating existence). Even the word *anima* means *spirit* in Latin. Our innate Nature is our spiritual essence. We even use the word *naturalized* when someone has been integrated into a new place with the intention to help make it better. Let's get *Natural*ized again and treat the world like we know how important it is to be able to drink from the streams, eat the sacred plants, and be in right relationship with that which is *our* Nature.

As your IntuWitchin unfolds, your interconnectedness with all things grows, generating more love for yourself and changing your relationship to reality.

The UNIVERSAL LAW *of* INTUWITCHIN

Swiss psychiatrist Carl Jung, whose work has been foundational in anthropology, psychology, and philosophy, recognized that the greatest way for us to understand ourselves, and our species, behaviors, and existence is by understanding the deeper meanings in myth and legend. Stories about magik contain the truest knowledge of our origins and capacity as human beings.

Believing in magik is not a silly, childlike way of behaving, nor is it just for fairy tales. It is a remembrance of our own supernatural ability to wield the energetic forces of creation. The nature of reality is governed by 12 Universal Laws (recorded on the ancient alchemical text the *Emerald Tablet* of Thoth, aka Hermes Trismegistus) at play through every fiber in the fabric of existence. The first and most important law is that of Oneness, which states everything is interconnected. The Law of Attraction is the most popular, generally considered a modern manifestation technique. But these laws are just two pieces of the rhythmic, vibrational puzzle we call *life on Earth*. Together, the Universal Laws describe and explain balance and energy, cause and effect, destruction, reflection, and rebirth—creating order out of chaos.

Embodying the Law of Oneness to attain enlightenment is not easy. For the sake of expediting your journey to living the most magikal life possible, let's focus on the Law of Correspondence. Often referred to by alchemists as the Law of Similarity, the essence of metaphor, it states that every occurrence in our lives is mirrored elsewhere in the cosmos. Its ancient idiom is "As above, so below; as within, so without." Anything happening in the microcosm of your life is a reflection of the macrocosm of the Universe and vice versa. IntuWitchin is your personal relationship with the Law of Correspondence revealing communication to you through every experience.

IntuWitchin carries the codes of recognizing that our bodies are made from the same Elements as Earth. Our muscles are the clay and mud, our bones the stones of Her mountains, our breath the wind in Her trees, our blood the waters of Her rivers, and the electricity making our hearts beat is the fire of sunlight inside. An effortlessly functioning system with spiritual soul vibration animating it all. We can use each of these elements to heal their corresponding associations in ourselves. IntuWitchin is a road map to show you how.

Appropriately, this book has been written all over the world. Beginning in Antarctica via Argentina, I transcribed these words for you from meadows through the highlands of Scotland, waterfalls in Wales, and jungles of Costa Rica. I wrote with the Mediterranean Sea lapping at my feet, and finished up in the snowy and majestic Rocky Mountains. My hope is that IntuWitchin plays an integral role in uncovering your own greatest magik by accessing the preeminent symbolic language that speaks to the primordial potential in our DNA. Living in alignment with our ancient wisdom liberates us from limitation so we trust and feel confident in ourselves and our spiritual gifts, reconnecting us to our true Nature and letting us know that we are deeply worthy of all our dreams coming true.

Much separation from the Earth and one another has been caused by poor leadership. Simply *believing* in magik is an act of rebellion against the governance of our modern world. But a multitude of studies being done on creativity, problem solving, lifetime achievements, and personal fulfillment are proving that magikal thinking is exactly what we need. In his book *Spellbound*, Daniel Lieberman shared a creativity assessment done on children who scored *twice* as high after being exposed to the possibility of magik in a scene from the *Harry Potter* series as opposed to those whose clips didn't include magik. Turns out, not believing in the supernatural is incredibly detrimental to our performance and well-being spiritually, emotionally, and professionally.

When we look around, it's blatantly obvious the world is *so* ready for a more magikal perspective! Considering how obsessed we are with fantasy and sci-fi, it stands to reason that buried beneath all the venom of villains who victimized us, we *know* we have the potential to access magik in our real, everyday lives. We yearn for a glimpse inside a magikal Universe to remind us that our own power is not just a metaphor made for fantasy. Despite being dragged through the trenches by major religions and a society that discourage magikal thinking in favor of rationality, we remain captivated by the mystery. We simply can't get enough magik.

Now, I haven't learned to levitate (I made someone else do it once, though!) and I've never sent a glowing Patronus out of my body, but there is much more to magik than what is generally presented today.

What I have learned is my purpose: living in service to my superpowers by being a PerMissionary for people reclaiming their True Nature. I can hold solid energetic boundaries, maintaining my sense of self wherever I go. I have turned lessons into blessings—the Blessons. Magik enchanted me with wild fulfillment and pleasure, allowing me to wield and embody elemental abundance to actualize gifts of groundedness *and* flow in my life. Everything I have discovered is possible for you too.

The Universe is constantly reminding us of our magikal powers, only it speaks the oldest and purest language of all. Elements and symbols bridge dimensions of consciousness, with infinite and multifaceted significance. We say "a picture is worth a thousand words" because there are simply things that cannot be contained or described linguistically to fully illustrate a scene or sentiment to another.

We perceive the world through our senses, then get caught in logical thinking as if that's all there is. But symbolism speaks through the mystery within us. Each of our individual life's journeys creates unique psychological responses to and relationships with it. Plato's philosophy was that we all possess infinite preexisting wisdom at birth; we simply remember it as we learn. He theorized that we descend spiritually through the influence of the seven major planetary spheres in our solar system, receiving the intelligence of their associated God's or Goddess's frequency.

When you look back, we have lived by and studied magikal archetypal energy far longer than *anything* else. Magik—its myth, lore, and legends—isn't outside of us, but imparts what's *inside* of us. Carl Jung used the stories of Sky Gods, Earth Spirits, and mystical creatures as an explanation for our neurological behavior. Magikal artistry, help from wild animals, and love that turns a vicious beast into a handsome prince are all representations of the hidden realms of our inner world, messages from IntuWitchin.

I got into spirituality through quantum physics. The scientific approach can *describe* chemical interactions and neural network activity, yet even the most highly specialized doctors don't have a full grasp of what's happening. Can you imagine how much energy it would take to stay constantly aware that our reality is in fact an illusion created by quantum particles bumping up against one another? That no matter how solid we perceive an object to be, in actuality, it's not even there? Sounds exhausting. Science has absolutely brought unprecedented ease and convenience to us, technology delegating menial tasks to machines, but doing less in life seems to be making us feel like less. Magik asks more from us. Magik is yearning for engagement and interaction, for us to play with it again.

Your IntuWitchin is a recollection of what your soul has always known, inviting you to receive reflections from the world around you to recall your power from its primordial origins and acknowledge your blessings. I am living proof magik is real, within and all around us, just waiting for us to make it our own again. The intention of this book is to guide you to that magik within yourself.

YOU ARE MAGIK

✳ ················· ✳ ················· ✳

You may be wondering why I call it magik—as a witch, spelling is one of my specialties. With IntuWitchin, everything carries a deeper meaning; it's all intentional. Making my own way, with words and everything else, has made life far more magikal than trying to follow the flock and societal prescriptions. The *K* is to differentiate from the magic performed by illusionists pulling rabbits out of hats and a nod to the ka, or the energetic body the ancient Egyptians saw as our soul or Higher Self.

I personally don't identify with traditional witchy labels like Wiccan or Pagan. The amalgamation of remembrance within me from studying many ancient wisdom traditions has carved and sculpted this approach to IntuWitchin. I have sat at the feet of Hupa elders, Egyptologists, Ram Dass, and redwood trees, and what I have learned is that magik, in its essence, is healing. I've watched too many ceremonialists deny the importance of this truth in ritual communities, resulting in the need for more healing. Many people get uncomfortable with that word, as if it implies there's something wrong, but we'll heal that limiting belief too. Healing is necessary for magik. It is the process of uprooting whatever has prevented us from believing in ourselves indubitably. When we heal our programming and conditioning to return to our original essence, we can wield whatever magik we want.

My personal area of expertise is Transfiguration—yes, the course at Hogwarts is a real discipline. In fact, all the classes mentioned in the Wizarding World are. That's one of my favorite correspondences from our famous "fictional" fantasy. Transfiguration is the magik of transforming one thing into another. This is the essence of *all* mainstream personal development and spiritual practice, from yoga to Tony Robbins to biohacking and human optimization. Changing rigidity to flexibility, disease to vitality, and fear into faith. It is internal, spiritual alchemy, turning those hard lessons into blessings. My personal journey, mission, and greatest gifts lie in the metamorphosis of self from one version into the most magikal iteration possible. An unhappy, unhealthy girl terrified of her potential, unwilling to escape a suffocating comfort zone, became a powerful, purpose-fulfilled woman living fantasy as reality, surrounded by soul allies and guided by Goddess Herself, as the living Earth.

Who might you become after some spiritual Transfiguration?

IntuWitchin is the distillation of lifelong learning through personal transfiguration. Morphing trials into triumphs, pain into power, and your mess into your message and medicine. Alchemy was the ancient study of literally and metaphorically turning lead into gold; IntuWitchin is inner alchemy. Shifting a disempowering belief that's weighed you down into initiative for innovation, a painful memory into motivation, or a wounded inner child into a confident, joyful adult—this is the gold we treasure in life. Whoever your ideal version of yourself is, IntuWitchin is your eternal inner guidance showing you how to become them. The word *decide*, the same suffix as *homicide*, means to kill off one half. So when we decide something, we are literally allowing the other possibility to die. Your most magikal life is waiting for you if you decide to claim it.

This book will show you how to transfigure yourself and your mindset to make magik every day, with only the tools you've always had: your body, mind, and spirit. I will illustrate my own Earth-based, Goddess-guided magikal path, hoping it inspires you to find and follow your own. Thousands of people have learned my fundamentals for living through Witch School, part of my online academy for Magikal Artistry. The more I share these skills, the stronger my IntuWitchin grows and more magikal my own life becomes.

BECOMING A *SOURCE*ROUS

Before we dive in, let's slay some common misconceptions about magik, super*natural* abilities, and intuitive information. First, you do not have to be "special," shamanically trained, reliant upon religion, or bitten by a radioactive spider to access magik and your powerful IntuWitchin. The only bat wings involved here might come fluttering in a dream, carrying the message that it's time to let go of old thinking and bring in the new. All that is required of you is openness and willingness to divine greater meaning in life.

We're told witches are evil, heartless child-eaters—yikes. But *witch* (the same origin as *Wicca*, *wicked*, and *wizard* from old German and Scottish) means *wise*, *wisdom*, *or one who sees or knows*, while *craft* refers to developing *strength* or *skill*. WitchCraft, therefore, is simply about strengthening the skill of wielding your wisdom. Being a witch, then, isn't about *what* you practice; it's *how you live.* How do you integrate and embody the wisdom you've gained from all your trials, tribulations, and triumphs into the character you play in life?

My witchery doesn't involve "casting spells" as much as remembering every word we speak is a spell. My approach to magik and manifestation applies personal exploration to provide a more embodied, experiential energy to the craft. After all, spells are just blueprints for correspondence designed to help us achieve or receive goals and desires. And IntuWitchin, the language that this book will help you become fluent in, simply requires a shift in awareness, an opening to possibility. As you learn to source your creative life force energy from the Universe itself, you become a *Source*rous. From the old French, *source* means *to rise*, while the suffix *-ous* means to be *abounding in, or full of.* To be a Sourcerous, therefore, is to rise into your own abundant fullness and wholeness. Discovering how to activate the source of power within you to become the visionary leader of your life. This is the basis for one of my immersive online emodiment offerings of the same name.

Even when things seem like they're falling apart, the Universe is telling you a story, and making yours more exciting, giving you a perfect comeback opportunity. In every good hero's journey, the pitfalls, pain, and peak life experiences each serve healing and evolution, contributing to our blossoming. The more you engage and interact with IntuWitchin, the safer you'll feel in your body and the more you will appreciate what a gift it is to be connected to the Earth.

Cultivating magik and IntuWitchin is a lifelong process. Each day brings new possibilities to devote ourselves to practicing personal power. There is no prescription or set of "steps" to follow other than to listen deeply. My role is to empower *your* craft of implementing rituals in your everyday life, no matter where you are on the path. Luckily, IntuWitchin is less precise than baking. I'm horrible at baking because I love to improvise. My IntuWitchin always serves me when mixing garlic with caramelized lemon, but the rigid, regimented precision of cakery makes most of my baked goods rather disappointing. IntuWitchin is the opposite—based on the moment, it's impossible for it to fail. The only "secret" is trusting yourself enough to wing it. Improvise, honey—be spontaneous and write your own rules.

The only imperative of IntuWitchin is: *NO* comparing yourself to others. Some people hear their IntuWitchin's voice in the shower, others while sitting in silence. There are those who achieve goals in rapid succession and keep climbing higher, while their brothers learn acceptance and contentment in simplicity. Your journey is unique to you.

The FUNDAMENTALS of INTUWITCHIN

We'll use many tools along the way, but no eye of newt or toe of frog is required, though they both carry important messages about our human form and subconscious feelings. Amphibians live between earth and water, walking the line of material and emotional worlds. The fundamental building blocks of life are the essential elements of IntuWitchin, each fractalizing into beacons for us to follow. Let me show you the keys to unlocking hidden gems of treasure within you.

✵ **Earth:** The soil, stones, crystals, flowers, trees, and seeds represent your body, relationships, and physical, material reality. The body is a map throughout this quest, our physical vessels each reflecting the Earth, Herself. Composed of the same minerals, elements, and Matter, which comes from the Latin for "Mother," we must treat both our bodies, and Mother Earth's body, with love. Where could you take better care of either? Listen to the symphony of cells within, honoring their service by doing what makes them feel best. Change your life by changing your Earthly habits.

✵ **Water:** Holds the memories, our emotions, creativity, and sexuality. Connect with Her in the wild. In rains, rivers, lakes, and oceans, she runs free. If you don't have wild waters nearby: you are made of water—your blood, sweat, and tears, juice from lips or between thighs, your joy or sadness, gratitude or rage. The waters just want you to *feel.*

⁂ **Fire:** It is your light, your strength, forged in the flames. Your willpower, drive, motivation, and life force energy. Fire and light transform. Bask in the blaze with the movement of your body, illuminated awareness, your radiant shining, and the glow of your taper. Where do you need to take more action? Ignite the fires of your passion or stop burning the candle at both ends?

⁂ **Air:** The breath of life, our music and poetry, expression of essence spoken in words, ways, and beliefs. Air writes the story of our lives through what we say and how we say it. We call it *spelling*, for our words are spells we cast, the foundational formation of our world weaving the web of our destiny—which is the original meaning of *word*, as I'll explain. What thoughts create your reality? What beliefs inform your experience or response to the world? How are you telling the Universe what you do and don't want?

⁂ **Spirit:** The ethers, vibration, and frequency of your ineffable you-ness. The space between it all, the song and sound of your soul, describing God/Goddess/Divine/Universe, or the spark inside all life. That which *anima*tes us, making us who we are. The element of essence itself and through line of them all. Quantum entanglement dictates that a particle of sound emitted from us can impact the molecules of a star on the other side of the Universe, harkening back to the Law of Oneness. Spirit matters.

⁂ **Song:** Our way of attuning to and serenading with our vibrational frequency. Different levels of resonance can heal by receiving or reciprocating. When you get a song stuck in your head with disempowering or disrespectful lyrics, that can do more damage to your subconscious opinion of yourself than you are aware. Throughout this journey, be mindful of the music you listen to and pay attention to lyrics that might just be messages from the Universe. Song alone can transform us with its reprogramming power.

⚜ **Elementals:** Dragons, fairies, mermaids, unicorns, and mythical creatures represent both the magik of the Earth and our own spiritual gifts. They can be called upon in the wilds of Nature—forever in forests, creeks, and oceans—as angelic guides. They can perform psychic surgery on your body to break you free from limitations and bring realms of imagination into reality. These have been some of the most rewarding relationships in my life, holding wisdom of what humans have forgotten, serving our evolution as constant reminders when we allow them in.

⚜ **Timing:** Action requires rest; summer is followed by winter. There are times to open and others to close. How do we feel when the moon waxes and wanes, is dark or bright and full? What cycle and season call to you? Some days we'll rise like the sun beaming bright or spend nights in ceremony beneath a blanket of stars. The ancient science of astrology dictates an optional schedule to amplify our energy, honor our strengths, and guide our healing. Letting go of *shoulds* and *supposed tos* optimizes how we operate to organize our lives in harmony with Universal rhythm.

⚜ **Weirdness:** This book asks you to disrupt your programming and embrace your eccentricity! Be authentically you. It's guaranteed to bring more magik. Regardless of what anyone says, your uniqueness is designed by the Divine and is a facet of it. If people think you are weird, you're on the right track. In my experience, the ones who love your weirdness are the ones who matter and will be there with you no matter what.

⚜ **Cauldron:** The womb is a cosmically connected cauldron inside of you. Not just for birthing babies but infusing life into all your creations. No matter your gender identity or biology, IntuWitchin unites the energetic portal in you with the Great Cosmic Womb that births us all. A kitchen cauldron, a cave in the Earth, or an alpine lake can all represent the creative and rebirthing powers of Womb Wisdom.

✻ **Journal:** On the subject of spelling, journaling has been scientifically proven to support mental health, and I encourage you to start a journal if you haven't already. Journals are like best friends. They safeguard our most cherished thoughts and reflections, hold us in our self-discovery, and help us uncover the invitations and initiations that call us forward. The insights gained from recording your synchronicities and experiences with IntuWitchin supports the crafting of your most magikal life.

INTUWITCHIN *in* ACTION

✻ ················· ✻ ················· ✻

The ancient cultures of First Nations people tell stories of Nature's generosity and care for us and our love and reverence in return. But most of us grew up with a very different story. One where receiving the gifts of Nature's bounty leads to being cast out of her Edenic garden. With IntuWitchin, we are welcomed home to ourselves and are an integral part of Her verdant fields and abundant orchards.

Indigenous traditions across the globe share Creation stories of how their sacred plants, like sweetgrass, blessed them. Plants have been evolving for hundreds of millions of years, before we even existed, their unfathomable intelligence and healing wisdom guiding us at every turn. Plants will often make themselves known to you when they have an antidote to your ailments.

The entire pharmacopoeia of our medicine came from Nature until J. D. Rockefeller, the oil magnate, discovered you could turn petrochemicals into pharmaceuticals, and he used his financial influence to eradicate all ancient Natural remedies from our medical system.

By acknowledging how we've been manipulated and being willing to heal, the Universe becomes our greatest support. You can walk outside and call up to the sky or down to the Earth like you would your closest confidant, and it will answer. Sometimes it might take a moment to get back to you, but it's *always* there, in the Stone People (boulders and mountains), Standing Ones (trees), and breath that unify us all.

The modern world has wired us for anxiety and depression, to anticipate stress even when it's not actually present. With IntuWitchin, we reclaim power over those stresses. Unlike blatant messages on social media, the Universe speaks in subtlety and signs, whispering winds. Those that are just for you and don't mean anything to anyone else are often the most special.

I'll illustrate IntuWitchin in action with stories from my own journey. Let me show you what I mean.

Several years into my IntuWitchin practice, I was in Mexico with a huge group of friends for Día de los Muertos, the cross-quarter celebration between the autumnal equinox and winter solstice (around the time of Halloween and Samhain), when Mexican people traditionally honor their ancestors. My grandmother Elva's birthday had just passed—she'd died at 100, eight years prior. I wanted to honor her and the tradition of intentionally communing with ancestors after making a YouTube video about how to celebrate. Cooking your loved ones' favorite dishes with a plate for them on the altar is one of the most time-honored Día de los Muertos customs. I closed with, "My noni made us the most delicious English short ribs, which I called 'stringy beef.' I'll have to find a plant-based substitute!"

When we got back from the Día de los Muertos parade, a friend at the hotel restaurant was finishing dinner. I sat down with him, and he asked, "Want the last bite of this? It's really good."

"What is it?" I asked.

"The best short ribs I've ever had."

Immediately, I got teary-eyed. It was my noni, come to say hello. I made an exception to my diet for this nostalgic nibble and savored every flavor before sharing Elva's story with my friends. Others spoke about their grandparents, and we made our own spontaneous ancestor-honoring ceremony. Elva made every holiday and meal magikal because of her dedication to the "food is love" mantra. She was reaching through the veil, sharing her presence, her love alive in my veins.

We can brush off these little "coincidences," and pretend they're insignificant. But when you choose to listen, though often invisible to others, the Universe is always giving you signs that are meaningful to you.

I am so excited to show you the magikal world no one teaches us to see that has been right before your eyes your entire life. You are embarking on a journey of becoming your most magikal self, and this book covers subjects that have been widely relegated to fairy tales—which science and spirituality alike are now revealing to be inspiring personal-development stories of the past, offering encoded reminders of our innate supernatural gifts, and metaphors for magik.

My wish for you is to establish a solid foundation upon which you can build a temple devoted to yourself. You will have so much new information at your fingertips by the time you finish reading, nourishing knowledge I hope you're inspired to spread far and wide so these teachings ripple out among your family, friends, and ultimately our global community.

Practice — AltarCraft

Your first IntuWitchin assignment is to build yourself an altar for your intentions. AltarCraft is one of my favorite IntuWitchin practices, a beautiful opening for the journey in this book. By creating an intentional space holding, representing, and enhancing the energies of what we're calling into our lives, we express our deep desires and core values. Every altar is different depending on how much space, creativity, and time you have to build it.

First, find a base for your altar. It doesn't need to be large or elaborate; you'll make it special no matter where it is. Maybe it's a small table, a bookcase shelf, or even on a stack of cherished coffee-table books covered with a cloth. You can put it on the floor, but some traditions say that's disrespectful to the energy. If that's your only option, put a cloth down to give your altar items something comfortable to rest upon.

Before you receive any more information, see what draws you in and calls to be included in your sacred space. Listen to your inner voice. Every item you choose has a purpose. Add any elements that feel important for you to connect with. What represents fire, water, air, Earth, and Spirit for you? Candles, incense, smudging herbs, seashells, a chalice, crystals, sticks, abandoned birds' nests (I have several altars with them), singing bowls, photographs, art, animal pelts—anything can contribute. This is *your* intentional creation space.

Chapter 1

Dive
IntuWitchin

IntuWitchin bears a playful resemblance to *intuition*. Yet the deeper aim is to illuminate intricate subtleties personal to you in a vastly rich Universal language. Learning to communicate in this tongue, once native to us all, is IntuWitchin, the aliveness animating each and every one of our unique spirits, in harmony with the elements of creation, our planet, and the infinite consciousness of the Universe.

Our very language is embedded with implications of intuitive energy informing our actions, such as when we say "A stroke of genius," "I don't know what got into me," or "What possessed him to do that?" While discussing a creative project, the muse is a force outside of us that we must wait for to grace our doorstep, blessing us. Intuition indicates an ability to receive extrasensory Universal information, while IntuWitchin necessitates response—*acting upon* the messages you receive, which requires us to become fluent in the symbolic language of Nature, learning how to interpret messages from dreams, conversations, animals, our bodies, and all of life in general. It is consciously engaging with the world around you through *perceiving* information, and grounds the collection of your life's experiences and lessons learned to support you in making magik. Making life magikal puts the *Witch* in *IntuWitchin*.

Information and knowledge are conceptual until they are assimilated into our habituated actions, becoming wisdom. Embodying the wisdom we've gathered throughout our life is what makes us a witch. Only with that trust and faith in your own wisdom can you truly begin to believe in your ability to make actual magik, reclaiming your inherent gifts through a constant and consistent connection to the cosmos and world around you. In any given situation, strive to be increasingly aware of living in alignment with your, and *the*, truth.

Here's a subtle distinction between an intuitive hit and the underlying invitation of IntuWitchin. Your *intuition* might hint that a man you're dating can't be trusted. You keep seeing him anyway, only to find out he's been using the same lines with you and several other women. (Been there!) Perhaps a friend comes to tell you she's experiencing a guy doing this to her, and you want to brush it off: "It's just a coincidence; my guy would never do that to *me*." Your IntuWitchin is the little voice that knows your friend's story is Universal intervention, encouraging your inclination to not only abandon ship but actually cut him off. Standing up for yourself with strong boundaries sheds light on the larger lesson being presented to you, asking you to receive its wisdom. Did your dad behave similarly? Is this the final straw that pushes you to excavate and completely rise out of a pattern of unworthiness? Maybe you treated someone this way in the past, and now you're seeing how hurtful it is. This shift in awareness comes when you tap into your magikal guidance system.

In future chapters, I'll share my favorite ways to ask your IntuWitchin directly for guidance, but the basic tools it works with are:

❊ **Inspiration:** As if it's breathed into you, the message comes in a quick spark, suddenly or "out of the blue," with a little voice that says: "Notice this, mention that, turn here." You have a sense you should do something, and when you follow through and act on it, you're always glad you did. It can ride the subtle edge between excitement and fear, leaning just on the side of the more pleasantly exhilarating feeling.

✥ **Information/Interpretation:** Everything is information, so everything is an opportunity for divination; that is, intentional interpretation. Use every opportunity to interpret the information so you understand which way to go or how best to respond.

✥ **In Service:** When you have to make a choice, your Intu-Witchin will always guide you toward the action most aligned with who you are destined to become. Why? Because this action is most in service to your own growth and healing, which is, in turn, in service to Earth and all beings. The choices won't always be easy. If in doubt, ask, "Is this helping me become who I am meant to be?" or "Why am I afraid of this? Who will I be if I do it anyway?"

✥ **Inner Nature:** As the elements express themselves through us, how could you express or embody the rising mountains or flowing waters? IntuWitchin is the intonation of our innate eternal urge toward liberation and freedom. Usually the only thing stopping you from listening is an outdated belief. Take the opportunity to invoke your True Nature in those moments, without societal conditioning. Ask yourself: "What part of me is afraid of taking a leap? What am I worried will happen? What would I do if I believed I was beautiful, worthy, powerful, and who I dream to be?" and "What action would I take if no one ever told me I couldn't, shouldn't, or wasn't good enough?"

Connecting us to everything, IntuWitchin is walking forward, generating harmony between us and Nature, other people, and this pristine planet we live on. It is a magikal ideology for navigating life through the song of our soul's essence, driving how we relate to reality and ultimately helping us understand what God(dess) is inviting us to see, asking us to learn, calling us to be, and guiding us where to go.

WHEN *the* FLOW *of* INTUWITCHIN IS DAMMED

✳·····················✳·····················✳

If we are all equipped with a magikal inner GPS, why can so few of us hear the voice of its direction? Humanity has muted this masterful voice, collectively wounded by separation from the Earth and our own divinity. Severing our personal power prevents us from trusting ourselves, making IntuWitchin nearly impossible to perceive. This existential pain keeps us from claiming our desires and gifts, feeling worthy of love and acceptance, and following our true path. We're terrified of straying from what society prescribes we "should" do.

Hiding and shrinking ourselves to fit into a box of what's "acceptable" is a trauma response stemming from fear of abandonment or rejection. Though our need for safety rises from the instinctual will to survive, concrete jungles have far fewer lions than the Serengeti. Yet the impulse to belong by whatever means necessary is deeply ingrained in our collective psyche. Whether unsafety expressing our magikal selves comes from being teased or bullied, shamed by religion, or punished by parents, it has affected us all.

The scars of these experiences manifest in the ego—the part of us overidentified with our humanness who forgets we are pieces of the infinite Universe. From the Latin meaning *I*, the human-identified ego urges us to stay quiet, not to be bold or shine too bright, so we're "safe" from what has caused us pain again. We go along with what the mean girls say is "cool," even if we disagree, because our ego is afraid of rejection.

Fear fuels the ego, but unless we're *really* facing life or death, it is the ultimate block to our magik. Because IntuWitchin *will* ask you to do scary things—to take the kind of risks that lead to achieving greatness.

When it does, the first step is recognizing the fear. Notice the story it's running, its sensations in your body. Then ask: "Is my ego telling me not to do what I'm afraid of?" Because fear (unless your physical safety is in danger) is generally a sign there's a breakthrough on the other side. Ask your body how to distinguish between a threat and an invitation for expansion.

Acting upon IntuWitchin is much easier with loving support. But when seeking counsel on your awakening journey, be careful who you call. Unless you've got an epic, spiritual, risk-taking mom, she'll likely talk you back into your comfort zone. Like your ego, her job is to keep you safe! Someone who is having a shitty time in life might be jealous of your blessings, and they may fear you'll leave them behind. You might have to. Make sure you examine and admire how anyone you take advice from lives their life. Do they take risks that spiritually expand them in a commendable way? If so, and their counsel resonates, great!

I'm very familiar with the voice of fear and smallness saying I'll be judged or rejected for being my magikal self. Though it played a leading role in my young adulthood, it's no longer sitting in the director's seat authoring my life's story.

Until fifth grade, I was in a very hippie charter school called Equinox. An open curriculum focused on imagination and creative arts fostered a healthy appreciation for our natural magikal capacities. Transitioning to public school was a rude awakening. I was a loser! We'd been a family; there were no cliques in elementary school! My self-expression became fuel for torment and bullying—magik was for babies and weirdos; it wasn't real. I found myself in constant battle with societal sabotage. Survival meant shutting my magik down and adapting to be "acceptable." Eventually I succumbed to their version of "reality," which felt more like my nightmare.

By the time I reached high school, I was completely disconnected from my IntuWitchin and had let go of all the dreams for my life. I spent my time numbing the pain from the exhaustive effort of trying to fit in with people who would never understand the life I was destined for. I blacked out on booze nearly every weekend, my young, impressionable mind poisoned by music that painted women as stupid, useless fuck toys rather than portals of creative power. Alcohol was a momentary escape from how lost I felt severed from my magik, but you better believe I always felt even worse the next day. So the cycle continued.

Inside, my magikal self withered away. I was striving to be liked by girls who didn't actually care about who I was, because no one cared who *they* were. Not because they were stupid, but because no one had taught *them* they could be more. Misery became my norm, and after sharing my dreams had gotten me ridiculed, I was terrified of success. Standing out meant you thought you were better than everyone, and success equaled rejection and humiliation. When you think back, can you pinpoint the moments you, too, might have shrunk yourself in order to fit in? The anguish and stress this creates in our bodies is one of the most uncomfortable sensations I've ever felt. Like Nature, we're not meant to be stuck in a box; we're meant to root deep so we can rise up!

We all carry pain from our past, being shamed for our sexual or creative expression, punished for speaking our mind, or simply beaten down by life. How thoroughly these experiences inform our adulthood—and impact our ability to access and act on IntuWitchin—is only recently beginning to be understood. Imagine if sexuality wasn't shamed and we were taught how to reclaim our pleasure after abuse or molestation. How different might the world be if we'd learned since childhood how to unlock emotional blockages built over time to dam up the sadness inside us? There are many people sharing this knowledge, but global awareness and access to resources is so limited, many people just don't know there's a way out of the hurt we've accumulated.

As a society, we've also abandoned honoring rites of passage that bid farewell to one stage of life and welcome us into another. Rites of passage were once ceremonial initiations, deeply involved and experiential quests or rituals designed for an individual to consciously step forward into a new version of themselves, surrounded and supported by their community. Now, without the acknowledgment of what a profound transition it is from dependent teenager to autonomous and self-responsible adult, young people, rife with anxiety and depression, can experience the onset of severe mental illness. This world-shaking experience overrides their capacity to cope and function.

One of the most important transitions in any person's life, especially for women, is from person to parent—Maiden to Mother. Yet the only marker we have for this transformation, baby showers, focuses on games and giving gifts. There is no real acknowledgment that you're becoming someone different—no longer sovereign, responsible only for yourself. You're becoming the sole source of survival for a helpless being now completely and utterly dependent upon you.

T-shirts and baby bottles are emblazoned with slogans about "good moms do this; bad moms do that," with no mention of how to mother *oneself* through this massive change, let alone advise trusting IntuWitchin to guide you rather than stressing over comparison.

If a new mom hasn't strengthened the muscle of listening, she might not hear that voice saying, "Skip the laundry and go take a nap" or "Call Rachel. She'll watch the baby so you can go to yoga." Instead, the *should*s and *supposed to*s take charge: "You're supposed to be grateful. I can't believe you're angry with your child." "A good mom would not leave her baby right now. You have your whole life to do yoga."

On an even deeper level, women have been disconnected from knowing ourselves as the Goddess. She of 10,000 names, the Great Mother, has been taken out of our consciousness. Once upon a time, priestesses were a ruling class, leaders in their own right. Like the Oracles of Delphi and Daughters of Isis, they had power, magik, and were sought-after, exemplary feminine nobility. If we don't know how to trust the Great Mother, the Goddess inside, guiding us, the overwhelm of having to figure it all out on our own can be far more damaging to our child than taking an hour away for ourselves. We then model to them that the correct behavior is self-abandonment. We are saying: "Don't value yourself, tend to your mental health, listen to your inner guidance, or refill and refuel yourself before giving to others." This is why generations of people simply don't know how to love and care for themselves.

I've had plenty of moments where choosing what's best for myself felt scary or impossible: "Oh shit, is this a good idea?" "Am I really worthy of saying yes to this?" Like writing this book! I knew I needed to share my knowledge but then tortured myself by doubting that it would be as impactful and magikal as I envisaged. Thank Goddess I pushed through. Can you remember a moment when you heard that voice igniting those questions inside of you? A moment you needed to rest but almost forced yourself not to? A time where you felt unsure of your ability but ended up being so grateful you took the leap?

The most important thing to take away from this section is that voices who say you can't trust your inner knowing and that magik isn't real are lying. Whether you've internalized them from parents, preachers, or peers, those voices are your ego trying to keep you trapped in the presumed "safety" of your comfort zone. IntuWitchin will drag your ass out of that comfort zone whether you're skipping and giggling or kicking and screaming. I've tried both ways! But Holy Goddess, when you welcome it into your world, the miracles that occur are astounding.

HOW INTUWITCHIN MANIFESTS *for* YOU

As I touched on in the introduction, IntuWitchin is different for each of us. You know those people who can just do something easily that feels impossible to you? My partner and I are like that. My sense of direction is impeccable, but my organization not so much; he's the opposite. Depending on how your mind works and what you are physically and mentally able to do, your IntuWitchin will find the best ways to connect with you, requiring little more than your attention.

If you learn better by listening—an auditory learner—you'll likely have an easier time hearing the voice of your IntuWitchin when it "speaks" to you. If you're a visual learner, you might need to read or see something modeled before you understand it. You'll notice signs, get visions, or have an IntuWitchin color letting you know when it's trying to get your attention. When that hue surrounds a particular choice you're making (you'll know when it happens), you're clear that it's your inner wisdom speaking and not another *should* in disguise.

For kinesthetic learners, or those who are more sensual, your sense of touch, emotions, or sensitivity to energy might light up. There will always be some element of "feeling" when tuning in, whether it's a reaction to a voice, an image, a color, or the difference between sensations of contraction (usually a no) and expansion (a yes) in your body.

Regardless of how it arises for you, IntuWitchin can carry the texture of *compulsion* with it. Perhaps this will feel like an exciting leap into the unknown, or maybe the subtlest hint of "I have to do this," even if you're terrified. As we familiarize ourselves with our inner wisdom, we have to accept that fear often accompanies it. It's scary doing what you want when it hasn't been safe before. But now you get to be responsible for making the distinction between genuine fear and the ego keeping you safe . . . and small.

Regardless of how it speaks to you, developing and improving your IntuWitchin helps you magnetize your mission and learn to work your magik.

If you're reading this book, you're likely leaps and bounds ahead of many. Thank the Goddess for you! Disconnection from Nature and our wisdom is causing rampant disease, obesity, mental illness, and record-high rates of suicide. We are yearning for new magikal ways to exist.

It might *seem* easier to pretend you don't have Divine power coursing through you, but it's far less fulfilling. I could have settled for the life we're all sold, the one we're supposed to have, but that was never the life for me. Disconnecting from my magik to fit into society's box felt wrong on every level. I wasn't really living at all; I was slowly dying.

Until I let myself be reborn.

The day I reconnected to my IntuWitchin changed everything, starting me on a journey of becoming myself again. Finding my inner wild child saved me from self-imposed imprisonment. Nurturing the magikal being who'd been locked in a cage, buried in the recesses of my psyche, turned me into a Witch. Healing Her allowed me to flourish, thrive, and reclaim my wisdom.

For years after leaving, I avoided my small Northern Californian hometown. But when my New York boyfriend wanted to quit modeling to become a star in Los Angeles, something (my IntuWitchin) told me it was time to go back to my West Coast roots. I accepted his invitation and returned to the Golden State. After so long in the concrete jungle, despite growing up in one of Earth's most pristine, mystical environments, I'd forgotten the importance of connecting with Nature.

Questions about the meaning of life were brewing beneath my surface-level existence, but without much response. Frustrated, I felt another one of those unfamiliar tingles telling me the oldest and largest living beings on the planet, the redwood trees of my homeland, might have some answers for me. Now I was just an hour's flight away, so I ventured north and asked my dad to take me to the forest. We began walking among the old-growth trees, something we'd done plenty when I was a kid, but with a new level of attention and appreciation.

For the first time in years, as I was awestruck, gazing up at these ancient beings, my mind was quiet enough to remember I *had* an IntuWitchin. I could *feel* God in the Nature surrounding me, *hearing* the wisdom of Earth. There's nothing like a sunny day in those trees, stretching far beyond view and reaching up 400 feet into the heavens. I'd been surrounded by man-made skyscrapers for nearly a decade, forgetting what true majesty was. There is no greater visual feast or more magnificent temple than that infinite spectrum of green illuminated by golden beams of light shimmering through rainbow prismatic wisps of mist hanging in their soaring canopy.

Redwood forests get 40 percent of their water from fog, holding that moisture in their furry bark, perpetually perfuming the air with petrichor, the smell of fresh Earth after rain. It is easier and entirely more enjoyable to walk among them barefoot. The needles that have fallen from high branches decompose to create the softest, richest soil, known as *black gold*. This is where the origin of the word *humility* comes from, not shrinking but knowing the alchemy of humus, the forest floor's regenerative recycling system. We, too, are meant to let go of things that will feed us in the future. Red roots ripple throughout the ground beneath you. Most people think the tallest trees have the deepest roots, but they don't. Instead, redwoods spread far and wide, weaving a web of interdependence solidifying their stable foundations.

One day, on the Cathedral Trees Trail, I walked past a sunbleached trunk. Most redwoods are a rich rusty brown, blackened with fire scars or green with moss. I stood beneath it in wonder and closed my eyes as something unexplainable occurred.

It was as if the tree absorbed my consciousness into it. I *was* the redwood. I could feel my roots holding and pushing into the earth. I was 300 feet tall. My heart became heartwood, united with its center. My limbs reached through the fog, clouds, and sky. My hands intertwined with the branches of my family, my brothers and sisters, my community. I sensed our collaboration, working together in loving harmony.

My dad said I was swaying like Michael Jackson in the "Thriller" video. In that moment, this tree, or all of them, communicated to me, the forest transmitting a message through my roots that went far beyond words:

"This is why you come from here. Like us, you can lift your head and heart high, reach for the stars, and rise to the sky, as long as you keep your roots firmly planted, grounded on and in the Earth, with your community holding you."

The experience was psychedelic, yet I was clear and sober. After that, I never looked back. This magikal moment would mark the true beginning of my spiritual awakening, a process that continued to unfold for the next decade.

A month or so later, I was supposed to pick up my awful boyfriend from the airport, and instead, I stayed at home watching *Game of Thrones* with some new friends. We'd gotten in yet another fight before he took off, and I just couldn't get myself to leave a fun environment with people who made me feel good to spend another second with him. Maybe it was the strength of the trees that finally gave me permission to "stand up" for myself; maybe it was the sensation of the deep, supportive connections in their roots. I don't know why I didn't do it, but it was worth it. I chose me, and we didn't speak for *two years* after that night.

The trees had changed me. I couldn't let him drag me down anymore; it was time to rise, reach for something higher. I'd imprinted a new cellular blueprint for how I wanted to feel, individually and in kinship with others. It took a year to find my soul family, but the shift in my awareness, boundaries, and desires that day is what led me to them.

After Christmas dinner a few years later, I went out to sing with friends. In my childhood, rabies had wiped out a flourishing gray fox population, and two decades later, they were finally starting to thrive again. As I drove, my eye caught a stripe of black on the side of the road. Though I hadn't seen one in years, instantly I instinctively knew what it was. Never having picked up roadkill before, I have no idea what compelled me to U-turn twice. I pulled over, my headlights illuminating her beautiful body, lifeless on the pavement. I got out, not knowing why I was standing there. Until an inexplicable initiation occurred.

As the redwood tree had incorporated me into it, so Mother Nature Herself entered me. She animated my body and bent to lift the lithe form.

My mind screamed in protest, "No, this is gross. I don't want to touch it."

Her Spirit shouted, reprimanding, "This is *sacred*!"

I could feel Her using my arms to scoop up the fox, placing her gently in my back seat.

The next day, no one, including my dad—an avid hunter—would help me. His taxidermist refused, saying foxes give off a horrible scent, and advised against skinning it. I almost returned Her to the Earth when a doctor friend pulled into the driveway and nonchalantly said, "Animal flesh should separate from muscle much easier than ours."

My IntuWitchin was in the driver's seat. I grabbed a sharp filet knife and decided I had nothing to fear. I made my first cut at her neck, her coat smoothly peeling away from her muscles, a wave of remembrance washing over me. It was as if the wisdom of all our ancestors, who used every pelt for a purpose, relayed the recognition of my WitchCraft.

In my soul, I'd done this a thousand times. It was the next greatest induction to my magik that never would have happened without surrendering to the Goddess's guidance, lifting her in honor. The primal thrill coursing through me as I sliced through fascia in awe of her tiny but mighty muscles was an unparalleled experience. I didn't spill a single drop of blood and left the rest of her fully intact for the critters. Three months later I returned for her bones, perfectly cleaned by the circle of life.

Her fur adorns my altar to this day, perpetually upholding her medicine and the magik of IntuWitchin.

Which isn't always a straight direction, as you can see. But there are many practical tools to help. You may be drawn to perform certain rituals, astrology, or tarot, or "just know" which color candle, herbs, or oils to use in spell work. All of a sudden, bada-bing-bada-bang-bada-boom, or bibbity-bobbity-boo, and you're making magik too!

Every time I returned home to the redwoods, my IntuWitchin was lit up like it had been in my childhood, more and more magik emerging. My inner witch was reawakening, but I'd still never performed an actual "spell." In springtime, after the fox, the perfect chance presented itself. I learned about Singing Alive in Hawaii two weeks later. Having been working on healing the childhood wounds that kept me from singing, despite how much I loved to do it, my soul felt something awaiting me there. But with $200 in my bank account, it seemed impossible.

With no idea if it would work, I tried a candle magik spell a fellow witch had shared. I went to a local apothecary, got a red spell candle (for deeply rooted power and infinite abundance of the redwoods), carved intentions into it with my fingernail, rubbed oil from bottom to top, dressed it with herbs from my spice cabinet, and sat in meditation until it went out.

The next day I signed my first big-ticket coaching client and was off to Hawaii. I couldn't believe it! Magik was real. I found courage in sharing my voice in a whole new way that weekend, serving as a launchpad for the trajectory and direction of my life. I send praise to the Great Mother and Goddess within me. A kumu, or Hawaiian elder, told me their dragon legends, and I learned native Hawaiian chants with accompanying hula movements, telling a story of the magikal island. I baptized myself in the turquoise ocean and sacred rivers knowing, yet again, I was reborn.

I hope this gives you insight into the limitless gifts, power, and abilities that have been obscured from our conscious minds simmering just beneath the surface.

CONFIDENCE MEANS TRUST

When we can trust ourselves we remember to trust the Universe—and our innate capacity for divining its wisdom and information.

There's a lot of noise in the world. The opinions alone, from people disappointed in themselves for not following their dreams, can drown out our truth. Plus with distractions of social media, constant comparison, and advertisements—hearing our inner wisdom's voice is hard enough, but trusting it? Being courageous and original enough to act upon those little whispers? That can feel nearly impossible!

As children we're taught to trust other people's *should*s for our lives over our own intuitive knowing, learning we're unworthy of having our spiritual needs met. To overcome this, we have to mend the damage from those programs. It took heart-rending inner-child healing to receive the redwood magik and abundance spell work.

At age seven, I wanted to be a singer—until I overheard my "biggest fan," my dad, say, "I can't listen to that screeching anymore." He was just joking with my mom, but little me was crushed, and I threw that dream away. In fact, I quit voice lessons and didn't sing for nearly 20 years, until IntuWitchin led me to my first song circles and kirtan, devotional singing in Sanskrit. The retreat in Hawaii rewarded me for my reconciliation. I take voice lessons now, and that micro trauma still rears its head almost every session. But I keep pushing through because it feels just as good to sing as it did when I was seven, maybe better.

Spiritual healing is one of the most challenging paths you'll ever take, but the most worth it! Giving yourself permission to be the witch, wizard, or superhero of your story is only half the battle; you must release what's hindered your magik to fully access IntuWitchin. Facing our darkness can be terrifying. It's a lot easier to watch Netflix and numb with substances, shopping, or scrolling. Yet for IntuWitchin to guide you, you must believe in your power and be in service to it. That power will heal you from the inside out, and no one can ever take it from you.

Your IntuWitchin might guide you to particular places to support your regeneration. Perhaps with tingling when you find a workshop, practice, or teacher that truly speaks to you. Genius loci, or *spirit of place*, can be so profound, and you'll keep getting nudges to visit locations that hold harmonic codes for you—trust them. Sedona, Greece, and Australia are some of those special places for me, each one visited on a whim when someone suggested it or asked me to join them. Every time I go, I receive a major activation that supports me rising to the next level. You also generally find incredible soul family when you RSVP to those invitations.

Maintaining confidence throughout this process can be excruciating. Whether introverted or extroverted, we all want to feel proud of who we are. That's why placing trust and faith in the unknown is so challenging—we've been taught confidence is reserved for a select few who look a certain way or have attained specific things. But that's all part of the illusion.

Confidence comes from *confidere* in Latin, meaning *trust* or *to trust in the benevolence of*. Like our closest confidant, only one letter different, is our most trusted friend. To be truly confident cosmic creators, we have to trust our IntuWitchin and let it show us the way. It takes immense initiative to let go of old, deeply ingrained habits and trust who we are, where we are, and why we're here. Confidence is about having faith in the benevolence of the Universe, even in the most challenging moments. It is only when we feel that zing of electricity from our inner knowing and ignore the invitation that we have regrets.

As if trusting ourselves wasn't difficult enough, we also need to free ourselves from the mental prisons society locks us in. The *should*s we're surrounded by, rules that keep us on the straight and narrow, prohibit us from being authentically ourselves. I am living proof that believing wholeheartedly in yourself, even in the direst straits, no matter what anyone has to say, is the real secret to success.

If people call you weird, thank the Goddess. Weirdness is the real confidence because we're trusting ourselves! Weird comes from the old German *wyrd*, the root of both *word* and *weird*, which meant *destiny*. Weirdos speak and embody our truth no matter what. We're moving in the direction of our fate or destiny rather than following the flock. I say the weirder, the better! Getting called weird for following your IntuWitchin is a high honor. It means you're not ignoring the call. You feel the vibration and pick it up enthusiastically with a "Yes, Goddess, let's do this!"

However, owning our weirdness can feel like we're going it alone. Without our spiritual family, we can get caught in a web of old ways, habits, and relationships that aren't in alignment with our true desires. If we distance ourselves from the people we engaged in those outdated behaviors with, we can feel lonely, making commitment to our growth feel isolating. But aloneness has magik too.

The origin of the word *alone* is a conjunction of *All One*. Remember that first Universal Law? When we are alone, we have the opportunity to remember we are one with everything, always. If you feel alone, try connecting with the elements around you: the wind of your breath, the flow of your emotional waters, the Earth of your body, or the fire of your beating heart. It might take practice, but loneliness can always be remedied by the remembrance that you're not alone, not really. You are all one with everything and everyone. You are profoundly and powerfully connected to this planet and the Universe around it.

SIGNS *and* SYMBOLS

⸻⸻⸻⸻⸻⸻

Trusting the guidance for next best steps is instinctive once you've identified your blocks and begun healing your inner child. But IntuWitchin doesn't always make sense when it "speaks." Learning to work with it means learning to interpret its messages in resonance with you. Here are some examples from my practice.

A few years ago, I worked with an amazing man named Alan who had recently lost his wife. Their daughter was 11, and he was raising her, plus several older kids, on his own. He came to me to heal after the loss and figure out how to care for himself and his children. During a session, I led him to communicate with his wife through his subconscious. My psychic gifts generally provide some clues as to where a client is in a session;

I'll get glimpses or sensations of their inner environment, and Alan was walking through a beautiful forest.

All of a sudden, I saw a bear in front of him on the path. I tried to shoo it away psychically: "Sorry, bear friend, we're busy. He wants to talk to his wife." But the bear was persistent. It didn't leave my field of vision and energetically just wasn't taking no for an answer. Remember, this is all happening in my own mind while I'm leading him through a meditation *on the phone.* It was as if the bear was saying, "Put me in, coach. I got this." Utterly befuddled, I finally gave in and invited Alan to "see the beautiful bear beside you on the path."

That session was one of the most transformative moments of his life. He had seen a bear in his yard that morning, and bears were his wife's spirit animal. It held his hands in its paws, which then became her hands. After a healing conversation with his wife, we wrapped up the session, and Alan wiped tears from his eyes with an old T-shirt on the chair next to him. Right as we were about to hang up, he said, "Oh my God, I thought this was a rag. Jenn got me this shirt years ago. Before she died, she told me to get rid of it, and I thought I had. . . . But it's right here. That was really her. I can feel her."

Too often we brush aside our IntuWitchin—but when we give in and listen, we receive what we were meant to. Another time, I walked into a friend's house and heard water running.

I wonder who's showering, I thought.

I walked upstairs to her bedroom and went to ask, but part of me reasoned, "She lives with people. Someone's in the shower. They'll join after if they want." This whole dialogue ran in my head as we greeted each other.

My IntuWitchin didn't shout; she hardly ever does. She is rarely as clear as "Hi, Mia. It's your inner guidance speaking. It's time for you to turn left, even though GPS says right." She prefers her mysterious murmurs. The thought seemed totally meaningless, and I had no logical explanation for it. Forty-five minutes later, as my friend and I were sitting by the fire, she gasped, jumped up, and yelled, "Oh my God, the tub!" and sprinted to the bathroom.

Repairing her living room ceiling cost $10,000 because *I* didn't listen to my IntuWitchin. Her bathtub overflowed for an hour into the rooms below. But the real message was more than just telling my friend to turn off the water. As we'll discuss, water represents our emotions, and she was incredibly sad that day. The overflowing bath represented something much deeper.

The living room ceiling is the bathroom floor. Floors represent foundations beneath us; ceilings protective (or limiting) roofs above us. The lights—taken out by the bathtub for a week— illuminate darkness, or "shed light" on situations. That evening, her "emotions" (the bathwater) flooded her stable foundation (the floor) to the point that it had to be completely removed and rebuilt (some personal transformation required!). The protection or limitation in the living room was damaged, and the lights (her ability to see through the darkness she was experiencing) were cut off.

Discovering the deeper meaning in mundane moments allows us to gain insight and make significant changes in our lives. As you will see, every experience can have this much significance, the web of wisdom intricately woven within and all around you.

One summer, I noticed a sprinkling of tiny red clovers had popped up in my yard. I'd been enjoying them for a few days when the gardeners came to mow the lawn. I panicked, gasping, "Oh my God, I have to save the clover!" I went outside, frantically picking the little blossoms. One of the gardeners saw me and started helping enthusiastically. When he brought his calloused palms to me in offering, they were overflowing with the sweet fairy flowers. As he handed them to me, he smiled like he knew they were precious but didn't say anything.

The following week at a retreat in Mexico, I sat overlooking the ocean with a woman who specialized in womb health. She was sharing herbal wisdom for female reproductive and sexual wellness, explaining how yoni steaming, which is like a tea facial for your pussy, can support endometriosis and fertility challenges. I wasn't experiencing these issues, so I asked, "What's the best yoni-steaming herb for regular maintenance?" Her response was so perfectly synchronistic.

"Red clover."

My jaw dropped. "Wow. I've got two huge jars of them sitting in my kitchen."

Thanks, IntuWitchin. Now I knew why I'd been compelled to rescue them. Imagine if I hadn't listened. An entire yard of red clover could've been totally wiped out. I might not have needed them to heal a specific issue, but the Universe was giving me a gift to reward me for *simply listening*.

IntuWitchin is not one-size-fits-all. I can't tell you "It will be like this," "These are the moments it shows up," or "This is what the message is for you." You just never know! The one thing I do know is that when you start listening, you will always be rewarded. Your IntuWitchin, the voice of your Higher Self and the Divine, *wants* to be connected to you. It's part of you, and you are part of it.

This simple ritual provides an astonishing amount of information to optimize the following lessons and invitations of IntuWitchin. Stand in front of a mirror and look directly into your left eye for a minimum of five minutes—if you can, go longer. Notice what thoughts you have about yourself, any discomfort that arises while just being present, facing yourself. Can you relax into the experience? Do you feel like looking away? Why?

Step it up by repeating affirmations like "I love you," "I am powerful," or "You are / I am beautiful" over and over. Is it hard or easy to say? Do you believe it when you tell yourself / hear these acknowledgments?

Our left side is receiving energy. Generally people look to the right side, which is more dominant. Shifting that pattern of behavior can have a big impact. The eyes are the windows to the soul, so this is a place where you can truly see yourself. Once you get the old stories out of the way, the Divine unconditional love of the Universe flows over, through, and *to* you.

Try this for a minimum of five minutes each day for one week and see how you feel. Each of the following chapters helps you overcome the challenge of truly seeing, valuing, or appreciating yourself. The more you engage with these practices, the more any armor you've built up to protect yourself and your magik will fall away.

This is one of the quickest and easiest ways to clear the channel for your IntuWitchin's emergence. The goal is to empower you to tap into the needs of your body and soul and determine which actions will lead to becoming the most confident, powerful version of yourself.

At first, it might be difficult to access the body's subtle energies and ways of communicating. Don't get discouraged if you don't receive an answer. We can't force or put pressure on inner wisdom; this is meant to be a beautiful and enjoyable experience. Keep trying until it feels clear, because soon it will.

You can make this as magikal, ritualistic, or ceremonial as you want. Call in your angels and guides or have some divination cards on hand—anything you feel will support you. Most importantly, do this process when it feels *right* for you, and create whatever makes you feel safe.

You can find a "resource" to connect with if you get overwhelmed, anxious, or uncomfortable in your body. This can be a physical part of you: "My hands keep me safe." If you get nervous, send breath and attention to your hands to recalibrate. Or it could be the green of the trees, the Earth below, the sound of your sighing exhales. Your resource can be energetic, or even just a statement to yourself. I love to use the mantra "I am *in the Hand of the Goddess*," which was the title of my favorite book as a kid and has gained more and more significance for me every year.

Find a quiet place to begin, ideally in Nature, or with Her elements close by (plants, a bowl of water, breeze through a window, or sunlight on your skin). Drums emulate the first sound we ever heard, our mother's heartbeat, so perhaps play some soft drum music to support you dropping in. Close your eyes and bring yourself into a calm, meditative state.

Begin to feel into your body, breathing deeply. Follow your breath in and out. Notice the sounds and smells around you, the temperature of the air. Create as much sensual awareness in your imagination from your external environment as possible.

Now shift the exploration from external sensations to internal sensations.

What is alive in your body? Is there pain, stuck energy, or an emotion that's asking to be felt?

Once you have focused your attention within, scan your entire body with your awareness, starting at the top of your head. Envision a waterfall of light cascading over you, traveling through your chakras (your body's energy centers), entering from the crown of your head, dropping down to illuminate what's present.

Notice: Does your mind feel still and calm like the glassy surface of a lake? Or is it chaotic, fuzzy, and frenetic?

Is your heart beating slowly and rhythmically, or is it racing? Is there tingling in your hands? Density in your stomach, excitement in your pleasure center?

What's going on in your body? Be curious. There is no right or wrong way to feel. Whatever is just is.

Once you've connected to your bodily sensations, ask:

"Where does my IntuWitchin live?"

Let the answer arise, paying attention to how your body responds. It might be warmth or a tingling in that area, an instant sensation, signal, or awareness of a specific location you see, feel, or hear.

Now ask:

"What color represents it?"

Tune in to that area of the body or however you experience the guidance of your inner wisdom and let that place, or your entire field of awareness, show you the color.

Now ask:

"Is there a texture of energy I can attune to, connect with, and utilize to better know my guidance system and inner wisdom?"

If you haven't received any responses to the previous questions, it might be because sensation is key for you. IntuWitchin speaks in pleasant sensations over contracted or painful ones, but there can be discomfort if it's unfamiliar or pushing you to expand. For example, "It feels soft and warm" or "It's like lightning running through my body," or "It feels like heaviness but not sad. It's as if this voice carries weight for me." Your body and IntuWitchin will know the best way for you and you alone.

Perhaps you hear a voice in response: the soft nurturing coo of the Goddess or the strong, empowered timbre of the warrior. Simply allow the archetype, frequency, or location of your IntuWitchin to present itself. Remember, it shows up in a myriad of ways because we all operate differently. If you hear it, great! If you see it, great! If you feel it, great! However it shows up is the way it's meant to be.

Now ask the part of you that is certain and self-assured to show itself to you energetically. Ask this part:

"How can I know when you are trying to get my attention?"

"When will I know you are inviting me forward?"

"What is the distinction between you and fear?"

Let yourself simply be aware of how the answers present themselves.

Establish an intentional exchange with this version of you. The better you get to know it, the more permission you will give it to guide you for the rest of your days.

When you feel complete, find a safe place to let this energy live within your body so you can call upon it and keep cultivating this connection.

Thank it, celebrate it for showing up, and close your practice by holding yourself in stillness until you are ready to return.

Chapter 2

Reclaiming
the Witch
from the Wound

Before we go any further and get into the juice of working with our IntuWitchin, it's important to understand the biggest block to acting on our inner wisdom and making magik in the world: the Witch Wound. All humans have been imprinted with this spiritual injury resulting from the severing between us and our greatest power: the unique magik and wisdom of oneness with all of life. The source of our IntuWitchin.

In our everyday lives, the Witch Wound manifests as a deep-seated, almost primal fear and loathing of anything that seems "weird" about ourselves, others, our dreams, desires, beliefs, behaviors, or the invitations life presents us.

Healing this wound requires finding and feeling it with courage and compassion. Our Witch Wound manifests in habits like people-pleasing, agreeing just to prevent rocking the boat, and avoiding our power or uniqueness, stress, anxiety, or anger. If you crave deep intimacy in friendships or romantic relationships, but you just don't trust people, this could be the cause. Perhaps you push people away, resist putting yourself and your gifts out there, or have a hard time expressing your feelings. Can you feel how it lives inside you?

If the Witch Wound ruled our reality, we would be alone in little huts in the woods, afraid to leave or be seen. Thank the Goddess we're revivifying so we can experience the magikal gifts, like love and sisterhood, that life has to offer.

Yes, I use *Goddess* intentionally. The last 2,000-plus years saw a massive transition from Earth-based spirituality worshipping multiple deities of all genders to monotheistic religions' single, punitive, masculine "God," marking the defamation of witches. Even though I had very little religious upbringing, I used to avoid using the word *God* because it just didn't feel right. How could I talk about such an unfathomable aspect of life? Part of me always felt the immense magnitude of the *concept* of God, even though I didn't understand it. Clearly, I never resonated with the idea of some bearded dude looking down from the clouds, hoping to smite me for having fun.

When I heard thunderclaps rolling through the Rocky Mountains as a kid, it felt like God was up to something in the sky. Perhaps rearranging the almighty furniture? But all I could see, hear, feel, or smell were the storm clouds, rain, flashing bolts of lightning illuminating purple peaks at midnight, and thunder itself. These awesome acts of nature were God to me.

These days, my relationship with God(dess) is the heart of my IntuWitchin practice. I choose to remember God is in my every breath, though there are plenty of breaths I forget. God is what makes the trees grow, transforming acorns into beautiful, majestic oaks. God expresses itself to infinity through the planets and stars and every one of us. When I am aligned with my IntuWitchin, I am in communication with God. *Constantly.*

To me, God is the Divine Universal energy of Creation and the most forgiving, insightful, and supportive presence. When I chose to see God as *all things* rather than one specific entity, I released the negative connotation or association with the word and the Divine itself. It no longer represented a negative, punitive aspect of religion. In my own life, I use *God* and *Goddess* interchangeably, giving a nod to the womb of life when I thank the Goddess.

Prior to organized religion, everyone had access to God and was inherently linked with the Divine; it was a natural resource like air or water. In this transition, libraries full of esoteric scripture were ransacked and burned, ancient temples were confiscated or destroyed, and churches were built from their rubble, forcing people to worship differently than they ever had in the familiar sacred places they had always known. God was no longer *everything* and became *one* very limited thing.

Anybody using Nature for healing and magik-making—living their IntuWitchin—was branded "evil" and condemned to a painful, humiliating death. While the European "witch trials" of the 16th and 17th centuries are a notorious example, every ancient and Indigenous society had healers—shamans, curanderas, rishis, priestesses, medicine men and women—who were all but eliminated. They were branded "witches" and eradicated in a global genocide that effectively wiped out generations of Earth-based wisdom and left a gaping open wound worldwide.

Though the Roman Empire was once the most widespread polytheistic pagan population, the history gets a little murky around the advent of Christianity and the conversion of such a massive group. Originally a sect of Judaism, Christianity became its own distinct religious ideology in the second century. Much of the actual written history has been destroyed in favor of the Bible's allegorical account, but the transition from everyone worshipping sun gods to only worshipping the *son* of God was quite rapid relative to human history.

The conquest of Britain in 43 C.E. saw a beautiful synergistic worship of equivalent Gods in Romano-British practice. Both Earth and elemental pagan traditions—Sulis of the Celtic and Minerva of the Roman—became one, honored in the hot springs of Bath. But when Emperor Constantine's rule began in 306, his rapid change of heart regarding pagan worship is obvious evidence of corruption. Originally, he encouraged pagans to tolerate their new Christian neighbors but quickly renounced his inclusive edict to further the agenda of the Vatican, imploring

Christians to do away with pagans. Ancient temples through-out the world were seized and converted into churches.

In 380 C.E., Roman Catholicism became the Empire's official religion. By the 6th century the Catholic Church had control of the Roman political system. The papacy gained absolute rule in the 15th century, "coincidentally" right as transatlantic voyages became common. Until the Current Era, we *all*—Europe, Africa, Oceania, Central and South America—were Indigenous, Earth-based tribal civilizations. But colonization, rampantly expanding in the 1400s, disrupted ancient magik worldwide. All the gold in the Vatican was pillaged from South America, annihilating Mayan, Incan, and Taino people to pilfer their land and resources. The fact that the official languages of the entire continent are Spanish and Portuguese, European languages, elucidates the eradication of natural traditions, dialects and culture, unfathomably altering the course of history. The monotheistic religions, once a vast minority, so violently persecuted anyone practicing ancient, nature-based worship that the tides were forced to turn. The decline of our species had begun, IntuWitchin lost in its wake.

This persecution lives on today. We must do all we can to shift our course toward healing. Whatever your background, dark history taints the human lineage, and lives in our DNA.

This genocide was part of the global transition from feudalism to capitalism. Wild, pristinely unsullied environments became "savage" lands to be conquered and plundered. People had been free to cultivate land as they saw fit; no one could "own" Earth. Women occupied positions of prominence, and "healers" of all modalities were held in high regard. But within two centuries, a new ruling class used a combination of violence and fear-based coercion to assume power over the masses. Now the resources of the Natural world were fenced off and sold to the highest bidder, often with money stolen from the original inhabitants of the land itself—the origins of extractive capitalism decimating our planet and its people. The Dutch East India Company "purchased" the island of Manhattan for a ludicriously low sum from the local Lenape people who believed everyone had rights to the land and it could never be bought or sold.

For people to acquiesce to the severing of this relationship with Earth, they had to be convinced that Nature and those connected to Her were *dangerous* and must be tamed. This represented another fatal blow for witches—the wise women (men/queer/nonbinary people) who knew how to work *with* Nature to peacefully coexist with plants, wild beasts, and elements of the nonhuman world.

The multitude of rationalizations that could brand someone a witch in times past is mind-boggling. Many were elderly women, often widows whose husbands had died and left them large plots of land, a home with a deep well, or a hefty herd of livestock. They were victimized by jealous, conniving neighbors accusing them of witchcraft to poach their resources. Some were mentally ill, others had bodily disfigurement; anyone in any way deemed "different" could be marked as a witch.

Menstrual blood—the liquid of creation used in countless ancient rituals as the elixir of life, the original blood of Christ, shed without violence—became evil, dirty, and shameful. Any expression of sexual energy outside of procreation, for pleasure or enjoyment, was forbidden, only to be engaged with for making more workers to enslave and build the systems we see today. This meant queer people, liberated women, or anyone with different levels of income, beauty, desirability, intelligence, or physical capacity risked being accused of witchcraft and hung, burned, or drowned for it.

Witches were tortured to put the *fear of God* into anyone who dared step out of line. This started with a rumor that witches couldn't bear the touch of iron. To prove malfeasance, torturers used a tool called the *pear of anguish*. At scorching temperatures, it was inserted vaginally to mutilate the accused. It worked perfectly with the rumor they'd started that witches couldn't bear the touch of iron. When forced onto an iron chair, the accused witch would cry out in pain, and the crowd, oblivious to the violating wound beneath her skirts, was instantly convinced of her guilt. No wonder survival instincts kick in, denying our Intu-Witchin. The real evil in that scenario is clear.

It's a lot, I know. Family trauma and schoolyard bullies are one thing. But when brutality like this remains in our genetic memory as a result of our magik, reclaiming its power is the fastest track to healing.

When I said we *all* carry the remnants of the Witch Wound, I'm including white, straight, cisgender men too. I believe it's ultimately because of this wound, wherever the fear of God outside oneself began in religion, that men carried out these atrocities, initiating capitalist land and power grabs (i.e., patriarchy). It was a man's duty to protect and provide for his family. How it must have felt, as a man then, to watch your mother, sister, daughter, or wife be accused of witchcraft and burned alive. The harm to the sense of self in men forced to complicity in these acts must have been devastating. This is the root of "toxic masculinity" that manifests in misogyny and violence among men today. Men were taught to stand by when their families were torn apart because their child or spouse was "evil." There's a reason rape is still used as an act of war; men are "protectors," and when they are unable to protect the women they love, they lash out and fight. Hurt people will inflict pain on others because they don't know how to handle it themselves.

There are about 100 different rabbit holes we could go down right now, and I know they're all deep. In short, part of the work of IntuWitchin is being the best ancestors we can possibly be for our descendants by honoring the pain of those who came before us and healing ourselves so we in turn heal our lineage. Let us write new stories with more happily-ever-afters for future generations.

The world is changing. At long last, witches are coming out of the broom closet, finding one another in communities and on social media. As the global climate shifts, we're starting to heal this wound in ourselves and others. The wisdom of witches is awakening within us again.

The INNER WITCH HUNTER

✳·······························✳·······························✳

I call my own internalized toxic patriarchy the "Witch Hunter." Taking in the shaming, punitive voices of parents, teachers, and leaders—repeated by our ego, convincing us to shut down our self-expression and stay small and "safe"—which becomes our inner Witch Hunter, who fears our IntuWitchin and wants us to do the same.

The Witch Hunter's wrath can still plague me in the most peaceful, natural environments, until I am totally overcome by the fear someone is coming to "get me." It told me, "You're a failure. You're pathetic," and "You'll never make it, so don't even try." So I didn't try. I let years pass me by in misery because I believed this voice was right. On the other side of the coin was, "If you do it and succeed, you're dead." It can sound outrageous out of context, but these were real consequences for witches in every lineage.

The Witch Hunter's libel makes you afraid to be who you are, trying to tell you that if you say, do, or are *X, Y,* or *Z,* no one will accept or love you and it could cost you your life.

Can you identify this voice in you?

What is the story that makes you procrastinate, eat poorly, avoid intimacy, fear friendship, or dislike yourself?

What have you wanted to do that the Witch Hunter talked you out of?

Who have you longed to be that the Witch Hunter said was unacceptable or disgusting?

Don't listen to those lies; don't let them win. Let's excavate some inner Witch Hunter manifestations so we can confront and heal from its influence.

Compliance

To access the energy that lights up your soul, connects you to your essence, and ignites the Divine spark within, follow your IntuWitchin. Because for generations of witches, accessing that spark made you a danger to the status quo, too dangerous to be tolerated.

Have you ever wondered why so much of what is labeled "sinful" by organized religions is also lots of fun? People who know how to have fun—*real* fun, not using substances to numb, mask, or escape pain—are empowered in their sovereignty. Fun people are dangerous because, like a candle, their flame ignites others. They aren't concerned with what other people think, do, or want; they magnetize joy wherever they go. Happy people are much less easily manipulated than people who feel like "something is missing," because they're already fulfilled. Stripped of their fun, people were coerced into thinking someone or something outside of them, like a spiritual figurehead or religion, held the key to their fulfillment and salvation.

The truth is, we're the only ones who can save ourselves. We're responsible for lighting that spark within, and we can do so through fun, play, and being our wildest, weirdest selves. Remember, *weird* means *destiny*. We all want to follow our destinies, but our inner Witch Hunter often causes self sabotage, insisting it is safer to fit into society's definition of *good*. Consider that for 2,000 years, anyone who was a weirdo or went against the grain was liable to be branded a witch, immediately endangering their life. Accepting the program, then, became the only way to survive. If the alternative is death, compliance—however maddening—becomes a way of life. This is how dictators and oppressive rulers have built their empires since time immemorial.

Compliance could mean anything from biting your tongue when you want to say something, worried people will think you're stupid or reject you, to not wearing, doing, or being what you want so you aren't made fun of. Or, like me, staying small rather than striving for success because you want to fit in. The only way to disrupt these patterns is to start following your heart, which begins with baby steps.

One of the greatest gifts of social media is you can find a wonderful weirdo who lives their life completely differently than everyone in your immediate circle. You get to watch them exist on their own terms, resonating and role-modeling for you, helping you reprogram the belief that going your own way just gets you in trouble and giving you permission to try on new habits.

I get messages all the time saying, "I wasn't going to _____, but I heard this voice in my head say, 'What would Mia do?'" I *love* that! Find whoever that person is for you and let them be your inspiration and motivation for saying, "No more hiding. I only comply with myself and God(dess)."

It's challenging to follow your magikal destiny. When you blaze a trail, you get a lot of fire in your face. But our IntuWitchin is our inner lighthouse. We are always guiding ourselves home no matter how lost we feel or how dark the storm.

Fear of Nature

Nature is the home of the Goddess, where she speaks directly to us. We remember who we are in Her quiet. We hear the songs of our soul and Hers. Of *course* our inner Witch Hunter uses its strongest weapon, fear, to prevent us from reuniting with Nature. The Witch Hunter can be so nefarious that even I can still almost talk myself out of replenishing in the most nourishing place for me.

We mask the terror of spending quiet time in Nature with all kinds of justifications: it's too hot or cold, it's raining, it takes too long to get there, we have more "important" things to do, it's a waste of time, or, like many of us were conditioned to think, "I don't want to get dirty." But deep down, underneath all the excuses, is fear created by the Witch Hunters. Because Nature was once where we sustainably harvested all our resources: water from springs, medicines from herbs, and food from wild plants and animals.

A clear example of how we fear our own life force energy is the vulnerability—both physical and emotional—we feel being naked in nature. This is literally our *most natural* state, yet we've evolved to be on guard or even adamantly opposed to it.

It was in Crete when I first experienced the nourishing empowerment overriding this resistance to simply *trust* in Nature. Crete, the largest Greek island, has a long and storied history of priestess-led civilization and mythology.

After I arrived at a magikal farm, I cold-plunged in the fairy waterfalls nestled in chestnut forests, picked avocados and oranges from trees I climbed, and felt utterly nourished by the land. I slept 16 hours the first night. The next day, while hiking in the wildflower-decorated hills nearby, my Intu-Witchin whispered: "Read the sign. There is something here for you. . . ."

A little church of the 99 Fathers had been built in 1894 upon, and from the ruins of, a 9,000-year-old temple to Artemis. This momentous honorarium to Her had been destroyed. Stones of her ancient sanctuary—etched with description of worship, prayers, and invocations to Her—were lost. I could feel in the Earth, She had called me for a reason.

I was entirely alone, feeling completely safe and free when She suggested I finish the hike topless. I'm a pretty wild woman, but being half naked solo in a strange place and knowing in my bones I was utterly protected by this sacred environment was a Divine gift I'd never experienced before. The higher I climbed, the more the mountain, plants, and birds spoke to me. A great earthen gate hewn from cliffside rose, evidence of how much life had been imbued in the very stones of the entrance. These ancient walls lined someplace majestic. As I crested the top of the hill, basking in panoramic views of turquoise waters and marble canyons around the partially buried temple, the presence of potent priestess magik fortified in the very ground overwhelmed me.

I inhaled myself open to the next direction. Again, my IntuWitchin whispered on the wind, "Come, lay your skin down upon me. Stay until you hear my song." I stripped off my remaining clothes and lay down face-first on the Earth, third eye to the ground, ears upon the periwinkle blossoms, where I remained for four hours. I let my nervous system melt, cell by cell, into the soft meadow floor. She asked me to stay, so I did. This period of deep listening turned out to be one of the most inspiring experiences of my life.

I'd never tasted the texture of *trust* so viscerally, mentally, physically, and spiritually, *simultaneously*! To let myself get that quiet, reveling in oneness, receiving guidance I knew wholeheartedly I could follow. My body surrendered, fully held, unified with Nature. She knew I was in service to Her, trusting my devotion, my enthusiasm, and my weird. I didn't know what spring would bring but felt a fire in my belly, a tsunami of inspiration brewing, ready to make waves in the world. She would take care of me, unapologetic and untamed, like She knew I would take care of Her and Her wild. Though the pandemic would shut the world down just two weeks later, this was only three months before I started Witch School, my life's most magikal turn yet.

Nature was once our global house of worship, the holiest of temples. Now most sacred sites have been ruined or had churches built on top of them. Organized religion prevented worship in remembrance of our own Divine Nature as a reflection of Hers, changing the holy days (holidays), astrologically and cosmically aligned, into Christian observances using the metaphor of the sun and life itself to be Jesus's story rather than Nature's. That's why Christmas, originally the winter solstice celebration (the rebirth of the *Sun* came to represent the birth of Christ, the *Son*), is now four days later. Easter, named for the Celtic Goddess of rebirth, Ostara, originally honored the resurrection of life on Earth (baby bunnies being born, chicks hatching, and the green of life returning) with the spring equinox. Even spending time in darkness, one of the most relaxing and recharging things for us to experience, a return to the womb, has become something to fear.

The inner Witch Hunter is the voice that says Nature is "gross" or "dirty." That our inner wilderness is something we should fear. We get expensive mud baths and clay masks at spas but freak out when the Earth serves them to us on a stone platter. The Witch Hunter can talk you out of a dip in the ocean and say a spring-fed waterfall is too cold or there might be spiders in the hollowed-out tree you hear calling—all of which have happened to me. Finally, one day, I fought off its claws and crawled 30 feet into a burned-out redwood. It was pitch-black everywhere except when I turned back toward the light at the entrance of its fallen roots. Webs catching on my face again and again, I kept going. I forced myself to stay inside that hollowed heartwood for 20 minutes in meditation to overcome my fear and acquiescence to the Witch Hunter. When I finished, I turned toward the light and saw a massive spider dropping down on a single silken strand from the top of the cavity, but I just watched in awe, thanked the Creator for Her lessons, and eventually crawled past the spider with respect. Spiders' webs spun with silk are sacred, a metaphor for how we weave our realities. First Nations people of the Americas honor the Goddess Grandmother Spider.

The Earth remains our body; water, our blood; air, our breath; fire, our energy; and Spirit, our soul. Working with these elements in and all around us reawakens the Witch and our IntuWitchin.

If you live near national, state/provincial parks, or Nature areas, go explore them! Swim in rivers, lakes, and streams; scramble up boulders; and climb up mountains, down valleys, and across meadows, rain or shine! Within an hour of most major cities, gorgeous Nature can be found. I'd lived in LA for years before a friend and I took a camping trip to the Angeles National Forest. *One hour* from the bustling metropolis is pristine wilderness with waterfalls and swimming holes, silent nights and starry skies. I couldn't believe how long I'd taken to open my eyes to beauty that had been right there all along.

If you live in a big city, like so many of my clients have, start spending time daily reconnecting with Nature in your local parks and green zones. Remove your shoes, feel the Earth beneath your feet. Focus on the elemental sensations: wind rustling, sunlight warming you, scents in the air, the wonder of birds serenading you even in the concrete jungle. Slow your breathing, take in your surroundings with presence. Mother Earth doesn't need an apology for how long it's been—She'll always welcome you home to Her open arms, elated to see you. Let Her hold you.

Find a tree, rock, or flower that calls to you and sit with it. Notice the bark, leaves, colors, textures. How do you feel focusing your attention on this living being—rather than on your phone—for one minute? Bring a journal and record your experience. Maybe you'll have a beautiful realization or message from the Natural world, but note any stories that try to talk you out of it or tell you what you're doing is silly. That's the Witch Hunter. Embraced by Nature, your nervous system will settle into regulation with the harmonic frequencies of Earth, and those stories instinctively unravel.

Ridiculing the Woo-Woo

In many Disney movies, the witch is evil, a greedy corrupter of innocence, while princesses are depicted in harmony with the wild world and its creatures, often with a cherished familiar. Those princesses are nodding to our wild, authentic spiritual potential, which can be awakened through primal affiliation with Nature and Her fantastic beasts. This is classic Witch Hunter thinking, projecting their poor behavior onto us, portraying an adversarial conflict between the two elements of *our* Nature and desire for freedom from the civilized life of material success the princesses most often try to escape.

Pocahontas has Flit *and* Meeko, Mulan has Mushu (we'll talk about dragons later), and Jasmine has Rajah. Tigers are associated with courage, willpower, trusting yourself and your primal instincts (the recipe for IntuWitchin). Hummingbirds can fly in every direction while kissing flowers, harkening to adaptability and joyful blossoming. Each familiar animal is a metaphor for Her sovereign truth. Princesses are pitted *against* witches, but that's who they are.

Because of this harmonious Natural attachment, and the challenge of keeping earthen homes rodent-free, witches' familiars were often cats. One of Minerva McGonagall's most iconic aspects is Transfiguration into a cat, an age-old association with witchery. I finally understood this when my familiar, Minerva (named for the Roman Goddess of wisdom *and* in McGonagall's honor), a tiny but mighty, fluffy black cat, found me. Without a leash, she hikes and climbs mountains, explores edges of creeks when I cold-plunge, has an entire vocabulary of chirps and chortles, and radiates empress power. She reminds me to revere my own wild feline Nature in every moment, avoiding me anytime my vibration is off, an extension of my True Nature.

Egyptians said black cats were endowed with magikal powers; other cultures worshipped them as Gods—until the 14th century, when their companions began to burn en masse. Witches were said to become cats to accomplish supernatural deeds under the cover of darkness, as their silent paws make them easy to miss as they roam like inky shadows at night. Many cats were killed during the Black Death plague under the pretense they were harbingers of the devil, spreading the disease. In actuality, they were helping kill the rodents that were carrying the illness through sewers and pantries. Witches and our black cats were the scapegoats for centuries, starting superstitions that still stand today.

It is no coincidence all things magikal have come to be labeled childish, idiotic, crazy, and woo-woo. People are blown away when they see my cat following (or leading) me down a trail. I wanted a magikal relationship with my familiar; I believed it was possible, and it is. Fantastical beliefs became cause for concern. You have to be "serious" to be respectable, or "get anywhere" in the world. But as discussed, the *disdain* for magikal thinking is actually what's "new age." Because if we truly knew how magikal we are, no one would be over-working to build extractive empires for other people. We would be peacefully tending to our land, manifesting everything we desire and require, treating other people with kindness and respect.

Imagine being torn from your home for healing an ailing child, having a fertile and abundant field, or taking a walk with your friend in the forest. During the millennia of actual witch hunts, it was safer to shut our magik down. The inherited trauma dictates our lives today.

For example, when I was first really building my business and my team asked me to make sales videos, even though I know the power of this work, sometimes I would fully shut down. Spiritual entrepreneurship can be incapacitating. I don't want to sell to people, partly because I just want you to feel called to hop in the cauldron with me—but mostly because my ancestors could have been killed just for talking about these tools. I used to get so nervous on social media. Sharing my magikal information, even simply identifying with a word that would have meant my demise not long ago, can make me subconsciously want to hide. Panicked, I wouldn't create for weeks, while the Witch Hunter spewed outrage at my audacity for speaking about my healing gifts and offerings. "How dare you?! Who do you think you are?!"

Once upon a time, you had to know how to follow the feathers, whirls of bark, and spirals woven in moss to find me and my little forest-witch cabin remedies. Now here I am, sharing my healing balm for your spirit with the world. It's scary.

So I banish the Witch Hunter by blasting through my own edges. After five years of developing a very deep yet very personal relationship to my moon time, painting, face masks, and blood rituals were normal practices for me. Finally, the Goddess wanted this intimate information shared with the world. I'd known my IntuWitchin's message was coming but pretended not to. The Cancer full moon would illuminate a dark side I had never let be seen. Cancer rules our blood, emotions, and creativity, the Great Mother and Healer archetype, ruled by the moon Herself.

The energy was as aligned as could be, and She was loud and clear: "This time, when you paint yourself with blood, don't hide. You have to show the world." I could feel the Witch Hunter's claws inside me. Would I keep choosing to be the version of myself who guards the most sacred practice in my life like a secret? Or would I share it, *knowing* I could serve to empower hundreds of thousands of women to release the patriarchal programming that their blood was shameful, dirty, or gross.

I got ready, dressed head to toe in red, and filmed against stark white snow contrasting the deep crimson blood I drew across my cheeks, anointing my third eye, and down my chin. I edited as fast as I could, not wanting to leave a single moment for doubt or chickening out. Pressing "post" was one of the most vulnerable moments of my life. And guess what: after consistent growth over the last few years, that post was the first time I *lost* followers, hundreds of them, in fact, within the next day. I had a choice: Was I going to let the Witch Hunter win?

No, I'm not hiding anymore! I can't ignore my IntuWitchin just to make sure I'm approved of and accepted by people. The following moon cycle, She wanted more: "Now acknowledge the rejection." I started the video with "Hundreds of people unfollowed me when I painted my face in moon blood. . . ." And guess what. Hundreds more unfollowed me *again*, but that video got half a million views and 40,000 shares. The ripple effect of activating that many women is such a blessing and the duty of my life.

How often do we let one terrible thought outweigh the blessings of our bravery? How often do we completely ignore the good to just focus on the bad? These are the ultimate opportunities for us to rewire the neural pathways of outdated programs, because any action that overrides the inner Witch Hunter and results in responses you were afraid of (rejection, abandonment, judgment) does *not* mean you made the wrong choice. It's a chance to choose who you want to be, reclaim your freedom and power from society's prescription, to be the Hero(ine) your inner child always needed.

The Witch Hunter will say, "*See?!* I *told* you! You're an idiot. You're disgusting. People hate you." But that's because you've loosened its grip on you, and it's afraid you're stepping over the threshold into someone new. The version of you who's willing to be seen is reborn, but the deeply ingrained patterns might momentarily linger, testing if you'll fall back into them. Sometimes you will, and that's okay. You can use the blueprint of pride in yourself, courage, and boldness to start rebuilding and rewriting your new stories, invigorating your IntuWitchin.

Painting moon blood on your face for Instagram is extreme— overcoming limiting beliefs doesn't have to be. Practice privately by doing solo ceremonies or rituals with trusted friends to recall your magik. Whatever makes you afraid to do so unravels either way. In the following chapters, I'll share how to work with these beliefs to wreak havoc on the wiles of the Witch Hunter. Remember, you are not alone in this endeavor. Every step we take is integral to rewriting the story for our future in honor of our witchy ancestors.

Biting Your Tongue

One of the Witch Wound's deepest challenges to being ourselves is in speaking our truth. The power to express ourselves authentically was systematically and strategically stripped from us by the original Witch Hunters. Our songs weren't safe to be sung, as singing anything other than specific church-authorized hymns to God was deemed evil and temptation of the devil. Speaking out against the atrocities being committed meant you would be the next victim. So we stopped saying what we think and how we really feel. We now choke down our emotions and our ideas and stay quiet in the face of injustice for fear the perpetrators will turn against us. The response to the inner Witch Hunter is shutting ourselves up or down. We see this on our childhood playgrounds all too often. Bullies beat up someone smaller, younger, or different from them, and no one comes to their defense, too afraid to receive the same treatment. Evolutionarily, survival of the fittest became survival of the quietest.

The ancestral and genetically inherited Witch Wound manifests as blockage in our throat chakra. I hear from my students and clients sentiments such as:

"It's like I'm being strangled."

"Something is clawing at my throat."

"My throat literally closes up when I try to speak."

Have you ever experienced any of these sensations when trying to tell someone how you feel, standing up for what's right when no one else will, or sharing in front of an audience? Some people get terrible sore throats if they're required to do public speaking—in meetings, leading classes, giving talks. Maybe you strain your neck and can barely move from the energetic discomfort you're experiencing at the sheer thought of speaking before a group. Take a moment to think about your emotional response to expressing yourself—whether in intimate relationships, to authority like parents or teachers, or to groups of strangers. How has the Witch Wound impacted your voice?

Thank the Goddess there is hope for healing and it's one of the sweetest salves for our souls. The panacea for patriarchal programming in our voice is simply speaking or singing the song of your spirit. Begin by telling a trusted friend you feel safe with something you haven't been able to share before. It doesn't have to be your deepest, darkest secret, but perhaps a dream you've never revealed. My salvation came in sacred songs. Kirtan, the devotional singing of Sanskrit mantras, and sinking into song circles praising the Goddess and the Earth with simple melodies worked wonders. Just letting my voice stretch and shine healed parts of my soul I'd buried so deeply, I'd forgotten they even existed.

There are many healers who can help you with personal expression and unlocking your voice. It's one of the main spiritual maladies people come to me for help with because I've made such strides with my own unapologetic expression. I work with a vocal coach, Anye, who had me sobbing like a baby during our first several sessions surrendering to where the Witch Wound was hidden in me. The Witch Hunter showed up as my dad (responding to my inner seven-year-old's wound), and while I wept, we channeled a whole song begging for him to treat me differently.

One of the main things spiritual entrepreneurs and clients come to me for is healing their Witch Wound to unashamedly express themselves and share their gifts. We explore their subconscious mind to reprogram the core memory or first moment they shut down their voice. Working with the inner child to see how the wound presents itself symbolically whether they were shamed or punished for speaking up. Then we can fulfill their needs with love or listening and figure out how the adult self can nurture that suffering to move forward. A good healer in this realm follows the energy letting the song of your soul guide the session, whatever that looks like.

Sexual Repression

Have you ever considered why that which creates all life and brought each and every one of us into the world has been demonized, commodified, shamed, and repressed in humanity but particularly in women? How the most free and natural form of pleasure and creativity has become dirty (and not in the good way)? It just doesn't add up. Repeat after me: there is *nothing* wrong with my sexuality.

There is nothing wrong with your desires, your kinks, and the way you find pleasure.

Our sexuality is the other expression most affected by the Witch Wound. Sex is one of the fastest and easiest ways to connect to Spirit—the literal embodiment of life force energy animating all things. When we are fully connected to our sexuality, we can reach higher states of consciousness, heal and liberate ourselves from painful conditioning, and manifest our dreams. Sex is truly magik! Which is exactly why the Witch Hunter shows up in the body and bedroom doing everything it can to repress our natural sexual expression, cockblocking our pleasure, sensual enjoyment, connection, and the Divine Universal energy we can access through sex.

The patriarchy turned women's naturally seductive form into a vessel of the devil. The residual impact of this—no matter your religion or background—can make you feel a lack of safety in, or hatred of, your own body. Depending on your programming, the Witch Hunter might arrive while you're making love, telling you sex is dangerous or disgusting, that you should be ashamed, you're going to hell, your desires or fantasies are repulsive, or if you act on them, you'll be punished for this "sin."

There's another valid theory about how women's sexuality and reproductivity came to be controlled by patriarchy and why the witch hunts were part of this. Witches, often women, knew how to work with the herbs and cycles of the moon to control reproduction. And one of the core tenets of many organized religions is to "go forth and multiply," deeming all non-procreative sex, including queer sex and sex outside of marriage, evil. This is further reason why the LGBTQIA+ community knows the voice of the Witch Hunter well.

Those who inflict pain upon others through sexual violence are responding to their inner Witch Hunter. They feel "wrong," "bad," and isolated in their shame (as shame does to everyone) and lash out as an attempt to reclaim power by having power *over* another.

Take a moment to consider what beliefs you've had about sex. Do you feel worthy of your pleasure? Do you enjoy experiencing your body, or do you find yourself disassociating and thinking about anything but the present moment and your sensations? Are you able to surrender and receive worship from another, or do you only engage in a performative way? Again, everyone experiences their wounds differently, and we often don't even realize their roots.

Sexual healing comes in infinite forms. And while there are many amazing healers out there, there are also many who take advantage of people, so be very aware if you're seeking support in this area. Personally, a self-pleasure practice was what really worked for me. Remember, pleasure doesn't just mean orgasm. This is about learning the sweet spots on your own body and what feels good to you.

Privacy and safety, where no one can hear or walk in on you (unless that's what you're into), are key for this kind of work. If you've experienced trauma, you can be your own healer by taking your time and showing your body how it deserves to be treated. Rewrite the story through tenderness, deep listening, and the exact kind of touch you desire. Start with just understanding what sensations your body enjoys. Do you like an oil massage with hard pressure on your thighs? Feathers and light, tickling caresses around your neck and collar bone? Will candles and a warm bath relax you enough to feel open to receiving love from yourself?

Go slow, take your time, don't rush. Use your breath to excite or calm your nervous system. Long, deep breaths in through the nose and sighing out the mouth can send signals of safety and security to your brain if you get overwhelmed. We tend to hold our breath and keep silent when we feel like we're in danger, so make all the sound you want! If you want to amplify your energy, quicken your breathing through your mouth, the way you would after a sprint or while exercising. But it's *not* a sprint; it's a marathon. It might take months or years of this practice to even be able to shift the energy and touch from sensual to sexual, and that's *okay*! This is about gently retraining your body to be able to express its boundaries, needs, and desires and have them honored and fulfilled with respect. You are the one who can show it what that looks and feels like, to set the standard for a partner to uphold the same level of reverence.

SACRED SISTERHOOD

Perhaps the most healing salve to my Witch Wound has been the sacredness of my sisterhood. It is not in the female nature to compete; flowers bloom beside all others. Consider that, in Nature, males compete for mates, but females generally cooperate or cohabitate with each other. I would not be the witch I am today without the women who held my hand when I felt alone, healed my heart with their love when it felt broken, or showed me how to hold my head high when I was hiding who I truly am. This sisterhood applies to all friendships, no matter gender identity; feminine energy bonds in a particular way that bears mentioning.

My friends are the sisters I never had. We share the secrets of our greatest gifts and darkest depths. We've heard each other's climatic roars in pleasure rituals and found a breadth of intimacy I've never seen before in female friendship. This is sacred sisterhood, where every part of you is safe to be seen and expressed with other women and you are celebrated for your success because they're climbing the mountain by your side. Where you are loved fiercely but also called forward and given the necessary feedback (you might not want to hear!) to grow into all you're capable of being.

Too many of us have never experienced such friendships. At my retreats, we constantly hear, "I've only known you a few days, but I've never had sisters like this before." This is because many women, despite all our unique gifts and powers, so magikal in our own ways, tend to gang up on and go against each other. From undermining another's success or strengths or fighting over boys to starting rumors or talking shit about someone you actually want to be friends with, it can feel like a constant competition. How often have you truly felt like you *belonged* in a group?

Save yourself by naming another. Understanding the Witch Wound has also helped me understand the divisions that exist among us: often, if a woman was accused of being a witch, the only way she could halt her torture or save her own life was by giving the name of another "witch" (sister, cousin, friend, or neighbor). The legacy of these trade-offs is the source of the sisterhood wound and much competition among women. In addition, the very activities that once bonded us—healing with herbs, performing moon rituals, telling each other's fortunes by the stars in the sky—became warrant for arrest and murder. No wonder we learned it was safer to step out of our sacred circles and distance ourselves from those who engaged in them. When the Witch Hunters were in town, gathering beneath the moon together was a death sentence. We've been separated from and made to fear each other ever since, leaving us subconsciously skeptical of sisterhood.

The Witch Hunter can tell you other women aren't trustworthy, convince you you're the only one who feels like this, you're alone in your experience, or like you should talk badly about others behind their back. It can make you feel unworthy in comparison, envying their success rather than knowing they are showing you what's possible for you, too! The Witch Hunter can toxify your relationships through judgment of clothes, bodies, lifestyle, choices, or willingness to take risks, when you are longing for that kind of courage yourself. Whenever we judge another, there is always an opportunity to untangle how that same judgment is rooted in us. Is it because we don't like that part of who we are or wish we could be *more* like them?

The Witch Hunter infiltrates female friendship through an unwillingness to repair ruptures. If we have an argument, it can be challenging to take responsibility or apologize. Oftentimes both involved parties avoid doing so altogether. When this is the case, one disagreement means the end of the relationship. Repair matters to me. When I take time to remedy misunderstandings or disconnection, the friendship can become much deeper. Just as scar tissue is stronger than regular tissue, our bonds are fortified by making it through something. Witnessing another's wounds makes us better able to take care of them, and vice versa, in the future. The old way is to use their shadow or weakness against them. Not anymore. When we team up, take care of each other, and work together, we are unfuckwithable and unstoppable!

Following my IntuWitchin is one of the greatest ways I've healed my sisterhood and Witch Wounds, leading to massive growth in my relationships. If you feel like someone's energy is toxic, they might not be the right friend for you. But check in with yourself: Is it actually a judgment cast by your ego to keep you from what could become a deep connection? If you're subconsciously creating a narrative because of an inner feeling of unworthiness, could it be your own toxicity you're being asked to heal? As you connect with your soul family, witness any judgment or negative stories that arise toward others. Ask yourself, "What are they triggering in me?" "Is my resistance or rejection of them representative of something I am resisting or rejecting within myself?"

If your IntuWitchin guides you to reach out to someone, do it! When I first met one of my best friends, Rachel, we would see each other at parties and laugh and enjoy each other's company but never really drop in or spend time one-on-one. Finally, I reached out to her and said, "Hey, I would really love to get to know you better. Would you want to hang out just us sometime?"

She responded with a resounding "Yes!" For nearly a decade, she has been one of the strongest examples of this love I could have ever imagined. Sometimes it takes you being brave. I know many people aren't as extroverted as I am, but if the other person isn't either, you might miss out on a relationship that could change the course of your life! I know rejection hurts, but you've got nothing to lose by giving it a shot.

I met virtually all of my soul sisters (and brothers) by saying yes—to an event, an adventure, a workshop, a lecture, a yoga class, teacher training, or a ceremony I may never have gone to on my own. I don't drink, so it was sound baths or breath work, festivals and Burning Man, or full moon rituals, never bars or clubs. I have grown with my group of Goddesses in ways we could never have foreseen 10 years ago, all because we said yes to finding each other.

INTUWITCHIN *for* HEALING *the* WITCH WOUND

✳ .... ✳ .... ✳

The key to healing the Witch Wound with IntuWitchin starts by noticing when and how it affects your life. Are you holding yourself back from an action you've heard over and over that you should take? Have you stayed in a relationship or a job you know isn't right for you far longer than you should? At its core, the Witch Wound is an injury to our sovereignty of expression, sexuality, and eternal, creative energy. Sovereignty means knowing no one else owns you, your responses, your desires, or your life in any way. It prevents anything from possessing or having power over you. The original witches were truly sovereign, which is why they were considered a threat.

IntuWitchin asks you to live the answer to the question: How can I be most authentic, my freest and most magikal, empowered self, in any given situation? If you're feeling stuck, trapped, confused, or resentful toward another, that's your inner Witch Hunter speaking! And if you are *being* the Witch Hunter toward anyone, which we've seen a lot in social media cancel culture, there is an opportunity to heal whatever is allowing that mob mentality to infiltrate your sovereignty. Ask yourself: "What is my intention with this action, these words? What needs nurturing inside me that is lashing out?"

Though it can be the source of our greatest sorrow, this anguish represents an opportunity. This is our spiritual curriculum to become the witches we have always dreamed we could be. If you see it silencing you, speak up, sing out. If you see it shrinking you, shine bright, share your light! If you see it weakening you, stand strong and tall. Above all, allow your IntuWitchin to illuminate the path for alchemizing your Witch Wound.

RE-WITCHING OUR WORDS

As you know, I love "spelling" and am a big believer in words weaving our destiny. The Witch Wound has also turned certain words with powerful origins against women, further indicating its presence in our society.

✻ *Hysteria* and *hysterical* come from the Greek *hustera*, meaning *womb* or *of the womb*. Our wombs are the sacred gateway to infinite Source energy; being "hysterical" should mean being highly creative, attuned, powerful, and connected to our pleasure. But it has come to mean *crazy* or *out of control*, with hysteria even once being a diagnosis of mental illness in women.

✻ *Vagina*. *Vagina*, meaning *sheath for a sword*, was recorded as the medical term for a woman's genitals during the height of the witch burnings, in the 1500s to 1600s. Listen, my pussy is not available for violence—only magik, love, and reverence. She is a cosmic cauldron, a pleasure portal, but *never* the home of a weapon. I believe the word *vagina* has played a more significant role in our rape culture than we've ever acknowledged.

✻ *Mafia*. The first recorded use of the word *Mafia* was in 1668 Sicilian witch trials. It referred to "bold and ambitious" women who had been through rites of initiation. That's right, witches! *Ma, mama, madre,* as in almost every language, means *mother*. *Daughter* in Italian is *figlia*, pronounced *filia*. The *I* nearly silent, trickling down, and ma-*fia* were daughters of the Great Mother, the Goddess. Of course, some of the most violent men on the planet would take a powerful not-to-be-fucked-with female title for themselves.

✻ *Lunatic*. From *luna*, meaning *moon*. Witches have always enjoyed embracing their wildness beneath Her fullness. The easiest state to access our IntuWitchin! But today, to be branded a "lunatic" is to be considered raving mad. For anybody who values the gifts of venturing into our own wild unknowns, we should all be bathing beneath the moonlight more often.

··········· ✳ JOURNAL PROMPTS ✳ ···········

Here are some writing prompts to clarify how the Witch Wound shows up in your life. This is the trailhead on the map to your healing.

Can you feel any blocks or resistance inside you?

Where is your life most impacted by them?

How do you make decisions based on fear or another's opinion?

How do you shrink to keep yourself safe or be accepted?

What are you afraid to say?

How do you lie to fit in?

How do you lose yourself in partnership? Do you people-please by sacrificing yourself? Do you perhaps allow another's desires or perspective to determine who or how you should be?

Where do you self sabotage most often? How is your ego trying to keep you safe?

··········· ✳ ···········

✳ *Practice* — Tend to Your Inner Witch

In order to energetically and spiritually move through the Witch Wound, try creating a safe and sacred space for yourself to feel into your own magik, tending to your inner witch. Build an altar within you to physically connect with your Intu-Witchin.

Considering the answers to any of the journal prompts above, does your body most need vocal, physical, sexual, or creative expression to start moving past this wound?

This can be a morning movement practice or solo dance party, a rage ritual out in the woods, or just fully expressing yourself—letting your voice be heard by saying all the things you've been holding back. Dance like nobody's watching, shout like no one is listening (because they aren't), or connect with your sexual energy in a way you've never allowed yourself to before. Just give yourself permission to embody any aspect of your personal flavor of witchery and see what arises.

As with any practice that can bring up strong emotions, remember to create safety in your space, have a resource you can rely on if it gets to be too much, and let yourself be held in the arms of the Goddess no matter what.

Chapter 3

Everything Is Information, Everything Is Divination

Divine is one of my absolute favorite words. Its origin comes from *heavenly, to shine, a sorcerer, to be of God, a seer.* As a noun it refers to *God/Goddess*, the forces of creation, and the eternal nature of our Universal reality. As a verb, from *to make out by supernatural insight*, it describes the art of interpretation and finding meaning, diving deep into the symbolic nature of the material realm. As an adjective, it is the elements of life that harken to heavenly enjoyment.

The fact we use the same word for *God* as we do for *Intu-Witchin* has Divine significance. Working with your Intu-Witchin is activating the Divine in you and divining every circumstance in your life.

There are many methods of divination. It all began with Augury, found in African, Celtic, Western, and South American spiritual and mystical traditions, which involves divining messages from the movement or patterns of the Natural world, like clouds, water, or animals, specifically birds. Practices such as astrology, tarot, numerology, and color magik all offer tools to help us communicate with our surroundings for taking aligned action.

I know some of you are thinking, *Well, I* don't *like the word* Divine.

For anybody who grew up with religious trauma, *Divine* connotations can be mostly the opposite. The Witch Wound concerning magik is that it is just another dogmatic, disciplinary, and restrictive religion. I totally get it. My intention is for you to find your own relationship with the Divine so you never need a middleman to help you connect to it. You can see the Divine in the eyes of loved ones, trees in your yard, birdsong, and the quiet moments in between. This chapter will show you how Divine your life is.

LIKE *a* PRAYER

From here on, you get to discover your own personal relationship to God. This is a huge part of healing the Witch Wound. Regardless of your previous views on or experiences with God(dess), Great Spirit, Creator, Nature, or Universal life force energy, the messenger of IntuWitchin interfaces with it however is most impactful and enjoyable for you.

Most of us only reached for this energy in need—praying for help, palms clasped, looking up toward the sky, pleading: "Oh, God, please help me! I'm sorry I never pray, but if you get me out of this, I swear I'll do anything." If you can talk to God(dess) daily, you are indubitably held in those situations!

Enter the "divination" of IntuWitchin, the constant conversation, always seeking and listening for messages from the Divine, creating a reciprocal, symbiotic relationship with Spirit. In my experience, this is all God(dess) wants from us.

The voice of the Allness is IntuWitchin speaking to us in a way we can actually understand—something I discovered in my final year of college. That same model boyfriend was a religious hypocrite: he was traumatized and abusive, a liar and cheater, but a self-proclaimed "good Christian boy." My heart still bears scars from cruel things he said and did. But despite his behavior, I have gratitude for him. He was the one who brought me back to California and, ultimately, to myself. Without much of a masculine role model in his life, he had a strong relationship to the Heavenly Father. Whenever he needed guidance, he would say, "I have to go talk to God." He'd close the door and have one-sided "conversations with God." I found myself in the other room wondering, "Who is he talking to?!" I knew people prayed, but I'd never heard a dialogue like being on the phone.

One day, right before graduation, I was feeling utterly dejected. I had alienated all my friends during our relationship and become one of those women I always pitied, sticking around with some asshole. Head down, I stared at the broken concrete beneath my feet, strolling past the brownstones of NYC's East Village, feeling like all hope was lost. Had I ruined my life already? In that moment, I figured maybe, just maybe, I was worthy of redemption, despite the horrible choices that had gotten me into this mess. I dragged my eyes to the sky with trepidation, glancing to make sure no one would hear me, and whispered, "Uh, God?"

Immediately, a gust of wind whipped through the trees, rustling their branches and sweeping down through my hair. Sunlight glimmered through the leaves shining on my face like a warm caress; the response was visceral. My body was over-whelmed with an all-encompassing ardor that seemed to say, "Yes? I'm right here. I'm always here. I've always been here. I'm everything, everywhere, all around you."

Awe and wonder pulsed throughout every cell; I felt alive for the first time since childhood. There was hope! There was an infinite Universe of possibilities just waiting for me to see them. And I, too, was worthy of a relationship with this infinite life force animating me and every living thing around me. I could receive its guidance and feel held in its unconditionally loving embrace. Life was still worth living. I was walking on air the rest of the day.

My first conversation with God shifted my entire trajectory—but not overnight. I wish I could say I went home, left the guy, and hopped onto the path of my purpose. I didn't.

We moved to LA together, remember? My journey took many twists and turns before I found myself and my mission, until finally, I could see, feel, and hear God all around me, supporting me every step of the way.

FOLLOWING *the* SIGNS

When we are immersed in the world of God(dess)'s creation versus the man-made concrete jungles most of us call home, it's a lot easier to feel our direct line to the Divine.

Sure, you can read signs on buildings, resonate with your yoga teacher's quote at the end of class, or get messages from bumper stickers and chalkboards in front of restaurants—the Universe absolutely communicates in these ways. However, when we're near trees, plants, oceans, and animals, there is no middleman; nothing between you and the source of that directive. The language itself is less about words and much more like lyrical illustrative poetry. And since God(dess) also made us humans, the Divine is communicating to us through all our experiences—the beautiful, the bad, and the ugly. So bless them: *bless* our pain, *bless* our shadows. They are the Divine in disguise. Events that occur in our lives are signs too. Remember the bathtub?

It would be easy if we were able to read the signs surrounding us without past pain and programming blurring our (psychic) vision. But for us, the art of Divination is a mystery we get to solve, guiding our healing based on how we react to a sign, symbol, or situation. The Universe creates instances that elicit intense emotional responses to get our attention. When you're triggered or upset, there is work to do on the issue. Your reaction is the impetus of the navigation system guiding you toward what's asking to be transformed or held in your psyche.

As you learn how your IntuWitchin communicates with you, do your best to remain unattached to these experiences.

They are not a personal attack on you; they're there to help you strengthen your resolve. Over time you'll discover that facing your wounds head-on lessens their charge and takes back any power they had over you.

I'll leave you with one final thing. You know I love spelling and the origins of words because they are powerful signs in and of themselves. Letters are symbols humans created to manifest our thoughts in the world. I discovered just how powerful they can be a year or so into my journey of self-discovery, when I decided to try an experiment.

A LETTER *from* MY HIGHER SELF

Inspired by a friend who swore by stream-of-consciousness writing, I started meditating for 15 minutes each morning to an "Access Your Higher Self Binaural Beats" YouTube video and then immediately wrote a "Higher Self letter." I did this every day for a year. This period became one of the most rapidly transformational of my life. Not because of the letter itself but because the days I actually *followed* the guidance I received changed my whole world. I've since shared the practice with thousands of people with outstanding results. I highly suggest you try it.

As you sit down to write each morning, state the following invocation either out loud or as the opening line: "I call upon my Highest Self to write to me, through me, anything I am meant to receive in this moment." You can get more specific about what you're looking for guidance on or who you're asking (e.g., Mother Earth, Athena, Mountain Spirits, and so on). Then take a deep breath, tune in to the vibration of your Higher Self, notice how contact with it feels, and let yourself write.

In this way, each day you will receive a letter from your IntuWitchin. I got guidance about how to show up, where to go, what to do, and every time I adhered, the most magikal things would happen.

I would meet exactly the right person to support me with something I needed. I'd receive a beautiful gift. I'd run into someone I missed who I'd been thinking about the day before. Each time I *listened* to the guidance I received in these letters, I was rewarded. The more I took action on what my Intu-Witchin shared with me, the stronger it got and the better my life became as it learned to trust me. I went from being broke and homeless to living a life abundant in community, wealth, friendship, joy, and fun.

WHAT DOES IT ALL MEAN?

How do you know what your IntuWitchin is actually saying to you? Until you've really gotten intimate with it, it can be challenging to grasp what your IntuWitchin is trying to tell you. It won't be as cut-and-dried as "Go there. Say this. Do that." The messages show up in different ways at different times for different people; our IntuWitchin relies on us to decipher the meaning in any given situation.

See if you can divine the meaning from this story:

Before my partner and I lived together, we were leaving his place the day before my birthday when I noticed a little green bag next to his backpack. I wondered what it was, felt an inkling to mention it, but figured he'd see it. The following morning, he was frantically searching through my room and closet. I always wake up before him, so I knew something was wrong.

"I can't find your present!" he said exasperatedly.

"What's it look like?"

"It's in a pretty green pouch."

I hesitated. "I saw it on your couch yesterday, next to your backpack. Did you grab it?"

Crestfallen, he deflated like a popped balloon. He'd forgotten my gift on our first birthday together and was so disappointed in himself for not having everything perfectly organized.

The next day at my birthday party, my friends placed love notes into a little bowl for me to read later. Before I went out the following morning, I looked at the bowl but didn't move it from my coffee table. When the housekeeper came to clean up later, I found all my love notes and affirmations in the trash.

The meaning I divined from this?

Birthdays are the sun (which represents our ability to shine and be powerfully regenerative forces on Earth), returning to where it was when you were born. Naturally, we all enjoy celebration during this time.

Gifts represent a physical exchange of love or appreciation. In general, the masculine is the giving energy (yang), while the feminine is the receptive energy (yin). Meanwhile, green is the color of abundance and the heart chakra.

Somehow I had blocked my ability to receive love and gifts on my birthday that year.

It's a clear message that helped me realize how many walls I had constructed and how closed-off I was even to people who truly cared for me. I am still working to dismantle these walls, and part of that was making sure my next birthday went differently. I had a magician, and instead of leaving notes, my friends told me all their favorite things about me to my face. Then we sang and danced and made candles together. It was just what I wanted!

Take a moment to think about a recent sticky situation in your life and look at all the different elements present. What greater significance was at play? How, where, and with whom did it occur? Can you see deeper meaning from the Universe?

DIVINATION TOOLS

As mentioned, many practices have been developed through the ages to help humans interpret messages from the Divine. Three of the most accessible (and fun!) divination tools are astrology, tarot, and numerology, and the popularity of these practices today is a sign of just how many people crave a deeper connection to IntuWitchin. There's tons of information about how to use them, but I like to make my own meanings out of what the stars and cards show me with my IntuWitchin.

✢ **Astrology.** We'll be digging into astrology (one of my favorite IntuWitchin practices) in another chapter, but let me give you a primer for using it in divination. Personally, I don't subscribe to the fatalistic fortune-telling type. Rather than getting overwhelmed with the complex and intricate science of transiting and conjunct planets, I use my IntuWitchin to see what the archetypal energy of each zodiac sign might be asking of me.

✢ **Tarot.** This complex system involves imagery, metaphor, and archetypes coming alive with a heavy dose of IntuWitchin in our interpretations. When I feel lost about a choice I need to make, I always reach for the cards. Every color, image, and symbol on a tarot card can contain substantial information. I work primarily with what the art represents for me to decode what's disguised in the deck.

I knock three times on a deck, the way you would when visiting someone's home, to ask permission for working with it. I shuffle the cards while thinking about my inquiry—if a card falls out while shuffling, I notice what I was thinking when it emerged. Then I hover my left hand (the "receptive" side) over the cards and wait until I feel a little tingle. I usually experience it in my palm, but sometimes it's in one of my fingers, and I'll use that finger to pull the card.

I try to keep my questions open-ended, like, "What do I need to learn/embody in order to receive this in my life?" "What needs to be released, healed, or let go of for me to be in alignment with this goal?" If I have a tough choice to make, I choose one card for each option.

To get familiar with how your IntuWitchin interacts with the cards, practice, practice, practice. Do readings for yourself, friends, and family. Get to know what the symbols mean and represent to *you*. What does a triangle, star, the moon, or particular animal mean? How you interpret these symbols is *allowed* to change over time. The more you learn and connect to your IntuWitchin, the more easily you will be able to feel what each color, shape, symbol, animal, or archetype has to say to you. Developing your relationship to imagery (a picture is worth a thousand words, after all) will allow you to divine how the cards are asking you to grow or go deeper.

⁂ **Numerology.** Like letters, numbers are a language of their own and are also symbols of Divination. Nicomachus of Gerasa, a Greek philosopher, said, "[Numbers are] immaterial, eternal, and without end, and it is their nature to persist ever the same and unchanging, abiding by their own essential being, and each one of them is called real in the proper sense, but things in the Natural world which are involved in birth and destruction, growth and diminution are seen to vary continually and while they are called real things, they are not actually real by their own nature for they do not abide for even the shortest moment in the same condition but are always passing over in all sorts of changes." In other words, numbers have an energy and their progression tells a story, just like the zodiac. Arithmancy—the special class Hermione takes in *Harry Potter*—is an ancient form of Gematria, the assignment of numerological value to letters, secretly encoding messages in words. Start connecting with numerology by learning your life path number. This number represents who we are archetypally, similar to your zodiac sign. In my case they're the same: my life path is 3, and I am also a Gemini, the third astrological sign. Implying a heavy dose of creative expression (what both 3s and Gemini embody).

Your life path number comes from adding all the digits of your birth date together. For example, if your birthday is July 21, 1994, it breaks down to $7 + 2 + 1 + 1 + 9 + 9 + 4 = 33$. Keep adding until you get a single digit: $3 + 3$ means your life path number is 6.

Each digit from 0 to 9 has significance that tells a story of Divine creation the same way fairy tales and myths describe our inner realms. The void is the birthplace of life and matter (from the Latin for *mother*), and we classify 0 as the beginning, before bursting forth into the Oneness of existence. If you look into the work of someone like Robert Edward Grant, it is blatantly obvious numbers are a complex dialect most of us have forgotten to speak. If each number carries its own archetypal energy, like the expression of their quantifiable soul—especially numbers that keep showing up—we can easily receive the messages they contain for us.

Repeating (or "angel") numbers are often your IntuWitchin communicating to you. Patterns such as 333 or 11:11 are another way God(dess) requests our attention. Perhaps you keep seeing 222 when you need support or guidance, 555 leads you to the right people and opportunities, or following 444 always results in magikal rewards from the Universe. When angel numbers appear, notice what you were thinking about, how you're feeling, and what's occurring around you, divining your own meaning for each series of numbers.

Here are the basics:

❶   The ineffable all, the spark, the visionary. Our transformation into existence, when nothing becomes something. One is the first Universal Law, our divinity, and unity with everything in the Universe. The willingness to be bold, blaze a new trail, start a movement, or go against herd mentality. One is the confidence, inspiration, and motivation required to take the first step, which can be a little wobbly and requires a leap of faith. *If you are a Life Path 1, ask yourself: "Am I living a visionary life?" "What step will bring my visions to fruition?" "Do I feel confident taking that leap of faith into the unknown or in the direction of my destiny? If not, what can I do to heal the fears or limiting beliefs that have kept me from becoming who I am meant to be?"*

❷ The solid balance when both feet touch the ground but also the split from oneness. Two can be a supportive number, the energy of equilibrium, understanding the reflective nature of reality. Two finds stability when firmly planted, trusting in the Earth beneath, but also represents individuation, as it is in the first separation from the All that an individual becomes two, and can signify conflict when imbalanced. *Life Path 2, ask yourself: "How balanced do I feel in my masculine and feminine expression, between my work and play?" "Do I feel like I'm standing firmly on the solid foundation of my life? Like I can trust my body and the Earth?" "How connected do I feel to the world around me?" "Am I balanced in my capacity to both give and receive support?"*

❸ The spirit and synergy—we are greater than the sum of our parts, as in 1 + 1 = 3. Mind, body, and spirit coming together as a unified being. Like the cosmic child born from two parents, the original duality, 3 is their fruit or creation. It is the relationship between others that becomes its own entity. The cycles of life, death, and rebirth and three phases of femininity: maiden, mother, matron. Three is creation via communication—weaving destiny through words (in connection with others)—carrying our unique, individual weirdness. *Life Path 3, ask yourself: "How harmoniously do my mind, body, and spirit function together?" "What am I here to create or share?" "How safe do I feel expressing myself, my desires, needs, boundaries, and dreams?" "Do the words I speak or the stories I tell myself and others align with who I want to be?"*

❹ The four elements are both literally and figuratively the building blocks of creation. Four doubles the energy of 2. It is the strong, solid legs of a table, shape of a square, and essential foundations of the world around us. Four seasons, moon phases, directions—our stability and fundamentals. Four ensures everything is organized and taken care of. *Life Path 4, ask yourself: "What is my relationship to structure?" "How connected do I feel to* *the elements? To the fundamental building blocks of creation?" "How do I manage myself, my life, work, and relationships to others?" "Do I give myself permission to cycle through my inner seasons and the elements, action of fire, and flow of water?"*

❺ The fifth element—vibration, essence itself—5 represents our soul, the ethereal, ineffable spark that animates each of us uniquely. The addition of Spirit brings life to Earthly creation, cementing the truth that this is also the realm of the Divine. Five speaks to our five senses, fingers, and toes, as well as that which comes from beyond the human world. Five represents energy honed into perfection or angelic resonance. *Life Path 5, ask yourself: "How is my life guided by and connected to my unique spirit?" "What is my relationship to the spiritual realms?" "How deeply connected to my senses and sensual Nature am I? What could I do to enhance my connection to them?"*

❻ The witchy number associated with our sixth sense, the sixth chakra of visionary capacity and imagination invites us to embody our fantasies, bring our imagination to fruition, and honor our visual creativity aesthetically with design or the arts. The original significance of the six-pointed star, or hexagram, was the alchemical union of masculine and feminine, the ascending and descending triangles, hence its link to the occult and fascination with all that resides beyond the veil. *Life Path 6, ask yourself: "How active is my sixth sense?" "Am I ready to expand my visionary capacity or psychic gifts?" "How much do I let my imagination run wild? Do I feel capable of bringing these dreams and visions to life?" "What occult or spiritual lineage might help me amplify these powers?"*

❼ The number of the Mystic and mystical arts, the union of four elements and synergy of Spirit's life, death, and rebirth cycles, 7 is linked to the crown chakra, uniting our human body to the cosmos. Seven has been sacred in many ancient traditions—such as why we have seven days named for the seven major planets. *Life Path 7, ask yourself:*

"What are the mystical experiences I've had in my life? How have I let them guide or transform me?" "What spiritual lineages or practices ignite my interest and inspire me most?" "What is my relationship to the Great Spirit, God/Goddess?" "If I look at my life in seven-year cycles, what has shifted and changed throughout them?" "How can I express my mysticism more in life?"

❽ The number of eternity, infinite abundance, and interconnectedness of all things. The figure 8 can be viewed as two circles on top of each other or two blossoms facing out and up, kissing each other's petals. On its side, 8 is an infinity symbol. The only number without any edges, it is entirely self-sustaining and represents our ability to generate everything we need. Throughout most cultures 8 is considered prosperous, benevolent, and lucky. *Life Path 8, ask yourself: "How do I define abundance? What is my relationship with it?" "Do I limit abundance to the singular financial expression or the true nature of infinite resources?" "How connected do I feel to the world and life blossoming around me?"*

❾ The completion of the cycle, the result of spiritual growth and the arc of this hero's journey, 9 is both the number of death and rebirth. It can represent the collective, coming together, or the celebration of a group accomplishment. Nine often asks us to be of service by working for the benefit of all beings. *Life Path 9, ask yourself: "How do I come together in collaboration with others?" "How has the cycle of death and rebirth flowed through my life?" "How do I show up for my community?" "What is my relationship to leadership in my friendships, family, work, partnerships, and life in general?"*

❿ As noted, 10 brings us back to the energy of 1, but it also represents the beginning of a new cycle. After the completion of 9, 10 begins again, letting 1 take the lead. It is a number of forward motion, still confident but with 0 bringing the emptiness, openness, and uncertainty of/for the next chapter. Ten was worshipped by many ancient mathematicians for exactly this reason.

If what I've shared about your Life Path Number doesn't resonate with you, Divine your own meaning! The key to interpreting these messages is always the same: What does that number mean to you? It's about what you experience when you feel into the energy of any sign or symbol. Nothing you find on Google, or my interpretations offered above, can override your own personal significance. How does it show up for you? Even the energy itself is less important than what your IntuWitchin says about the message it's trying to share. Notice your surroundings and bring attention to your inner world, and the meaning will reveal itself.

COLOR MAGIK

One of the most fundamental basics for divining your life is often left out of the discussion: color. Even though color informs our entire visual reality and can evoke powerful juxtapositions to our IntuWitchin, color magik is rarely considered.

Rainbows are pure awe-inspiring magik. The spectrum mirrored by our chakra system contains so much information for us. As such, everything from the clothes you wear and the color of your car to how you paint your nails can have magikal significance—if you choose color consciously. If you want to embody more of a particular energy, try wearing that color more often and see what happens!

One of my favorite ways to use color magik is in how I furnish my home. I called in my next levels of business and financial abundance by making deep emerald green and gold my base colors, then love and partnership by bringing rich ruby red and gem-toned accents in with pillows, curtains, and decor. These colors represent feeling wholeness and fulfillment for me through my deep connection to Nature, Earth, and sky.

Those of you who have seen my YouTube channel will be familiar with my green set and globe chair—a color that holds amazing synchronicity for me. While I was decorating, I picked up a crystal book and opened it to the page describing moss agate, a stone of connection to Mother Earth, deep creativity, new beginnings, and bringing prosperity to land. The next day I took the cushion of my chair in to have paint matched to it: Of course, I didn't need a custom one. It was the same as a color called moss agate. Perfect.

As always, each color's meaning will be unique to you, because even the chakra system's energetic association with the elements can oppose common sense. We think of water as blue, but the water element is held in the sexual organs of our sacral chakra, which is represented by the color orange. The throat chakra, associated with vibration and sound—which we think of as colorless—is actually represented by the color blue. With this in mind, connect with each color's archetypal energy to help you divine the message when it shows up in your life. Here are some general descriptions for color magik:

❁ **RED.** Red is power. The color of the root chakra's stability, foundation, and Earth element. The root rules basic survival needs and is the *foundation* for material abundance.

Red is also the color of blood—our life force. We associate red with passion, fire, motivation, and sex. Being called to paint a bedroom red suggests you are ready to explore your sexuality and ignite the fire of desire. Donning red for an important meeting or interview has also been proven to make people feel more confident. Matadors use red capes to torment bulls, while we "see red" when our blood is boiling in anger.

What does red mean to you? The redwood trees I grew up in make red the most rooted, primal color to me. But if you come from a tropical place, where red is fruits and flowers, perhaps it signifies "blossoming" to you.

When you see red, ask: "How powerful do I feel right now in my everyday life?" "Do I feel connected to the Earth? To my genitals?"

"What have I allowed to take power from me it's time to reclaim?"
"How safe and stable do I feel in my reality? In myself?"

✸ **ORANGE.** Orange is the spark of creativity, our sacral chakra, representing our capacity for manifestation and the kindling of new souls and projects being born. I like to think of the glowing orange surface of this womb water as it reflects during sunset or a sweet juicy peach on a summer afternoon.

Orange is associated with warmth and pleasure, sexual or otherwise, and happiness in general. Studies on color therapy show that orange makes us feel warm in a nourishing, cozy, welcoming, and inviting way. Being drawn to orange items of clothing could mean you are ready to allow yourself to be more joyful, ignite the flames of your creative passion, or bring a project to life.

For me, orange holds the emotional charge of bursting with joy, a zest for life. What is orange to you? How does it make you feel? When you see something orange, what comes alive in your body? For example, if your grandmother liked to make orange cake, then the taste, scent, flavor, and image of an orange could feel like she is speaking to you.

When you see orange, ask: "How am I relating to my sensuality and sexuality right now?" "How passionate do I feel about my life, my relationships, my work, myself, and how I show up in general?" "How comfortable do I feel experiencing emotions?" "Do I allow myself to feel the joy in my life?"

✸ **YELLOW.** Yellow is confidence. Representing the solar plexus chakra, yellow signifies our motivation, how we shine, and are driven forward, and how empowered we are, or not.

Yellow is the golden light of the sun, the dancing flames of fire, and relates to how we take action on a daily basis. In astrology, the sun represents our personality, our outward-facing energy, how we radiate our essence beyond ourselves. Yellow is generally thought of as a fun, happy color. Studies show yellow makes people feel joyful and hopeful. Many road signs communicate to us in yellow to help dictate our actions. Picking a yellow journal or painting a wall could support you beaming your light even brighter.

For me, yellow is the sweetness of honey, happy flowers, mornings when you jump out of bed ready to greet the day, our willingness or capacity to shine, and playful silliness. What does it mean to you? Is it brass instruments and jazz? Autumn leaves first changing? Excitement and exhilaration? Motivation to rise and the passion for your power?

When you see yellow, ask: "How am I shining (or not) right now?" "What is my relationship to my personal power?" "Am I taking aligned and inspired action in the direction of my dreams, desires, and goals?" "Do I feel worthy of laughter, silliness, and play?" "What would the most powerful version of myself look/ act/feel like, and how can I take the necessary steps to become that person?" "What is my level of motivation?"

�֍ **GREEN.** Green is abundance and harmony of the Natural world. My personal favorite, it is the color of the heart chakra and represents the beauty of the great green Earth.

This is why our money is green; green represents the lush, vibrant bounty of our food, forests, jungles, river valleys, and meadows. The color of Nature is profoundly healing, calming, and soothing. Spending time in green spaces has been shown to have long-lasting positive effects on brain matter, and wearing green-lensed glasses can even reduce chronic pain and ease anxiety. Being called to Nature likely means you are ready for more health, vibrancy, and aliveness. The heart chakra is represented by the air in our lungs and is reminiscent to me of love. Like air, and the abundance of Nature, love is all around us, but we build walls and imaginary borders, conditions to our love—this is mine vs. yours—when love is meant to be free, all-encompassing, and unconditional like the breath of life.

How does green make you feel? Green is my teacher since my wisdom comes from Mother Nature Herself. Perhaps green is grounded, Earthy energy, a healthy body from your favorite foods, vibrant aliveness, the flow of rivers, or true abundance.

When you see green, ask: "How connected to the Earth am I?"
"Are my actions in alignment with Her or am I consuming harm-
fully?" "What does abundance mean to me? How do I embody that
energy (or not)?" "How does my heart feel? What does it believe
about love, worthiness, or who I am? Is it open or closed to love?"

✥ **BLUE.** Blue is expression. The color of the fifth, or throat, chakra, representing the fifth element of sound and vibration.

Blue speaks (literally!) to our communication, genius, and how we share with the world. Blue is the sky and ocean, expansive and vast, like the possibilities we can speak into motion when we choose words with care and intention. Blue is the second most peaceful color but can also represent a forlorn emotional state. If you want to communicate a message of tranquility, wear something blue. When you feel this way on the inside, you will also project this vibration out into the world around you.

For me, blue is the color of water, reminding me to go with the flow, creating calm and serenity in my mind. Perhaps for you it is peace, a higher vision of the sky, or the power of the ocean.

When you see blue, ask: "Does my presence promote well-
being within me and all around me or not? Can I use it to do so?"
"Is the flow of my expression blocked or clear?" "Can I help heal
others, the planet, myself, my connection, or lack thereof, to Her?"
"Is my expression peaceful or not?"

✥ **PURPLE.** Purple is insight. It represents the third-eye chakra, has long been associated with royalty, sits at the end of the rainbow, and acts as a bridge between the material and spiritual realms. Purple combines red and blue, grounded connection to the Earth, with the high vibration of our expression.

The third-eye chakra represents our vision—not in terms of how we literally see but our *vision*ary capacity. It speaks to dreams, imagination, and the supernatural gifts and abilities we are all born with which are ours to cultivate. Purple can give us the courage to express our highest truth and follow our IntuWitchin, leading our lives the way we desire. We're all born with innate psychic gifts, and when we're drawn to purple, our physical body is ready to merge with our spiritual body, asking us to look at a situation using our mind's eye, our spiritual eye.

For me, purple is regal and raw like my berry-stained fingertips in summer. I think of the violet flame's powerful healing rays. Perhaps for you it's decadent, blossoming, a favorite family member, or your own royalty.

When you see purple, ask: "How can I develop a deeper relationship to spiritual power?" "How willing am I to dream big, have visionary ideas, and express them while remaining grounded?" "What challenge might life be asking me to take on—requiring courage I've been shying away from?" "How can I connect more deeply to my psychic and intuitive abilities and communicate from that confident knowing?"

✳ **WHITE.** White is the color of clarity and cosmic connection. It is associated with the crown chakra, representing the light that pours down on us from the heavens and the sun.

White is our union with the Divine, cascading onto and into us. Even though we perceive the sun as yellowish, especially at golden hour, it is actually white. It is often what people are requested to wear in spiritual ceremonies—free from the "material" connotations of the other colors, white offers a clear channel as the "absence" of color. A word on "purity" (associated with white): just because you like to get freaky does *not* mean you are impure. Purity is about the intentions of your heart and mind, the way you treat yourself and others, the impact you have on the world. When you're truly following your Intu-Witchin, all your actions will be pure.

I see white as inviting, a clean slate, a fresh perspective, the magik of freshly fallen snow. For others, the interpretations might be openness, innocence, the light of oneness, divinity, or connection to Source.

When you see white, ask: "How does white make me feel?" "Is my connection to the Divine strong and clear or murky and confused?" "How 'pure' are my intentions in the situation I'm facing?" "What thoughts, beliefs, and stories could I 'clear away,' allowing more kindness for myself and others?"

✲ **BLACK.** Black is the void, emptiness brimming with promise, nothingness, the eternal night and fertile soil in which seeds are planted. Black is where we all come from and where we will return. Black is the absence of light, the sky glistening with stars, and the womb.

The color black gets a bad rap and is often associated with negativity, even evil. But we must know our shadows so we can be guided back to the light. If we didn't know where we were falling short or where we were hurting, we wouldn't know how or what to heal. Black is the color of many a witchy robe, representing the magikal potential of venturing into the dark. For me, black is about eternal possibility, the creativity of womb energy, and potent growth through wisdom. We learn the most from having to find our way in the dark.

Other interpretations might be the depths of inky blackness in our eyes (the windows to our soul), getting lost in endlessness, an invitation to look at our shadows, a way to heal a painful belief we've been avoiding, or how to move through sticky, stuck energy.

When you see black, ask: "What are the stories I find myself telling about what the color black means?" "Have I been afraid of it, convinced it is truly the darkness rather than potential?" "When I wear black, how do I feel?" "What is my relationship to my shadow side, my darkness?" "What possibilities are waiting in the womb within me?"

I'll leave the colors in between up to you. Feel into the middle ground of turquoise (a marriage between green and blue), magenta (red and purple), and pink (red and white), subtle shades amalgamating two or more frequencies. What do they mean to you?

The most important thing to remember is that *you* are your greatest divination tool. Because you are Divine—made of the same elements and minerals as this planet—you, your body, thoughts, mind, actions, interactions, and adventures are all parts of the Divination map. The Universal Creator speaks in a language so far beyond human comprehension, even setting the intention to master this vocabulary sets you apart from most. And, if nothing else, it makes life that much more meaningful, allowing you to play the human game in a more interactive and engaging way.

My hope is that this chapter reminds you that everything really is information for you, delivered directly from the Universe. The simplest correspondences can become incredibly impactful when we recognize how much significance they have for us—and then take action based on our IntuWitchin's communication. When you let yourself be guided and inspired by them, relating to your reality with a greater perspective, you can fully step into and claim your most magikal life.

To connect to each of the colors and divine their significance, simply close your eyes and let your inner vision fill with the color you want to delve into. What objects of that color do you see? How does it make you feel?

If you are making a big decision, see if a particular color presents itself for each of your options. What do each of those colors represent to you and how might they be communicating guidance for your choice?

You can do this with new people too. If they have their energy *color*ed with warning, maybe trusting them isn't the best idea. If they show up as the color your IntuWitchin uses to connect with you, perhaps this friendship is a Divine appointment and part of your karmic destiny.

Practice — *Divining Your Life*

How can you decipher the underlying meaning or invitation in an experience you've had recently?

Pay attention to details. Think about the elements, people, words, colors, or numbers involved, anything that might signal greater significance to you.

What do those aspects mean to you? Write down any that stand out first and see how they relate to the others.

When in doubt, ask your IntuWitchin for guidance.

If you're working through a particular challenge, how might this situation relate to what you'd like to overcome?

Practice — *Channeled Writing*

Many practices and traditions use stream-of-consciousness or automatic writing.

Begin by centering yourself and connecting to whatever it is you're calling in. Envision the energy of nature, if you're not already in it. Embody the frequency of the Goddess or your Higher Self, whatever you're seeking guidance from and for, if anything in particular.

"I call upon X (my Higher Self, Mother Nature, the dragons). Please write to me, through me, anything I am meant to receive in this moment."

If it doesn't come easily at first, just start with, "I don't know what to write. I can't feel or hear anything coming to me." Keep going and eventually the message will emerge. Try this practice every day for a week at first, either calling upon the same energy or different ones.

Chapter 4

Moon Magik and Divine Timing

The concept of Divine Timing is concurrently comforting and confronting. I've accepted the confounding nature of this idea living by a simple adage I've found true. I've shared it with hundreds of thousands of people who find solace in it, and I hope you will too.

If something is meant to be, there's nothing you can do to fuck it up. It's meant to be, so it will be. If something is not meant to be, there's nothing you can do to make it happen because it's just not meant to be.

If you are meant to be with someone, no matter how many times you break up and make up, you will *end up* together. If you're not, you won't. If this weren't the case, and you could make things happen that were not meant to be, then (1) the entire continuum of reality would likely collapse and (2) to do so, you'd have to be some kind of all-powerful, ultra-dimensional space-time-bending God(dess), not likely to be reading this book because you'd already know everything.

Trusting this aphorism can require tremendous patience—not one of my strongest virtues, but I have found it to be absolutely accurate. As much as we'd all love to snap our fingers and instantaneously manifest our desires, that just isn't possible.

Honestly, what would be the point of doing anything? We would have nothing to strive or hope for. Which is why trusting in Divine Timing can be such a gift, though often a frustrating one.

Our IntuWitchin is our greatest ally, reminding us never to lose hope when pursuing our dreams and desires. As long as we listen and take the actions it guides us to, we'll never be led astray, even if those actions might take us farther from something we "think" we want. The Universe has its plan for us. Either way, we know that when we put our order in with the cosmic waitress, it comes eventually, even if there's a fire in the kitchen or she gets a little delayed.

I had my future all mapped out by the age of five, which is when I first hit the streets of New York City. As my patent-leathered foot stepped out of the taxi, I said, "Mommy, I'm gonna live here when I grow up." Fast-forward and 10 days out of high school, I did.

By 21, my young adult life felt pretty far from how I'd originally envisioned it. My luxury apartment was 27 stories above the ground, surrounded by nine million other people. "Spending time outside" meant hanging out on our manicured roof deck among potted trees. My feet hadn't connected to the grounded energy of the Earth since my childhood, running wild on the rocky Lost Coast of Northern California.

I'd given up on the magik I felt connected to as a kid, letting life pass me by. I'd spent nearly every night in college dancing till dawn, making good grades simply because of my marvelous memory. After graduation I spent nights binging on Netflix and sleeping the days away. I had no purpose. I was fully removed from a connection to Nature or the rhythm of life.

Looking back, I could berate myself for all those "wasted" years. But Divine Timing means everything happens *when it happens* for a reason. Even months of precious time you might feel you have "lost" to depression or the distraction of a toxic relationship (like I have) can contain powerful teachings you only understand when looking back. No matter what happens, the moments we've "lost" or "wasted" are never truly so. Rather, they are often what encourage and inspire us to seek the fulfillment, growth, and appreciation, which make our lives worth living. My therapist helping me acknowledge my pain is what motivated me to find my magik. My yoga teacher, Ally Bogard, says even a millimeter of adjustment in the body is like steering a ship: if you shift one iota to the right, at the end of your journey, you've ended up somewhere else entirely.

Have you heard of the butterfly effect? It's not just a great Ashton Kutcher movie; it's part of chaos theory in physics. As small of a change as the flapping of a butterfly's wings can have a large impact on circumstances long-term—circumstances we can't possibly foresee in the moment. The fact that butterflies are also born as one thing and then metamorphize, reborn as entirely different creatures within the same lifespan, feels incredibly significant.

Sure, I could have used all those months on Netflix for something more productive. But then I might not be *here*, right where I am, writing this book for you, having become my own metaphorical butterfly. Without the years I spent feeling disassociated from my true self, I would not know how precious it is to live a magikal life, or embody the importance of listening to and acting on my IntuWitchin. I would not have spent my days since making up for lost time by saying yes to everything it asks of me.

Fighting tooth and nail against time, an ineffable Universal force, creates far more suffering and chaos than not having what we're waiting for. Have you ever had a moment where you were tired of anticipating something to happen and maybe even gave up on it? Then something else occurs, and that original desire comes back around, except now you understand why it didn't happen before? Or perhaps you've pushed up against the forces of time to make something happen and ultimately wished you'd waited to let things play out?

If the answer is yes, you already know our IntuWitchin will always let us know when it is time to wait or time to act—even if the reason isn't immediately clear. Our job is to make sure our channel to receive is open and available so we can hear it.

ASTRO MAGIK

Luckily, we have an ancient, scientific system to help us optimize our own energetic alignment with the greater cosmological forces. It reminds us that what we are experiencing is always part of a much bigger story. This system is astrology, the oldest science on Earth. As I work with my IntuWitchin to design optimal rituals for wielding my reality like a wand, I am continuously astounded by how supportive and validating astrology can be.

Astrology is a study of our relationship to the Nature of Divine Timing itself, helping us decode the swirling interplay of the cosmos. The energies of our closest planetary bodies can either help or hinder our progress in life. When we experience the withholding of something we desire, it's often the Goddess/Universe giving us an opportunity to learn something. We can make sense of it all by tapping into the energetic transits of the planets in our solar system. For example, Saturn's cycles remind us that growth requires time to integrate our lessons, encouraging us to cultivate deep, trusting patience. No matter what the outer circumstances appear to imply, Saturn helps us stick the course as we work toward the arrival of our desire. When we know how to work with them, all the celestial cycles can empower us with necessary tools to trust in the circle of life. This is the magik of both astrology and Moon Time Manifestation.

Once upon a time, I was skeptical of astrology. *Seventeen* magazine's blurbs about Gemini (my sun sign) never really resonated. I'd written it off. When I looked up, I gazed in awe only at New York City's skyscrapers, ignoring the moon and stars that were virtually invisible behind the bright lights of the city.

When I learned that our bodies contain the same percentage of water as the Earth, and Her waters are magnetized by the moon, I began to see the celestial sway on our species differently. Sleep, hormone function, and excretion, so many processes in our bodies respond to our circadian rhythm—the relationship and reaction to the sun and moon's cycles on a daily and monthly basis. Our menstruation cycles are magnetized by the moon. Without hormonal influence from birth control or too much artificial light, we bleed and ovulate with the new and full moons—we are so connected to the cosmos. It's all perfectly organized! If the moon is that powerful, and the sun literally fuels life on Earth, how could the other planets not have an influential role on us? My mind opened to astro wisdom, and the more I learn, the more it draws me in.

The archetypes of the astrological zodiac as represented by the 12 signs have been utilized to study human nature since at least 3000 B.C. Before artificial lights drowned out their twinkle, the stars themselves showed or told us what energies they carried. I experienced this myself once while staring in awe at the starry sky of Sedona, Arizona. A particularly brilliant sparkling star had me wondering what it was. I felt it tell me, "I am, we are, Sirius."

Hmm, doubt it . . ., I thought to myself.

But I checked my stargazing app, SkyView, and it was in fact Sirius. A few weeks later, another message came from an incandescent star as if trying to make itself known to me. Its energy was like open arms welcoming me into an embrace, radiating benevolence. "I *am* Jupiter." I felt expansive receiving its message.

I pulled out SkyView again: it *was* Jupiter, known as the great benefic planet of growth, good fortune, and generosity. The message from my IntuWitchin? Recognize the magik expanding within you. You can trust and rely on it; it won't steer you wrong. In that moment, the expansion of both my faith in myself and my appreciation of the strength of my inner voice was otherworldly.

I was hooked. I have since learned that reestablishing a personal relationship to the sun, moon, stars, and constellations of the zodiac can radically attune your IntuWitchin to the cosmic, Universal forces speaking to us in each moment.

The PRIMAL TRIAD: SUN, MOON, RISING

If you've never had a full astrology reading, I highly recommend it. You'll feel like someone has made a map of your mind and personality, down to specific dates when challenging experiences occurred in your life. You will receive insights about how to enhance your gifts and heal your shadows and get a lot of answers to the big questions like "What is my purpose?" or "Why do I do this to myself / am I like this?" My mind is blown by every reading I have because the IntuWitchin of each astrologer sees and points out different things.

The greatest activation of astrology for me was with a reflexologist who read my zodiac chart and the significance of my fingerprints while massaging my feet. How could I refuse? The designs and ripples on your skin form like rocks beneath waterfalls, from the waves of amniotic fluid in the womb. I know, right? That's how we get our fingerprints! As you can imagine, the experience was nothing short of magikal, and it validated so much about why I am the way I am. She looked at the whorls of my middle finger and said, "Scorpio Moon? That's your Sorceress Witch, as a Spiritual CEO."

I was still resistant to the word *witch* then and longed to actualize successful conscious entrepreneurship but had no idea how. My fingerprints knew who I was before I did.

You can easily calculate your astrological makeup by googling "free birth chart." Your birth chart will show you the sign representing each planet in your chart. In addition to your sun sign, you also have a Venus (relationships/money) sign, a Mercury (communication/intellect) sign, a Saturn (karma/discipline) sign, and many more.

For now, let's focus on the Primal Triad: your sun, moon, and rising signs. These are the foundational elements of your astrological composition everything orbits around.

The sun signifies the overall theme or mission of your life, how you function, and your outward personality. It also represents your willpower, connected to the solar plexus chakra, and how you deal with adversity. The shining sun gives us life, and this sign shows how you shine in yours.

The moon represents your emotional realm, heart and soul, spiritual nature, and sexuality. The moon rules the subconscious mind, what longs to be felt, and what drives us beneath our conscious awareness. Governed by water, our moon sign shows how we experience our emotions and how we nurture ourselves and others. The moon rules the tides and cycles within us.

The ascendant or rising is the constellation that was peaking over the horizon as you emerged into this world. The ascendent represents the deeper truth of your soul, beyond what you might think you're "supposed to" be. The greatest influence on your life, it acts as a map or blueprint of the lessons you are here to learn, leading you to self-actualization, attaining your desires, and becoming the best and truest version of yourself. It is literally how you rise and ascend (go figure).

SIGNS *of* INTUWITCHIN

Once you know your sun, moon, and rising, check out these insights into how your IntuWitchin speaks to you. There are so many different opinions and methodologies with astrology. I'm sharing what has worked for and resonated with me, but remember, there's no formula like your own.

You can use the questions below as journal prompts or invitations for how to create your own rituals when the moon is in that sign.

ARIES

The Warrior, the Hero,
Standing for What's Right
Element: Fire
Planetary Ruler: Mars

The first sign of the zodiac is concerned with individuality and leading from a place of personal power, leaving logistics and reason to the earthier signs. New paths require the Aries energy of a naively confident young person who feels invincible in the face of any challenge or the trailblazer who stops at nothing to accomplish their aim. Aries's willingness to take initiative is unparalleled; the stubborn ram faces any adversity head-on, literally.

Aries sun, moon, or rising: The fastest way to strengthen your IntuWitchin is through action upon its suggestions. Get your blood pumping through strenuous physical activity, igniting IntuWitchin's spark. Wearing red or other fiery colors might be activating for you, or seeing someone else in red might be a message for you, urging you to take action in your own life. Working with flame in candle magik is a great way to amplify your manifestations.

In ritual: Aries's warrior energy means doing battle with the forces that have tried to keep you down or from actualizing your achievements. How can you use the fire element to face your inner and outer adversaries, focus on transformation, and get motivated?

TAURUS

The Empress, the Sensualist, the Beauty
and Manifestation of Nature
Element: Earth
Planetary Ruler: Venus

Taurus rules abundance in all material forms (finances, food, relationships, pleasure), beauty, love, and luxury. The Earthiest sign is the most powerfully bolstered by a connection to Mother Nature. Taurus shows how we appreciate and express our natural gifts. She represents personal preferences and aesthetics, our tastes in both art and gastronomy. In addition to financial wealth, Taurus speaks to what we value most. She invites us to let reflect those values in how we treat the abundance of Nature, what comfort and beauty are to us, and our connection to the majesty of our planet.

Taurus sun, moon, or rising: There is nothing better for a Taurus than a day out in Nature. You can hear yourself more clearly in a quiet, wild place. Taurus can get caught up in the glamor of material things, but it is Mother Earth and the Goddess who will always guide you. Any sensual embodiment practices, meditations for listening to your physical vessel, and herbal/plant magik will be wonderful for you.

In ritual: Taurus the Empress wants you to embody your True Nature *through* Nature. While sensual comfort and abundant beauty can be optimal conditions for activating your IntuWitchin, be unafraid of getting your hands, and everything else, dirty. What do you truly value in life? How can you plant the seeds for cultivating more of your own True Nature to blossom? How can you step more into your Divine Feminine Leadership and Creation? What patterns have made you feel unworthy of it?

GEMINI

*The Storyteller, the Shape-Shifter,
the Keeper of Memory*
Element: Air
Planetary Ruler: Mercury

Gemini governs intellect, communication, and the capacity to receive and reciprocate messages and reflections. Ideas and information echo back from the world around us, mirroring what is most important for us to see. The commonly referred to "two-faced" nature of Gemini is that our minds can work for us, or against us, bring us to heaven or hell, depending on how powerful we allow them to be over us. The most adaptable, youthful, and curious of the signs, Gemini communes with the cyclic, cosmic rhythm, showing how we utilize quick wit and thinking to assimilate our lessons through our voice and expression.

Gemini sun, moon, or rising: Gemini minds move so fast and are so multifaceted that they can talk themselves in or out of listening to their IntuWitchin with valid arguments for both sides. But only one will take you up the highest timeline and possibility to the Realms of the Gods. The other will take you straight to the Underworld, convincing you that you'll never escape your darkness. It is important for Gemini not to rush into things; if you're spinning or falling into a downward spiral, breath can help to bring clarity. Channeled writing, singing, and having a coach/mentor/therapist to externally process with can be incredibly impactful for Gemini IntuWitchin.

In ritual: Gemini align with the truth of the Divine intelligence to be the Knowledge Carrier. Are you telling yourself stories that help or hinder your connection to the Universal voice of your own inner wisdom? How can you create crystal clarity and remembrance of your IntuWitchin communicating with you?

CANCER

*The Great Mother, the Healer,
the Primordial Essence*

Element: Water
Planetary ruler: The Moon

Cancer nourishes in every way. Like the depths of oceans, she is the source of all life, the Mother. But if you get too close to her babies, watch out! Whether they are projects or friends, if you mess with her cubs, a fiercely protective mama bear emerges. The crab can protect itself with a hard shell, safeguarding the soft underbelly, keeping people at a distance. She's sensitive, receptive, and can get her big feelings hurt—or held—easily.

Cancer sun, moon, or rising: Depending on whether your emotional realms feel frozen or overflowing, Cancer Intu-Witchin asks you to regulate your tides or immerse yourself in water. Baths are a Cancer's happy, nurturing place, even more powerful when you're willing to get into refreshing wild waters in Nature. Embodiment of and communication from the Goddess are easily encouraged through receptivity and creativity.

In ritual: Cancer the Great Mother asks us to cleanse, purify, and heal ourselves. This is an opportunity to reparent yourself with the kind of support you required but perhaps never received as a child. What emotions most yearn for your love and embrace? How can you plant the seeds of new streams for creative expression, spiritual soothing, or permission to feel? What are the waters asking you to do to release any dams you may have built or thaw the frigidity within?

Ω

LEO

*The Leader, the Performer,
Sharing What Serves Our Species*
Element: Fire
Planetary ruler: The Sun

The archetype of the *benevolent* leader, Leo is who and what we are devoted to with our powerful creativity. The sign of the ego, Leo rules both self-expression and fertility, showing how and what we want to be known for and what we use our platform to obtain. The Leo darkness appears as arrogance and superiority when they forget shining is meant to shed light on others, not cast shadows—that's just a symptom. Leo loves to be adored and brings a childish playfulness to every endeavor (tantrums and all!).

Leo sun, moon, or rising: Leo IntuWitchin will guide you to achieve your dreams by using your time in the spotlight for the benefit of all beings. It will ensure the words you're speaking on that center stage lift others up rather than pedestal yourself. Ritual theater, archetype work, and inquiring deeply about the most important message for the world to hear can be profoundly activating for Leonine IntuWitchin.

In ritual: The Leader wants proof of your benevolence to bestow brilliant blessings upon you. How can you plant the seeds for shining light upon the service you are meant to provide to others and the global community? How courageous can your actions be to accomplish both what you desire and what brings good to the world?

VIRGO

The Control Freak, the Analyst,
Maintaining Efficiency and Efficacy
Element: Earth
Planetary Ruler: Mercury

The origin of the word *Virgo/virgin* meant *sovereign.* The vestal virgins were priestesses, sovereign women unto themselves who served the sacred fire of Vesta, Goddess of Hearth and Home—not innocents depriving themselves of the greatest Roman pleasure, another patriarchal myth changing the feminine frequency of power. Virgo rules order, logic, and the mundane routine of life, working hard to ensure everything is in its proper place. This sign rules self-care and habitual behavior, governing our daily practices of tending to the physical body and environment. When empowered, Virgo is of service without becoming a servant, but people-pleasing can be a Virgo's demise. Deeply connected to the natural order of the Universe, Virgo creates systems for our empowered liberation.

Virgo sun, moon, and rising: When your physical space is clear, so too is the voice of Virgo IntuWitchin. Ensuring health of mind, body, and environment through building altars, scheduling time for your routines/self-care, eating in the optimal way for your digestion, and balancing structure and flow to organize your life efficiently activate Virgo IntuWitchin. Any mental overanalysis can be quieted by getting into the body, followed by meditation.

In ritual: The Virgo devotee wants to see what you are dedicated to and to design your life around the service you are on the planet to provide. How can you develop enthusiastic discipline in this endeavor to serve every facet of your life? How must you surrender control to experience the inner and outer rewards for your service?

♎︎

LIBRA

The Judge, the Socialite, Relational Synergy
Element: Air
Planetary Ruler: Venus

Libra rules diplomacy, balance, justice, and rapport in relationships. This sign wants to create cooperation, resonance, and equanimity. Even when life isn't fair, Libra believes it *should* be and will do everything in its power to make it so for all parties involved (at least as they see it). Libra seeks harmony, whether with others or with the aesthetics of our environment. The only sign represented by an inanimate object, the heavenly scales, Libra's shadow can be concerned only with how interactions might have "something in it for me," being overly conceited, condescending, even disdainful, to the detriment of others.

Libra sun, moon, or rising: If you can't hear your Libra IntuWitchin, look for the area of your life that's unbalanced and bring it back into resonance. This sign needs equilibrium in every area: work and play, social and alone time, rest and action, care for self and others. Notice how you respect and revere the world around you. Do you do so harmoniously or with disregard for yourself? Libra is often guided to their greatest gifts and struggles through the reflections of romantic partnership.

In ritual: The Harmonizer wants you to see where you are unsteady and restabilize your relationship to reality. Notice whether you are overly involved and invested in others and how to bring your attention back to yourself. What seeds of commitment can you plant that will attune your life to the healthiest relationships in every context? What habits must you release that have kept you from resonant relationships or balance in your life?

SCORPIO

The Alchemist, the Witch,
Sex, and the Occult
Element: Water
Planetary Ruler: Pluto

Scorpio governs life, death, and rebirth, the revolution and fundamental pattern of life. Scorpio's deep intensity is unafraid of the darkness, ruling the occult and our personal transfiguration; they prefer profound intimacy to interacting on the surface. Scorpios are only lost if they refuse to embark on the journey into hidden spiritual depths. The alchemical motto "transform or die" keeps them evolving, the perpetual cycle always in motion. This sign gives us the courage to lean into discomfort, making us unstoppable like the forces of nature Herself.

Scorpio sun, moon, or rising: Scorpio IntuWitchin wants you to own your deepest magik and greatest power. For you to fearlessly face what must fall away to fuel your growth and expansion. As the most sexual sign, Scorpio luxuriates in lovemaking as a healing or manifestation practice. Using sexual energy for the transmutation of pain and the amplification of pleasure is perhaps the ultimate Scorpionic sortilege.

In ritual: The Alchemist wants you to acknowledge what must change within you to become who you are destined to be. Scorpio's concern is that you let old ways die and incorporate the impact of your experiences by rising like a phoenix from the ashes. Do this through something that shakes up your energy: dance, breath work, plant medicine—anything that moves you physically and challenges you emotionally. What must transform within me to become the most magikal version of myself? How can I change my perspective to see the blessings in disguise?

SAGITTARIUS

The Philosopher, the Adventurer,
Life's Search for Meaning
Element: Fire
Planetary Ruler: Jupiter

Sagittarius, the centaur, wields the directed energy of the archer with a voracious hunger for knowledge that runs like a wild horse. Sagittarians seek sage wisdom across the world, investigating the realm of self, tradition, culture, and God. Always asking the big questions, they will not give up until an answer that feels true or holds significance is revealed. The ruler of study, literature, teaching, and philosophy, Sagittarius would rather send its roots up into the ethers than be stuck in one place without exploring all there is to learn.

Sagittarius sun, moon, or rising: IntuWitchin comes from freeing your mind and acting as soon as inspiration strikes. Anyone who tries to limit your freedom will just lose you. If you need to "settle down" because of work or kids, keep your spark alive with new hobbies and books and always make sure you have your next adventure planned to look forward to. Even if that's just a road trip to a new place a few hours away, a change of scenery will always activate your IntuWitchin.

In ritual: The Sagittarius guru needs you to maintain your cyclical action for accessing your higher wisdom. That means resting and taking time to integrate each lesson learned or adventuring to new realms of consciousness—even if just in meditation. In what ways must you devote yourself to your own path and higher learning? Is there a hobby you've always wanted to try but never given a shot or a dormant passion you could reawaken? How can you release the shackles from your mind, body, or spirit to liberate your limitless self?

CAPRICORN

*The Great Father, the Builder,
Mission-Driven Success*
Element: Earth
Planetary Ruler: Saturn

Capricorn rules the hard work of devotion and commitment behind every one of our "successes," whether intense spiritual work or our professional pursuits. Capricorn gives us the strength to take small, daily steps toward achieving our goals, and consistent baby steps culminate in great accomplishment. No matter how challenging the terrain, we push ever onward to think and reach bigger and higher. Methodical and steadfast, Capricorn is the mountain, the mission, and the map, reminding us that if we keep putting one foot in front of the other, we can reach any pinnacle.

Capricorn sun, moon, or rising: Capricorns will have a hard time hearing their IntuWitchin and will never be satisfied with life until they have given themselves to their purpose. But once they do, that voice will be there guiding every step. There is no need for grand leaps of faith; you will fare better moving in well-thought-out increments. Capricorns must make sure they treat themselves the way a loving and kind father would. Watch out for the punitive patriarchal programming within that can make you feel like you're not doing enough—that is just shadow and not your truth.

In ritual: The boss wants you to be living in alignment with your legacy, taking the necessary actions to build what you came here for. What kind of life are you leading and what will it leave behind? What would your purpose ask of you right now? How are you procrastinating or taking steps backward?

♒

AQUARIUS

The Visionary Rebel, the Outlaw,
Innovation, and Ingenuity
Element: Air
Planetary Ruler: Uranus

Aquarius, the sign of the higher mind, brings people together and rules community, networks, and ideas. Aquarius helps us gather the best group to bring our visions to life by uplifting and empowering others while staying focused on the bird's-eye view or bigger picture and rising above emotional entanglements. The weirdo of the zodiac, Aquarius wants us to act into the future in the present—with new techniques, technologies, systems, and strategies—as if it were already happening now.

Aquarius sun, moon, or rising: To hear your IntuWitchin, you must be true to yourself. Make a promise to never betray what's most important to you for the sake of fitting in or receiving the approval of others. If you feel like something is "off" in your life, take note of how your behaviors or choices might be informed by someone else's opinion. Dealing with whatever belief is underlying that inclination will be the key to unlocking infinite inspiration.

In ritual: The Aquarius visionary wants you to breathe life into your big dreams, bringing your desires to fruition. Focused meditation can help send your spirit up into the Divine mind with specific intention. How can you start to *really* believe in yourself? To feel worthy of faith in yourself, what ways of deferring to others for approval must come to completion?

PISCES

The Mystic, the Devotee, the Artist
Element: Water
Planetary Ruler: Neptune

Pisces is the sign of the mystic, embodying an unconditional compassion and empathy for the suffering of others. The last sign in the zodiac, Pisces governs our spiritual evolution, blurring the lines between the Earthly realm and what lies beyond the veil. Pisces is our third eye, psychic and supernatural gifts, imagination, fantasy, and creativity. They can also be the most addictive or obsessive sign, as cosmic depths come with big magik—and great darkness.

Pisces sun, moon, and rising: Your IntuWitchin is intrinsically linked to your spirituality. The deeper your devotion to the Divine, the clearer the communication from your inner wisdom. As long as you don't let it drown you, sensitivity is strength, not weakness. The ocean of emotion within can be your greatest teacher or deepest fear, so notice how you relate to the waters and waves in your own life.

In ritual: The Pisces mystic just wants to feel your dedication to your own Divine Nature, to go with the ebbing and flowing of life. How can you plant the seeds for a deeper devotion? Who is the most mystical, magikal version of you and how can you embody that energy more? What ways are you feeling disempowered by life, like it's happening to you instead of through you? How can you wash away whatever is drowning you in doubt and disbelief?

Remember, the above are all suggestions. You will feel called to what is right to you; follow *that*. These archetypes are present within all of us and can be called upon or embodied whenever we need them, regardless of our birth chart. Each of these archetypes expresses a different facet of serving the highest good of all through your own interpersonal alchemical evolution.

MOON TIME MANIFESTATION
........................................................*

The cycles of the moon, as part of an astrological practice, are a powerful way to work with our IntuWitchin.

We get the word *month* from the moon cycle (as in "moonth"), which is technically about 29 days, the same as our moon cycle, or infradian rhythm. The patriarchal papacy changed the structure of moonths along with our holy days with the Gregorian calendar, further programming us to disconnect from Earth's natural cycles.

Every month, there is one new moon and one full moon, with rare exceptions because of our calendar days. The new moon comes in the same sign the sun is currently transiting, and the full moon will be in the opposite sign (e.g., in March/April, there will be an Aries new moon and a Libra full moon). Think of it like a clock. Just as 12 and 6 are opposites, it's the same with astrological signs. Opposing signs not only complement one another, but they tend to pick up where one leaves off or falls short, always offering medicine for each other—which is why we say "opposites attract."

The new moon is a time to plant seeds of what we want to blossom or bear fruit in our lives. Full moons represent the completion of the cycle. In addition, the waxing quarter moon (the halfway point as the new moon grows toward fullness) brings things to light, including new information to be integrated or patterns to be released. The waning quarter moon (halfway between the full moon and the next new moon) asks you to turn inward and reflect: How have you changed? In what ways did and didn't your new moon intentions come to fruition, and why? I generally let the full cycle of a sign move through before I get too concerned whether or not my intentions came to fruition. So if you get into the quarter moons, find what sign they're in and look back to your new moon intentions from that cycle.

New moon rituals are for clear intentions of setting energy or action in motion, and full moon rituals can be about harvest and celebration or release and completion. What's more, the new moon in each sign is linked to the full moon in the same sign that comes six months later (another reminder that our intentions often don't manifest instantaneously). The Taurus new moon is in April or May, during Taurus season, but the full moon in Taurus comes in October/November, when the sun is in its opposing sign of Scorpio. When you set new moon intentions, look back on them at the corresponding full moon and see what progress you've made.

The archetypal energies at play during new and full moons (represented by the signs the planets are in) guide how you craft your ritual intentions and point to what you're bringing forth in your life. As you understand these archetypes, connected to the greater planetary forces, you get clear on what you're asking for, or being asked of, by the Universe.

See how these archetypes are present in your life for your new and full moon rituals. The most surefire way to create sustainable transformation in ritual is amplifying or healing and releasing that particular archetype's presence or patterns in you.

Practice — *New Moon Ritual*

There is no one or right way to do a moon ritual. They're unique to you; each time you craft and perform a ritual, you'll learn new things. What's exciting is that by repeating them throughout the year and seasons, you'll notice how the energies of these archetypes play out in your life.

If your intentions are more specifically calling in something like a job, partner, home, or amount of money and it still hasn't manifested, it means there is more internal work to be done. What do you *really* need to commit to in your new moon ritual?

Do some serious inventory and inquiry around your beliefs and behaviors to know what's specifically being asked of you, and look at how you feel about yourself for not yet having your desire. That's where manifestation begins.

For example:

What do I say or believe about money?

How do I tend to my current home?

How do I feel about my body (the home of my spirit)?

Do I feel worthy of this dream career/home/partnership?

If yes, how might my behavior not be reflecting that belief in myself?

If not, what is the story I'm telling myself and what could I do to prove it wrong?

Writing down and speaking your intentions to anyone out loud holds you accountable and vice versa. Ask: "Who do I need to be to accomplish this mission?" "What is the Universe, Goddess, or Nature asking of me so I walk forward on the highest timeline?"

Reflect upon the most impactful ways your intentions can be set in motion, then design a ritual based on your responses. As a container for the creation of the ritual, consider the astrological indication of the new moon and see how it applies to your life.

Is the moon in an Earth (body/physical environment/ career), Water (emotions/sexuality/creativity), Fire (action/ transformation/power) or Air (mind/breath/communication/ expression) sign?

In what ways would you like to grow in relationship to this element?

Is the Earth encouraging you to get into your body, build an altar, or start a new career?

Is the water wishing you'd dial up your sensual pleasures, shed tears, or create a new project?

Is the air asking you to calm your mind through meditation, boost your brilliance with breath work, or communicate something you've been suppressing?

Is the fire forcing you out of your comfort zone, pushing you to act where you've been afraid, or transform an old pattern once and for all?

Often when I'm leading a new moon ritual I ask people to bring something to represent seeds of intention. These can be seeds themselves, beads, crystals, or the like. Planting those seeds, literally or symbolically, is a magikal way to connect with the Earth and allow Her to support your visions blooming. Embody the energy of planting these seeds through speaking, writing, invocation, proclamation, mirror work, or whatever else calls to you. As long as your seeds are organic and biodegradable, when you complete your ritual you can also take them outside and bury them beneath a tree. The bonus of physically putting the seeds in the Earth is that over time you'll see those seeds grow into something beautiful—in tandem with what your ritual is manifesting. Seeing that growth reminds you to nurture your request.

When I plant the seeds, I like to envision giving them all of their nutrients:

Empowering thoughts, words, and beliefs as I blow my breath onto them.

Encouraging emotions, feelings, and sensations as I imagine watering them.

Beaming sunlight of my own power into them.

And feeling my body, my commitment, as the fertile soil holding them as they grow.

✴ Practice   *Full Moon Ritual*

As with new moon rituals, the most important aspect of creating your ritual is bringing awareness to any shadows that are present within you according to the astrological energy of the moon. Whatever sign the full moon is delivering its wisdom through, we can ask ourselves:

What am I still doing that I know isn't serving me?

What ways of being am I allowing, from myself or others, that are asking to be let go?

What beliefs am I still subscribing to that are keeping me from accessing my wisdom, mission, vision, etc.?

For example, if you haven't been taking good care of your body, you can use a full moon ritual to release any blockages that are hindering you. In this case, your ritual might be an intense, fiery yoga class. Any new action taken around the full moon that opposes the former limiting belief is an embodied transformation of that behavior or pattern as an old cycle ends.

Your full moon ritual can also be connected to the preceding new moon ritual in that sign. For example, if I set intentions for transforming my emotions, sexual expression, or capacity to hold myself on the Scorpio new moon, I can take inventory on my progress when the full moon in Scorpio comes six months later, with questions like:

How devoted have I been to this endeavor?

What still needs to be shifted?

What sexual inhibitions remain?

Where am I still overpowered by my emotions?

What needs to be released so I can become the priestess I am meant to be?

I love full moon hikes and doing rituals out in nature under the mystical moonlight, bathed in Her silvery glow, so bright, I can follow my moon shadow, harkening to the time when her luminosity would draw us out beyond the fireside to explore our own primal wildness. Howling at the full moon is so cathartic, especially with your wolfpack—your trusted circle of friends.

There is something extra magikal about engaging in sacred rites under moonlight. I just experienced my first full moon in the snow and was awestruck by the shimmering, sparkling snowflakes. Everything was glistening as She reflected off the luminous landscape of white blanketing the ground.

When it comes to ritual and ceremony, regardless of the greater energies at play, your attention and intention are the two most important ingredients. The new moon might come at a time when we just *don't know* what we want to manifest, and it doesn't feel right to force it. So don't. If I don't have the energy or motivation for a big, formal ritual with myself, I just do something that communicates my intentions through embodiment to the Universe. One spring around the Aries new moon, when I was calling in my new house, rather than a specific ceremony, I just spent intentional time cleaning and sprucing up my Airbnb. It felt so much clearer, refreshed and revitalized, a reemergent energy through love and care to support calling in the next aligned home space, environment, and creative cocoon for my next chapter. Perhaps the invitation is to just sit with yourself and get clear on what's most important for you right now. That's a ritual too.

The only distinction to be made is whether you are being lazy or resistant, perhaps due to fear. If the voice of your inner Witch Hunter is telling you that a new moon ritual is "silly" or "not worth it," then you need to push through. And when we are feeling lethargic and unmotivated, getting up and moving can be the perfect medicine.

The MAGIK of DIVINE TIMING

As discussed, trusting the timing of the Universe is challenging. Acting on your IntuWitchin without knowing how or when you will know the outcome is even more so. Hopefully, you're beginning to see how aligning with the astrological cycles can help you work *with* the flow of the Universe. Studying the astrological transits (what planets are moving where and when) can provide information about the optimal timing for you to release or call in specific aspects of life. However, one of the greatest gifts of astrology is teaching us to trust in the greater Universal cosmic unfoldings.

Consider what you're calling into your life right now. Do you have the feeling you are being denied it, or are you waiting for the right time? Are you trying to force things because of what someone told you is "supposed" to happen or because you have a "deadline"? Maybe the current astrology isn't right, and you're trying to convince yourself: "It has to be on *this* day, because X planet is aligning with..."

Surrendering to Divine Timing means quieting these voices so you can trust what's occurring no matter what internal stories are running in your mind. If everything is truly occurring in Divine Timing, we actually have no idea when, where, or how *anything* is "supposed" to be. It's hard to trust and not feel frustrated or impatient when things aren't happening on our timeline, but your IntuWitchin will always let you know when the time is right.

Remember: everything happens *when it happens* for a reason.

Yes, it's important for us to be as aware of and harness the greater forces of time and timing, cycles and the seasons of nature. But we also have to be compassionate for ourselves as human beings and recognize we are still loved, worthy, and precious when we listen to our body's need to rest.

This is where Divine Timing, Fate, and destiny meet the concept of free will. Every moment of our lives is a *choice point*. IntuWitchin, ultimately, is your free will. It's your ability to act upon the information presented to you by the Universe. You are always able to ignore your intuitive invitations (a big mistake for me, every time), but when you RSVP, there seems to always be a metaphorical celebration waiting. Because as an emanation of the Universe, every time we choose to say yes, our trust in ourselves increases, and so does the ease of receiving those powerful proposals. As you learn to trust your IntuWitchin, you will begin to trust more deeply in Divine Timing. The moments you choose to pause become opportunities to gain clarity on the choices you're being asked to make. Is this leading to more of the same things I've already experienced? Will this bring greater ease or greater hardship?

As my partner always reminds me: *"Easy choices, hard life; hard choices, easy life."* Sometimes the easy choice (e.g., not having a difficult conversation or putting up an energetic boundary) actually creates more distress. Sometimes the harder choice (e.g., risking being seen as the weirdo!) paves the path toward our purpose. Every moment we have a choice of which timeline we want to flow with, which version of ourselves we want to be.

No matter what, you'll end up exactly where you're supposed to be when you're supposed to be there. You might get some bumps and bruises along the way or splash in a waterfall you would have otherwise missed. When we perceive through the lens of our personal growth and believe in the truth of Divine Timing, we can recognize that *all* is for our good.

Practice — *Archetypal Activation*

This practice involves embodying and amplifying any of the astrological archetypes (or whatever else tickles your fancy / would be supportive to your evolution) to call more of that energy in.

First, take a look at your life through the lens of these frequencies. Which archetype of the zodiac is your IntuWitchin asking you to embody?

Do you need to be more nurturing to yourself or others in your life? Perhaps Cancer is calling you to connect.

Have you been denying your purpose on the planet? Perhaps Capricorn is asking you to take your first steps up that mountain.

You can work with this energy for a day, week, or month until you feel it has coalesced into your being. Dress the way that archetype shows up for you; take actions inspired by them. In any given situation, ask: "What would Cancer/Capricorn/etc. do?" Make the expression of this archetype your North Star for as long as it feels supportive.

Chapter 5

Body Language

On a Tuesday afternoon, exactly one month after my sweet 16th birthday, I almost became an amputee. I was driving to a movie with my best friend after our boyfriends' baseball game. One minute we were changing lanes, the next, my vision filled with blue and yellow, the colors of tow trucks in our town. I swerved as hard as I could, he blasted through the back of my SUV, and we flipped and rolled six times, sliding across the median as my left arm dragged against the asphalt until we skidded to a halt.

When I got myself out of the car, the back of my hand was touching my forearm. All I could see was red blood and white bones. Shock took over, and I collapsed. Sixty percent of my arm was ground away, from elbow to middle finger, completely destroying my wrist. The doctors in the emergency room decided there was no way to save it; they'd have to amputate at the elbow. But the Goddess stepped in for my first miracle. My mom was racing down a hallway to find me when she bumped into our new neighbor—a doctor she'd welcomed to our street just a few days before. He "happened" to be there for a meeting (he worked at a different hospital). Seeing her panic, he asked what was wrong and immediately came to see me.

Though the ER doctors had already "made the call," he tested whether I could feel any of my fingers. My arm was a mangled mess, but I could still tell him which digit he pinched in one of the only lucid moments I had.

"She's still got feeling. You can't let a sixteen-year-old walk out of here without her arm. There's a microsurgery clinic in the Bay Area; they'll take care of this. Get me a helicopter."

A few hours later, I'd been medevac'd to San Francisco. My mom's neighborliness saved my arm that day.

That near-fatal car accident would teach me the true nature of body language. Every part of our bodies, each limb, organ, and function, offers us spiritual guidance we can use to heal ourselves and optimize our experience in the physical vessels that house our spirit. The most traumatic experience my body ever endured became an invitation from my IntuWitchin to step into my true self and reclaim my power.

Following IntuWitchin requires listening to your body's unique language of sensation that the Universe uses to communicate with you. In fact, before we learn how to use words, body language is all we know. As infants, we rely heavily on physical touch, exploration, and facial cues to communicate; without being attuned to what our body needs and finding ways to express it to our caregivers, we would not survive.

As we learn spoken language, our sensitivity to body language diminishes (the same way people's sense of smell and touch *increase* if they lose their sight). This is especially true in a world where technology means we are increasingly living in our heads. But our body remains a powerful tool for communication.

IntuWitchin speaks through sensations in our body every day with goose bumps, tension, contractions, or a chill down your spine; the emotions you feel rise or keep suppressed in your system; and other energetic feelings. Your five senses are how you take in the transmission of the world around you. Light, color, sound, scent, taste, touch, and temperature relay information received through your body. Pain and disease, too, convey a message declaring needs or desires to you the only way your body knows how.

In addition, every part of us has spiritual significance signaling to our IntuWitchin for healing. We use many body-related idioms, for good reason. "Carrying the weight of the world on your shoulders" describes feeling weighed down and overburdened, right? Shoulders are a primary location that hold tension. Do we need to literally or figuratively "take a load off" and notice where too much gets taken on?

Anyone who's experienced sciatica pain—caused by a pinched sciatic nerve running from the butt down the back of the leg—knows the true meaning of something being a "pain in the ass"! Sciatic pain can last for months, and there is no real "remedy" for it except to rest, be patient, and wait. Anything that relates to our nerves can be an invitation to look where we might be feeling *nerv*ous. Our nervous system is how our body responds to and receives information, reacting on a moment-by-moment basis to our surroundings.

Contemplate:

What is my relationship to my body like?

How does it speak to me?

Do I listen to my body's needs?

Do I prioritize health and self-care?

Do I tend to it with conscious awareness or mindlessly eat what I know isn't nourishing for me?

Have I forgotten to appreciate my body effortlessly functioning for me?

Now think of injury, pain, and illness. Where and how have you injured yourself or been ill? What was going on in your life? Did you receive the information or lesson your body was trying to teach you? Have you changed or grown as a result of that challenge? Is there anywhere in your body that causes you consistent or ongoing discomfort?

INTUWITCHIN BODY SCAN

When interpreting body language, remember to ask these questions:

Inspiration—What is life asking me to breathe through in my body?

Interpretation—What deeper message is concealed in this experience?

In Service—How would following through on this guidance be in service to me and the world?

Nature—How is your True Nature being revealed in this moment?

THERE'S *No* SUCH THING *as* AN ACCIDENT

I learned after my accident the liberation in divining deeper meaning from physical trauma or dire diagnosis. The darkest circumstances can be illuminated into awakening. In my case, it took nearly a decade before I was able to divine the spiritual significance in my archetypal heroine's journey. Once I had clawed myself tooth and nail out of the hole of my own misery, I could look back and see my loss with new eyes as a gift.

For years I felt like a tragic, helpless loser who would always be dependent on others because the Universe had punished me with this awful disfigurement. I couldn't accept the "You create your reality" mantra as it started circulating. It was bullshit; why would I have created this?! Being disfigured is the ultimate "otherness," double the Witch Wound! There's constant danger of being cast out, and I often was, unable to physically participate in activities I'd once taken for granted. The rock bottom of my hiding from and shutting down my magik just kept getting lower. I had to fight for my life. Many of us just give up, so if this is you right now, even though it feels like it, you are *not* alone.

My happily-ever-after took learning to live with fear of ridicule and being outcast, helping me follow my IntuWitchin, giving me permission to find my full weirdo. It's pretty wild when we can find the archetypal mythical tale of our most painful experiences.... Here's mine:

When the surgeons rebuilt me, they used the latissimus muscle from my back to cover the open bones of my arm. The largest muscle in the body, lats are used for pulling, supporting the spine, shoulder, and aiding rotation of the arm. They are our wings and what make our posture stand tall.

My *left* arm was damaged; the left side of the body relates to femininity and receptivity, how we allow ourselves to be loved. The left *arm* specifically is how we receive support and connection. I had but a shred left. My inner damsel was in serious distress! So the warrior within—represented by my sword-wielding right, or masculine side—stepped in to save the day. Now here I am healing the Wisdom Wound and working with our masculine patriarchal programming to take a rest, receive support, and feel deeply. You can't make this shit up.

I was already right-handed, thank the Goddess, but a completely incapacitated left side meant reliance on my right hand for *everything*, while it, too, had been severely weakened to save the left. *Everything* was exhausting. I used one hand to type 150-page high school term papers (so tedious), get dressed, tie shoes (so hard), put up my hair, and tend to the wound of the left. Those were dark days for me. I still wash my face with just one hand from the years I had no other choice.

My right arm was practically debilitated itself from overuse, but I hated asking for help. The agony far outweighed the physical stress and pain in my body. Learning to accept support was excruciatingly vulnerable and psychologically challenging to my fiercely independent nature. I resented feeling so "weak." Rage would course through me in a public bathroom, having to ask a woman at the sink if she could help me button or zip my jeans. I was mortified.

The serpentine scar on my arm and gaping skin graft on my leg had to be kept out of the sunlight for a whole year, warping into a story that I had to hide my *whole* self away. First I covered the scar with medical bandages, then long black sleeves so no one would see how damaged I really was. But what others thought actually didn't matter; I felt this deformation was a punishment, and self-hatred infected me like a poison.

When I'd come to LA, embarked on my spiritual journey, started working with my IntuWitchin—and hanging out with people whose love helped me become who I was meant to be—the message and the Blesson began to emerge.

Not only was it necessary for me to learn to ask for and receive help and support, but I hid my true self, ashamed of being "damaged" and "different." I dimmed my light, avoiding living the life I'd always known was meant for me—a very *different* one indeed.

It was a Blesson I had to learn in the most painful way. Though challenging, confronting my demons brought victorious transfiguration and guided me to my magik. If I hadn't been so mired in my own darkness, I never would have sought the light or realized my own ability to shine. Without being so lost and confused, I wouldn't have been so open, saying yes to any opportunity for healing, growth, spiritual transformation, or deep connection with conscious community.

I got to learn how to love myself, scars and all. Ultimately, the experience morphed into a magnificent triumph over my wounds of imperfection, limitation, and unworthiness. Now I see it as my dragon skin, a mark of the battle waged and won. This was my IntuWitchin using body language to get my attention in a way that brought me to my destiny.

MY BODY SPEAKS *to* ME

✳······················✳······················✳

As you've been reading, I imagine you've reflected on the relationship with your body and physical challenges you may have experienced. In this next section, you'll find insights into the spiritual significance of anatomy to help use IntuWitchin for interpreting your body's language.

One key to interpretation can be to think literally (more spelling!) about what the physical function of an aching body part is and how it might translate on a spiritual level: joints *join* two parts together, the nervous system can signify nervousness, etc. There is so much to this magikal vessel beyond what we can see. Let's take a closer look.

Crown: There's a reason many angelic representations surround the crown of the head with a halo. This part of the body connects us to the world above—the Spirit realm. It's the place where we plug into the Divine, into our light. If we have issues with or pain in our crown, we are likely being asked to create more of a conscious connection with the cosmos or creative forces of the Universe.

Brain: There's a lot going on here: it's the control center and where our thought processes take place. Are your thoughts empowering and kind or the opposite? Do you tend to be more stressed or more relaxed? Where a headache is located—front or back, left or right—can help you determine its cause. It's the same if you bump or injure your head. Perhaps there's something you aren't seeing clearly (the occipital lobe, located at the back of the head, controls vision), or maybe you just need to get up and move to shift your state of mind (the frontal lobe, aptly located at the front, controls movement and cognitive function).

Bones: Bones are the structure, the foundation that holds the body up and together, like tectonic plates upon which the mud and clay of our muscles exist. When we break a bone or they become brittle and frail, something in our structure needs healing or repair to maintain strenth and integrity. We are being asked to rebuild so we can move forward, stronger. Consider the source of any insecurity or instability. How can you work on fortifying your physical foundations?

Joints: Joints help our bodies move, flex, and flow with life. Not all joints function the same way—hips can go all the way around (most of us aren't prima ballerinas, so we've likely never experienced that), but knees and ankles can be destroyed if they twist too far to one side. Our joints show us which way to go and how far is safe. Any stiffness can represent rigidity or holding on too tightly to something. As with your bones, where the joint in question is located contains more info about what your Intu-Witchin is communicating to you.

Blood: The waters of life flow like rivers in our veins, pumped and fueled by fire, carrying air to every cell, nourishing our entire system. Iron is a mineral made of stardust, and our blood distributes this spiritual substance to us. Menstrual blood was the original holy anointment, where the definition of *Christ* comes from. If our arteries are hardened, or we have issues with our blood, it could be a signal of stagnation, emotional rigidity, disconnection from the cosmic web of life and our elemental Nature, or call for rebirth of sacred fertility.

Ears: Are you listening? How deeply? Are you truly paying attention to whispers of the Goddess, of the Earth? Blocked ears could be a sign you're blocking something out, while pain in the ear suggests a painful message you don't want to hear. Perhaps you need to listen to your body, your pain, your wounds. Or are you listening too much to external voices and opinions of others as they tell you what they think you should be? Ringing in the ears is a common phenomenon and can be our IntuWitchin trying to get our attention: What are you being asked to "listen to" in that moment? My dear sister Blu started going deaf in her twenties, and it ended up bringing online profound spiritual and psychic gifts that allowed her to listen to energy, body language, and the voice of her IntuWitchin in a way she never had before. She interpreted her deafness as an invitation to listen more deeply with her sixth sense.

Eyes: The eyes allow us to take in the world around us, and issues with vision can signal we are either "not seeing" something or we need to "look inward" to find the answers. Our eyes are the primary way we connect with others, yet we spend more time looking at our screens these days. If your vision feels blurred after too much screen time, the message is clear: look up!

Nose: Smell is the sense most directly connected to memory. Scents can calm, comfort, and excite, draw us in, turn us on, or repel and repulse us. If you have issues with your nose, is there something luring you in or repelling you? An itchy nose can be a sign a forgotten memory is trying to get your attention. As related to the element of air, a stuffy nose can be a block to our mental clarity. What are we breathing in? Are the thoughts of ourselves clear and pure? How are we breathing? Shallow or deep? Is that how our lives are being lived, just on the surface rather than diving into the richness reality has to offer?

Mouth and lips: Our tastes and the words we speak. Does a cold sore make us want to hide from other people? How do we do that in our communication? Chapped lips are a sign of dryness and lack of moisture. How are we limiting our emotions or creativity in the way we speak or nourish ourselves? "Bite your tongue" means to hold back what you're saying and carries with it the implication that your words are not appropriate. So when we accidentally (and often painfully) bite our tongue, depending on what's happening in the moment, we may be preventing ourselves from saying what we really feel, or we need to be a little more mindful about our expression.

Throat: The throat is where we express ourselves, take in the breath of life itself, and swallow our food that nourishes and sustains us. Losing your voice is pretty self-explanatory: a request to just be silent and listen more deeply, whether within or around you. Are you expressing yourself from your truth or from a need and desire to be seen? Or it could be showing you an extreme version of who you've been. Have you been strangling yourself with stories of unworthiness, and when you get that voice back, it's time to *speak up*? What are you meant to say?

Neck: The neck is what "holds our head up high," *speaking* to our confidence and self-worth. It determines the mobility of our head. If you've got a crick and can't turn to see what's around you, your perspective is limited. The neck is also a point of extreme vulnerability. Severing the spinal cord or carotid artery and blockage to our windpipe are some of the fastest ways our lives can end. As such, pain in the neck (especially in situations where our Witch Wound is being activated) can signify past lifetime wounds or injuries such as hanging or strangulation.

Heart: With 60 times more electromagnetic energy than the brain, the heart is what powers the body. It also represents how we offer love to ourselves and others. This makes it an alchemical instrument of the highest order, one with many meanings. Heart palpitations, or an irregularly beating or racing heart, can signify imbalance in giving and receiving love, stress around intimacy and connection, or that you are simply disconnected from the fundamental energy of life: your breath. If you feel pain or constriction around your heart, this is likely an unhealed wound from someone you love or in your relationship to loving yourself. Our hearts can also become guarded and numb from pain and heartache; any spiritual or emotional armor serves as protection for our hearts but also prevents us from *feeling*. There is *always* something underneath the mask of numbness that's trying to escape detection. Keep digging.

Arms: The heart is one of the first things to form in the womb, and then guess what happens: your arms sprout out from it like flowers. The arms, therefore, represent how we hold and comfort one another as well as how we lift things, and each other, up. As I discovered, injuring an arm could be a sign you need to let yourself be cared for, to receive support from others. It may mean that you have been carrying too heavy a load or that your ability to *give* love is being challenged.

Breasts: Breasts signify love and nourishment for our children; being nursed as infants is our first experience of receiving these things. Even if we weren't breastfed, our mother had full jugs of milk meant for us. Breast cancer has become so prevalent in the modern day. When I have spoken to women who've dealt with it, the most common theme they have admitted to is a suppression of love and nourishment for themselves or others. Moms will often give everything they have to their children and end up feeling drained and dried up—we could have an entire conversation about the beauty of a mother's selflessness and how it often exists in tandem with the toxic programming that she should put her own life aside for her children. This is simply *one* possible interpretation for issues with the breasts. Can we accept the invitation to heal our relationship with self-love and care?

Hands: Connected to our arms and heart, the hands express our love through what we make and hold in our lives. They are tools used for feeding ourselves, communicating through writing, art, and poetry and what we build. How much love do we bring into what we form and generate with our hands? If our hands are dry and chapped, are our emotions missing from our creations? Are we holding back love? How do you touch people and the world around you?

Gut: The microbiome in our gut is so intelligent, it's known as the "emotional brain." Many of us feel our IntuWitchin most strongly here—hence we are told to "follow our gut." Our gut can speak to us through butterflies, that sinking feeling, loss of appetite due to stress, or pain and discomfort. The prevalence of gut issues says so much about how disconnected most of us are from our IntuWitchin and body language. Maybe you're not "digesting" the information from your life very well. Perhaps lessons are coming through, but you haven't yet internalized them and found the Blesson. So much power exists in our gut, which is the chakra of our willpower, drive, and motivation.

Back: The back represents what is behind us but also what supports and lifts us up—or whether we bend over backward to support others. Back pain today is typically caused by sedentary lifestyles (not moving forward) or poor posture, hunched over our screens (not holding ourselves or our heads high). Are you holding on to something that's meant to be left behind? Are you prioritizing supporting others over yourself? If you have back pain, are you bringing your past too much into your present? Are you focusing on what could have been instead of looking to the future?

Spine: The spine keeps us upright, representing how we stand and what we stand for. It's our integrity. The bones of our spine have rivers running through them, so the health of our spine and posture relates to our emotional well-being. We have become a very "hunched over" society, looking at our phones, lying on couches, sitting at desks. Studies have shown we feel worse about ourselves in that position. This can signify a general weakness in our willingness to stand tall, stand up, for ourselves, for what's right, for the kind of world we want to live in. Your spine is a staff of energy connecting heaven and Earth.

Legs: Our roots represent how grounded and stable we are in our lives. They can reveal how solid we are in the Earthly and material world and our willingness to grow. Legs are our strength, foundation, what holds us up, and what we build upon. If you are having issues or pain in your legs, check in on your stability in any area of your life. Is there a place you feel particularly out of balance or where you are having trouble supporting yourself? Have you been resisting walking forward into a new version of yourself or expression in your life?

Knees: The knees let us move through the world. They help us climb, sit, and take leaps in our lives. The front-facing energy of the patella is balanced by a vulnerability behind the knee. We've all seen a gentle hit on the back of a knee cause someone to collapse. If you have knee issues, where are you not going with the flow and pivoting to where it feels like the Universe may be guiding you? Perhaps you're being stubborn and are unwilling to move in a new direction out of vulnerability. Are you being called to take a leap?

Feet: As the crown connects us to the heavens, our feet connect us to Earth, out to the finest tendrils of our root system, our little toes. Our bodies are bioelectrical, and bare feet absorb free electrons from Her planetary pulse to recharge our batteries. Our feet contain energetic meridians connected to every other part of our body. Each of the meridians in ancient Chinese medicine link different glands, organs, and functions to specific points in our feet. If you've never had a real reflexology foot massage, I highly recommend it!

Womb: The uterus, or womb, is where we get the word *woman. Man* comes from the Latin word *manas,* which means *mind,* so women are the *womb-mind.* This cosmic cauldron is quite literally a direct portal to the Divine, where new souls incarnate and enter this realm. Many people choose not to have children, so the creations in their cauldron are businesses, books, art, songs, and bountiful gardens. Issues with the womb speak to what your soul yearns to create and bring into the world and how you are birthing your purpose on Earth. If you are having pain in your womb, or perhaps even trouble getting pregnant, a profound remedy is giving your inner child the freedom to play and create in their favorite way. Do they like to draw, write epic stories, paint, bake, or play pretend? Remembering how you expressed yourself during this time can be deep medicine for womb issues in our adult lives. What stories are running in your head about your abilities and your work in the world?

Sacral chakra: The energetic womb on men is often referred to as the *hara* or *dantian.* Regardless of gender, your sacral chakra is the source of sexuality and creativity flowing with ferocity or being dammed up by blockages and limitations. Pain and shame here can often be healed by connecting to your sexual or creative energies in a conscious and conscientious way. If you're feeling sexually blocked, try a genital breath work practice: take long deep breaths, imagining your inhales and exhales entering and exiting through your genitals. Remember to create safety for yourself before engaging in this practice and simply notice what comes up for you without judgment. Engaging our sexuality, alone or with another person, can be a beautiful, sacred way to get your creative juices flowing.

Left side: Regardless of our gender expression, the left is the feminine side of the body. This is just more information for our IntuWitchin to work with. For example, if you hurt your left leg, perhaps you are feeling unstable, insecure in your femininity, or need to work on your receptivity. As I learned when I damaged my left arm, issues on this side of the body are almost always about learning to receive in some way and how we connect to the creative flow of the feminine.

Right side: In contrast, the right is the masculine side. If you hurt your right leg and legs are how we walk forward, this is a very "masculine" or action-oriented injury. Perhaps you are moving full steam ahead without much care for yourself, the world beneath your feet, or who you might have to be "walking on/over" to get where you're going.

A WORD *on* WEIGHT

First and foremost, I know weight can be an incredibly sensitive subject. Personally, I spent my middle school years getting called Jelly Roll, Jiggly Puff, and Water Buffalo, tormented for something I didn't know how to change. I was the classic chubby sidekick. Boys would call me and talk to me for hours about *other* girls, and I blamed and hated my body for keeping me from being the object of their desire.

Being "healthy" has nothing to do with the natural size of a person's body. I define healthy as being able to do whatever you want with your body, free from limitation. You can be happy at any size and say, "Fuck it, this is how I am!" And that's great. But if excess weight is preventing you from living the kind of life you want—running, playing, being active, feeling strong—then your IntuWitchin is speaking to you.

For example, I worked through a severe weight issue with a student at one of my retreats. Though she was a major proponent of the body-positivity movement, her *body* actually wanted something different for itself from her. It yearned to be able to dance, go on hikes, stretch and touch her toes, see her feet, and be more flexible literally and figuratively. I spoke to her about the spiritual significance of obesity and weight issues (the kind that prevent us from living our lives to the fullest)—excess weight on the front of our bodies in particular can be a *defense mechanism*, a block to intimacy, a shield or disguise to keep the world at bay.

When we have excessive weight loss, as with some eating disorders, it can stem from a variety of traumas, but it can also be a response to reclaiming control the sufferer feels was taken from them. They may feel unworthy of receiving nourishment and reject food because they reject themselves.

Meanwhile, feeling like you "can't do things" because of your size is also a way of resisting following your IntuWitchin down the scarier (and potentially more transformational!) paths it wants to lead you. We can use the above descriptions to determine significance of holding weight in a specific part of our bodies.

Weight has played a large role in my family lineage. See if you can recognize patterns in your own ancestry through this example: My dad was always super fit. He was a river guide and spent his time out in nature bronzed by the sun, rugged and wild. He also cheated on most of his partners and humiliated my mom when we were kids by sleeping with just about anyone who would have him, including our housekeeper. When their marriage fell apart and he tried to change his philandering ways with subsequent partners, his *guilt* had already started showing up as weight gain. Now in his seventies, he's got a *lot* of weight around his belly, and it's not from drinking beer!

When looking for the root, he realized weight gain is his spiritual defense mechanism to keep women at a distance so he can avoid temptation. It shields him, hiding his power and sacral center, subconsciously keeping him from utilizing his sexuality to be validated like he had his entire life. He makes himself what he deems "less desirable." His work would be to find an inner source of validation, to feel enough within and as himself regardless of affirmation from anyone else.

There are many different wounds and traumatic experiences that can manifest with bodily responses of weight gain as a protective mechanism. When I switched to public school in sixth grade and made the mistake of sharing my magikal dreams with my classmates, I was bombarded with scoffing ridicule. That's when I started hiding my magik and gaining protective weight.

It's been a journey to find what healthy means to me. Admittedly, my motivation was multifaceted when I first altered my eating habits in high school. I was sick of being considered the "ugly duckling." I desired to be desired—but I also wanted to feel strong and powerful. Once my body changed, however, I realized how much better I felt regardless of other people's opinions or standards. That in turn changed the motivation for maintaining my new physique. Now I eat clean and optimize my health with supplements and biohacking, yoga, weights, and Nature because they positively affect my energy, sleep, sex drive, skin vibrance, and overall mental health and well-being. I want to be able to climb mountains, backpack into deep canyons, swim under waterfalls, and be a clear, receptive channel for the voice of the Goddess.

There is no "should" when it comes to body size, so I invite you to assess yourself honestly. "Is this my truth? Is the expression of my essence in my body?" If it is, great!

The WISDOM of DISEASE

✳............................✳............................✳

What about when we are really sick? Is this our body language speaking to us, too? I believe so. Whatever is going on in your body, no matter how challenging, there will always be a message or deeper meaning available, which can open your eyes, heart, or perspective to feel inspired to transform your habits, lifestyle, or mindset in a way that aids in your recovery. However, it's important to note we can't always rely on IntuWitchin alone for healing. As a beneficiary of the Western medical system, I know firsthand (pun intended) that there are times when major intervention is the way. I would have been an amputee otherwise, and I am so grateful that wasn't my life path. (Thank you, Dr. Buntic!)

Here is a powerful example of how we *can* heal using our IntuWitchin. One of my dearest sisters is known as Dr. Bones. She's a doctor of Chinese medicine, but there's magik in her nickname, too. When she was diagnosed with a rare, advanced bone-marrow cancer, she chose to conquer it holistically and refused any Western treatment. She created a bone altar throughout her house and sat beside it every day, praying with the chemotherapy drugs she'd been given, asking them to bestow their medicinal benefits in the fight against her cancer without her actually having to *ingest* the chemicals. She never swallowed a single pill and has been cancer-free for four years.

You can create *miracles*.

The real message is letting your inner wisdom be your guide. Not everyone has the level of spiritual practice and connection to manage a miracle like Dr. Bones—and that's okay. Cultivating this level of belief in your own magik and inherent interconnectedness with source is a lifelong commitment. Let this simply inspire you to create a close relationship to your body so you always know what it needs.

One of my clients spent years subverting herself, believing she was unworthy of expressing her truth. She didn't feel safe around her abusive sister and mother, but she never complained or even so much as admitted the ways her mom had not shown up for her. Eventually, the pain she had carried inside for years manifested as Lyme disease.

After months of her being in my online programs, we finally started working privately together. Two weeks into our deep subconscious healing and reprogramming, I led her into a hypnotic trance to ask the wisdom of her body why the Lyme was present. Her childhood memories of family hardship instantly surfaced. When she gathered the courage to express what she'd repressed, her symptoms significantly lessened. She finally listened to her body, and the results were profound.

I believe autoimmune conditions like Lyme ask you to look at where and how you are attacking yourself internally, including the "attack" of shutting down your self-expression and magik. Staying quiet can generate layers of guilt, shame, or unworthiness buried in the subconscious. It is a form of self-sabotage, contributing to a cellular violence on the immune system. After all, *auto* literally means *self*: with these conditions, something in the self is attacking our immune or nervous system. These conditions are on the rise in large part because of our relationship to and separation from Mother Earth. Intentional by our leadership and due to ignorance individually, the habits of our species are attacking our home, destroying rainforests and soil. We are the bacteria upon Her skin, causing Her harm, and our bodies are reflections of Her body.

I've supported many clients through these kinds of ailments who miraculously heal as a result of listening to their IntuWitchin. There is always a spiritual solution to what ails us. Depending on the nature of the condition, the sickness itself might not "go away," but unpleasant signs and symptoms can lessen or even disappear. After all, illness is your body literally saying, "Something's not working. I need help." When we communicate in return, "I hear you, I love you, I'm here to support you," often the response from your body will be of genuinely pleasant surprise and gratitude.

If your body is not used to feeling safe or held by you, it may take time for it to trust you again. Can you hear it? Go at your own pace, with patience and tenderness, and it will respond.

YOUR BODY, YOUR INTUWITCHIN

As you learn to communicate with your body, it will become one of the greatest sources of wisdom and IntuWitchin in your life. But so many of us are disconnected from our bodies. If you walk on concrete day in and day out, like I did, living in New York City, it's going to be harder to hear the intuitive guidance of your body. The same goes for if you're constantly being stimulated by noise, light pollution, and notifications from your phone (turn them off!). It can take a while to recenter and find the voice of your body language again, so explore connecting to your vessel however feels best to you. Simply greeting your body in the morning the way you would a friend or partner as you wake up is a great way to start letting it know you're intent upon reestablishing a relationship.

"Hello, my beautiful body. It's so wonderful to wake up within you today! Thank you!" Take it one step further by asking it how it's doing and really taking the time to listen or feel its response. Maybe give yourself a hug.

I get up and go outside with my kitties first thing every day to breathe fresh air before turning my phone on. Then I do a yoga class and meditate (for me, a minimum of 22 minutes). This gives me an opportunity to transition between sleeping and waking slowly and consciously, connecting with the Earthly body, then feeling where I'm holding tension and giving my system what it asks of me. I take hikes and walk barefoot as much as I can. I like to send imaginary roots from my toes down into the Earth and energetically plug into the mycelial network to remember how interconnected we all are. In what ways can you start to get outside to feel the Earth, even if that's in your own backyard?

It is vital to learn the language of your body to enhance your IntuWitchin, so take time to connect with it every day. What I've shared here is a guide, but as always, what you receive from your body is what really matters.

Full-Body Breathing

Breathing directly into pain, imbalance, or disease in your body can help you connect to the deeper message.

Begin by setting the intention for spiritual inquiry.

Find a safe space to practice and breathe long and slow for a few minutes, focusing on the sensations in your body.

When you connect to any imbalance present, ask: "Where could this attacking energy come from?"

Let yourself experience the response from your body. Is the healing mental, emotional, spiritual, or physical? What can you do to provide for your body and soul?

Let your body show you the way.

Body Talk

Journaling or recording voice memos can be a great tool to receive your Divine assignments. Start by lying down with your journal nearby or starting a voice memo. I use Otter, a transcription app, because then I have what I say written down for me without having to get up.

Settle into your body, breathe deeply, and let yourself relax as much as you can. I like to envision myself sinking into the bed to the point where I become it.

Focus on whatever part of your body you intend to connect with or whatever asks for your attention. You can also just let the breath course through your entire being and see what arises.

Notice each sensation. You can speak it aloud or simply acknowledge it.

When you feel what's most present, start describing what you see, hear, feel, sense, or experience in that part of your body.

Ask it what it needs, and let yourself speak for it. For example: "The black, sticky energy shaped like an anvil in my stomach needs love and trust." Then go one step further, and ask it how it can experience love and trust from you right now. Let yourself speak for it again so you have the answer from your body recorded.

You can energetically respond to this—show it love in the way it desires or requires experiencing it in that moment. Let yourself be trustworthy by responding to its request.

Then ask what it needs from you moving forward.

Can you commit to giving your body what it needs? Make a promise to your body you will honor it by committing to taking that action, and stick to it to create love and trust between you.

Earth
Temple

Every morning at the dawn of my awakening, I would walk down Venice Beach to witness the multidimensional nature of reality through the elemental interplay in the first few inches of shoreline. I would dig my toes into the sand, burying my feet like roots sinking into the layer of solid, immovable ground beneath me. Connected to the deep Earth and my body, I would proclaim aloud, "I am Earth."

The rush of sand in motion sliding down the shore kissed my skin as it washed away in the waves, a whole separate dimension, powder from the stones far below fluctuating in the flow of water's own entirely different energy and element. Breathing into the cool liquid lapping at my roots, feeling its reflection in the rivers of blood pumping through my veins, I proclaimed, "I am water."

The clouds of sand whirling and dancing within the waters are a world of their own transfixing splendor. The foam and bubbles burst at the shore and slide down into the sea. I would inhale deeply into the wild winds whipping through my hair. "I am air."

Sunlight shone down upon it all, a reflection of the sky above, while simultaneously the shimmering surface covering boundless depths beneath. As the warmth caressed my cheeks, I breathed into the bright luminous radiance. "I am fire."

To me, the entire spectrum of human consciousness and reality was illustrated in this single intersection of Nature, of the elements. The experience of them all around me and within me, emerging from my soul, uniting with the Universal Spirit, was visceral. Reminding me we are influenced by and interacting with forces far greater than us in every moment. Our exploration of the elemental forces that connect to and direct our IntuWitchin begins with the Earth—for we are Earth in our very bones. Our skeletons are the stones of the mountains forming Her terrain. Our veins, the waterways like rivers on Her sacred skin. Earth fuels and guides IntuWitchin because She is the very source of it. Just as the flowers bloom, fruits flourish, and trees root to rise, so too do we blossom into our beauty, growing into our own glory. Our bodies are microcosmic temples of this holy, heavenly sanctuary. As such, how we treat Mother Earth directly reflects how we treat and feel about ourselves.

When we are disconnected from Earth—when our bare feet never touch the naked ground—we are disconnected from our own creative life force energy. We have disassociated from that which enlivens, nourishes, and sustains us and from the magik of our own bodies. We have become distant and detached from the cycles and seasons of Nature and life itself. This is a new development, unprecedented in the history of our species. No wonder we're unhappy. Never before have we so blatantly disregarded the reciprocity and reverence Mother Earth deserves. She's been patient with us naughty children, but every mama has her limit.

We are anxious, depressed, dissatisfied, and stressed. Given how few of us have regular access to Nature, feeling ungrounded and isolated is understandable. We've forgotten we are part of a collaborative ecosystem where everything is designed to support growth and collective well-being.

During my last two years of high school after my accident, just getting out of bed was a feat of great proportions. I didn't have the tools or awareness to integrate grieving all I'd lost, mourn the casualty of my previous life, or process the pain I was experiencing—mental, emotional, spiritual, and physical. In college, I got good grades, went to the fanciest New York nightclubs with all the "coolest" people, but I was utterly unglued. Crippled by anxiety, the path expected of me felt void of any enjoyment or substance.

I was disconnected from who I was, what I wanted, and how to take care of myself because I was disconnected from the Earth. I grew up on a majestic coastline, where the salty sea breeze wafts through a well-preserved old town plaza beneath the great redwood forest. My summers were spent running river rafts through clear green waters at the base of mountain canyons. I was always butt naked and shrieking in delight at some tiny wonder of Nature, whether frogs on the banks or anemones in tide pools. Now it had been years since I'd put my feet on the Earth. Surrounded by concrete, I was *bewildered*: everything felt so wrong.

Little did I know, the source of my bewilderment was literally needing to *be wilder*! To get outside, sit beneath a tree, or dance under a rainstorm. Reconnecting to my Nature-nurtured redwood roots led me home to my magik; the magik of the Earth. Wildness and being in wilderness awakened my purpose: to serve Mother Nature. Part of my mission is speaking on behalf of ancient trees, sacred waters, winds of change, and fires of transformation, devoted to humanity's spiritual rebirth. If I hadn't been so devastatingly lost, I would never have gone searching—so thank you, bewilderment.

My most important invitation for you as you connect to your IntuWitchin? Be *wilder*. Remaining separate from the Earth has repercussions for our overall health and well-being. But spending time in appreciation of the gifts and bounty of Nature brings you abundance beyond your wildest dreams because She is the source and expression of it.

Walk into a forest, a real forest that sprouted long before your grandparents, and you will feel how abundant the magik is. Forests teach us to work together, synergistically growing stronger as we root down to rise and reach for the skies. The more I have emulated this way of being, the better I feel and the more capable I am of manifesting magik. The more I thank the Earth, pray to Her, and spend time quietly falling in love with Her, allowing Her to hold me as my mother, lover, and teacher, the more She blesses me.

MOTHER NATURE'S REMEDIES

Trees are some of the wisest beings on Earth. Grandmother willow, resplendent redwoods, majestic mangoes, Himalayan cedars, Australian eucalyptus—arbors are always sharing wisdom with us, teaching us about nourishment, abundance, healing, and resilience when we stop to listen. Even young trees have hundreds of millions of years of evolutionary information in their DNA. Nature will be your greatest teacher if you let Her be.

The Latin name for redwood trees—*Sequoia sempervirens*—translates to eternal life. Not only are they evergreen, flourishing throughout all seasons for millennia, but they are the epitome of healing. When they are burned, they scar. When traumatized by human or environmental abuse, they create burl, magikal bud tissue that stimulates new growth. We learn so much from these beings who create new life in death. The redwoods teach us we are worthy of rising. We too are resilient, overcoming trauma and hardships as we grow in harmony with those around us.

I was reminded of this one September after an epic birthday bash in Southern California. Exhausted, I couldn't believe I was getting talked into a trip to Hawaii by another friend who wanted me to keep the festivities going at her celebratory weekend. Every time those islands had beckoned before, I'd grown in leaps and bounds. But traveling halfway across the world for two days seemed silly. The carbon emissions alone meant I almost brushed aside the voice of my IntuWitchin urging me to go.

Walking across a black sand beach that weekend, I came across an altar built to the crystalline spring water coursing through the mountain. I stopped to give thanks when a mango sapling caught my eye. It had been decapitated by a machete right as it had begun to sprout. But just beneath where it had been severed, new life was already bursting fervently forth. It spoke to me like one of those fearless kids who blow you away with a courage and nobility beyond their years, shrugging: "Nothing bad ever happens. It's all just part of life."

Nothing bad? I replied (in my head). With all the atrocities of the world?! Of course bad things happen!

"Nope. Every experience is just a different facet of life. This could have killed me. But rather than wither, I choose an alternative path."

Another nugget of Nature wisdom that made the whole trip worth it. How might this message be medicine for you? Can you think of a challenge you faced that inspired you to heal, adapt, and evolve to your changing circumstances?

Painful experiences (as I discovered after my accident) can remind us of our body's innate knowledge of how to heal. After all, scar tissue is stronger than regular tissue. It forms in our souls, too, reconstituting our resilience. When we stop resenting them, our wounds always result in regeneration and repair. The Earth's forests can be destroyed in flame, fire scars charred into the side of tree trunks, and She's reborn in spring, the recovery of the understory undeniable with unbelievable wildflowers. Every year sprouts burst from the ground, flowers blossom, trees reach higher. This is healing.

Once upon a time, my scars made me miserable. Now they mark me as a sacred warrior, reminders of battles waged and won, evidence of the power I've reclaimed over what was once my greatest weakness.

Nature provides a remedy for every ailment. Besides the incredible benefits of plant medicines themselves, the majority of pharmaceutical drugs are synthesized in laboratories from originally organic compounds, aka plants, which have benefits ranging from natural birth control to combating depression to rehabilitation. The tonics, tinctures, salves, and serums of our original medicine all came from plants. Mushrooms, one of the oldest species on Earth, not quite animal, not quite vegetable, can offer miraculous healing with psychedelic therapy using psilocybin. Ibogaine clinics in Mexico working to use the isolated form of the African vine iboga have had miraculous results with PTSD in veterans and recovery for drug abuse, mainly with alcohol and opioids. Plants are the pharmacopeia of our forefathers and the future.

Scientific studies on grounding, earthing, and forest bathing (all practices that recall our ancient origins of living in harmony and deep relationship with the Earth) affirm Nature as our greatest healer. Eco/Nature therapy has been proven to lower blood pressure and the production of stress hormones; boost mood, peace, and clarity; promote mental and general health; regulate the nervous system; and create an overall sense of spiritual well-being.

Is it any wonder living separate from Nature can result in the opposite and is the cause of many modern maladies, especially mental illness and disease? Would so many children be diagnosed with ADD/ADHD and overly medicated with psychostimulants and antipsychotics if they weren't spending their days staring at screens when their brains are designed to learn through playing and exploring in Nature? With our sedentary, city lifestyles, factory-produced food bearing little genetic and molecular resemblance to what the Earth crafted on Her own for us, hours spent sitting in traffic or glued to the TV, how is it any surprise we are riddled with depression and anxiety?

Being severed from our communal roots, and Natural traditions, the lifeblood of our own original, Indigenous populations, has traumatized us. But all is not lost: as Nature Herself reminds us, we are resilient. Being in Nature, feeling Her aliveness in yourself, is the embodied source of eternal life. This is abundance.

I've taken people out into Nature and watched Her transform their trauma into triumph time and again. At my retreats, we walk into the stillness and silence of forests, sinking into the sacred sanctuary of ancient trees, and immediately everything becomes clearer. Our nervous systems calm, and we remember She is the source of our truth, the inner voice of our IntuWitchin, and our own authentic Nature.

In one ritual, a woman who had never been held by her mom lay upon the land and felt Mother Earth envelop her in an unconditionally loving embrace. The epiphany that her mother didn't know how to give this kind of love to her—because she had never experienced it herself—made her weep. Wrapped in the whirlwind of remembering this love, the strongest she'd ever felt, from this Mother, who would always be there for her, reminded her she would never feel alone, unloved, or unworthy of affection again. That's some serious transfiguration.

Underneath our modern programming, noise, and distractions, the hum of the Earth drums, asking us to harmonize with Her song. Want to grow in relationships, creativity, or prosperity? Listen to the trees. Want to rise up? Climb mountains. Want to heal? Lie upon Her hallowed grounds, surrender, and let Her hold and guide you. Every Earthly environment offers unique spiritual medicine. I've lived by the adage that oceans are for healing, mountains are for rising, and forests are for growing abundance and connection. Each animal's essential expression also offers information for us. The wintery Rockies have been the consummate container for finishing this book and skyrocketing to the next level of my business. Having an expansive daylight view, particularly of natural landscapes and sky, increases alertness, productivity, and cognitive function, reduces stress and the sense of confinement, enhances learning, and radically boosts mood and well-being. Notice how differently each of these energies affect you.

The wisest being of all is the Mother we share. Like any good mom, she loves when you take time to value Her opinion and seek Her sage counsel. She'll always be there for you. Next time you find yourself confused or concerned, ask for Her insight. Listen, and watch your life transform before your eyes.

★ *Practice* — **Connect with the Earth**

Go outside somewhere quiet, turn off your phone, and take in your surroundings. You can do this in a local park, but even in big cities, it's not hard to get a few miles away. You'll be astounded at how much beauty is all around. Find your closest national or state park or nature preserve. I recommend forests, rivers, or lakes, but anywhere *natural* will do.

When you find a holy natural temple, in any environment, please be mindful. Don't climb on old trees. Walk as far from their roots as you can; keep them safe and sacred. The ancient ones in particular need your protection and preservation. Don't disrupt their life under the soil, but as you step across them, feel the root systems and mycelial network, your connection to them. Remember, they love you.

To begin, sit or stand—barefoot is best—and take in the colors all around you, the shape of the leaves, and the light, and then close your eyes as you breathe in the scent of clean air. Listen to the sounds of the wind in the trees or the lapping waters or the singing birds, and let the chatter of your mind fade away as you stretch your hearing to take it all in.

Then move into your sensations. Feel the sun and wind around you and the Earth beneath you. Let the energy of your roots from every fiber of your being travel down into the dirt and shale of Her muscles and connect with this living deity who provides us with everything. How does Her energy feel to you?

Ask any questions related to your own Earthly reality. Such as:

"How can I find my purpose?"

"What do I need to love within myself in order to attract the love of a romantic partner?"

"What is the message of this injury or disease?"

"How can I heal my self worth?"

"How can I release my anxiety?"

Journal on what comes up for you.

✦ Practice —— Feeling Your Roots

Next time you are walking in a forest, experiment with sending each tendril of energy from your bare feet diving into the ground, splitting like arms as it reaches the trees' roots, giving them a hug, sending them love through the mycelial network. Wrap your energetic "arms" around the roots as you connect. This is how plants experience connection and communication so they can receive our love much easier below the surface! I got this tip directly from the redwoods. Try it! Feel into the "roots" that grow from every toe and every fiber of your seat. Connect to Her, no matter how far away She feels. Sense your support from the source of all life. This is Earth medicine, present for us in every moment.

✦ Practice —— Thanking the Earth

One of my favorite easy Earth-reconnection recommendations is to simply talk to Her with your prayers; learn to sing Her songs. If you haven't found the joy in singing yet, just say thank you over and over. Put your hands on the Earth or raise them up to the sky: "Thank you. Thank you so much for my life." Lovingly tell a tree: "Thank you for making the air I breathe for me."

Nature has much to teach us in relationship to *abundance*. Far beyond money, abundance is a conscious vibration we can attune to through love, joy, community, nourishing food, *time*(!) to spend as we see fit, and enjoying our loved ones. The Earth gave birth to every being upon Her: trees, mountains, rivers, creatures, and elements, all of us a family. We *are* abundance because we came from Her. Eternal generation and creation is *Her* natural state, the original, epitomic expression of abundance. She doesn't panic when hundreds of apples or thousands of acorns fall and rot; they feed and fuel what comes next. When we are connected to our own life force, we too access and actualize abundance in perpetuity.

Severing our connection to Her separated us from our own innate worth. All humans once lived off the land, but extractive capitalism meant those in power took ownership of Her resources—including human beings—as an expression of her bounty. Suddenly, we had to earn our keep, working hard to be fed or have shelter. The ruling class turned people into *possessions*, measuring our merit in monetary terms—when, just like the rivers, trees, and animals, we are worthy of being here simply *because we exist.*

How many of us, despite earning "enough" to survive, truly feel fulfillment sustainably on a daily basis? Unless you've done your inner work, no number in your bank account can replace self-love and inner worth. But *how* do you cultivate inner worth? Acceptance of our inner emotional realm, and the peace that comes with being our authentic self, is actually the key to abundance.

Ignoring IntuWitchin implies to your body, mind, and spirit that "I don't matter. The external voices are more valuable than my inner knowing." These voices keep us living the opposite kind of life than we're destined for. Listening to and acting upon IntuWitchin demonstrates valuing and trusting yourself and the Universe. No amount of wealth, no high-status job, and no material possession can fill the void of disconnection from our true selves.

As we'll discuss with the fire element, action motivated by scarcity like "what I have / who I am is not enough" is very different from inspired action from our innate creative nature. Even obsession with transformation can eliminate the important integration and assimilation of new information. When we are too caught up in scarcity-driven deeds, without giving other elements their due, we can burn out. Mother Nature doesn't experience this drain because She is always connected to, and operating from, the innate intelligence of her Divine design. She takes a break during winter, not shaming or punishing Herself for slowing down and resting, preparing to blossom again in spring.

Personally, I have never been busier than I am now. Writing this book and the oracle deck that accompanies it; running a team; planning retreats; leading my most in-depth program, Sourcerous; finding a home in a new place; maintaining friendships and partnership *simultaneously*? The burnout potential looms beneath my back-to-back schedule. *Remembering my true Nature keeps me on track.* I take breaks outside, meditating naked beneath the trees on sunny days. I sleep in when I want, sit in the hot tub, work out, sing to myself and the Earth, and connect with my sisters on the phone or in person, thus preserving my motivation and inspiration for the mission I am on Earth to accomplish. It is my highest excitement to serve these creations, but I never push myself past my limits.

IntuWitchin's invitations, when we listen, always guide us toward accessing our inner resources. We give ourselves permission to rest, follow our instincts, eat, move, sleep, and love how we need to.

What do you feel compelled to accomplish or bring to life while you're on Earth? That which requires time, energy, commitment, devotion, and even "hard work" comes naturally when our cyclical Nature is balanced.

When more of us understand Earth's value rests in what we *receive* rather than what we *take* from Her, our entire species will evolve. Aligning our values with the true Nature of abundance growth, cooperation, regeneration, harmony, and an awareness of our inherent interconnectedness will heal humanity. IntuWitchin always reminds us to operate by *being* abundant, therefore drawing and attracting abundance to us so we feel safe, secure, and cared for by the Universe.

The greatest amplifier for my financial flourishing, increased inner and outer resources in every expression, is mindfulness of my footprint and environmental impact. I am as plastic-free as possible, and I avoid buying from major conglomerates like Walmart or Ikea, sweatshops, or factory farms. The production of polyester and plastic fabrics is some of the greatest damage done to our planet. It releases microplastics into our water, so do not partake in fast fashion. I don't ignore the lithium mining for our phones and laptops (Google it), and She thanks me, bestows burgeoning blessings on me, simply for small shifts in habitual behaviors and acknowledgment of, or apology for, Her pain.

Giving thanks and praise for Her is a major component to healing our relationship with innate abundance, reflecting the bountiful Earth. Gratitude is the most abundant frequency because it implies enoughness. The irony being that saying thank you for everything you already have in your life just makes the Universe want to give you more! This is the art of *appreciation*, which we use to describe the growth of financial investments because it builds and enhances the value of everything.

One of my teachers, Special Blackburn of Potionarium, said to me: "All we can offer the Earth (in thanks) are our songs and prayers. Shells, feathers, tobacco, sweetgrass, cedar, sage, altars from wood or stone: these can't be offered to Her; they're being given *back* to Her, *returning* home. Our voice, gratitude, and songs are all that truly come from us. The love of our soul is all we can share with Her."

After all, She made you to be you. So when you go out into Nature, just give thanks: "Wow!" or "You're so beautiful. I love you!"

SONGS OF THE SEASONS

Exploring each season's energetic expression is a wonderful way to understand our own cyclical Nature. Every elemental interval is elucidated through unique Natural illustration, corresponding to the cycles through different phases in our lives.

A "winter" phase could be more internal, needing rest, feeling quiet, in a reflective mode, or not very social. "I don't need to be creating; I need silence, stillness."

Winter IntuWitchin says: "Take a break. Trying to push new leaves out when it's cold and snowing is a waste of energy. I'm gestating and rejuvenating."

Spring succeeds winter. When life feels cold and dark, it's comforting to know warmer, sunnier times are ahead. "I am reborn. I made it through the darkness, I weathered the storm, I survived the seemingly endless cold nights to bring new life. Now I am blossoming with all the colors of the Goddess." (Venus is associated with the deep green and pale pinks of this season.)

Then summer comes in hot for celebrating life and abundance. "I'm in full bloom, baby. All my peaches and sweet, sumptuous fruits are bursting from the trees. We're thriving! Get outside. I'm bright and sunny till 10 P.M.! Come dance and sing, laugh, and play with me. I'm sizzling, sweaty, and gorgeous."

Finally fall, the harvest phase, arrives. Autumn is for acknowledgment. "I have given my all to my creations. I watched them bear fruit and fuel my people/students/creatures. Here is my last output before it's time to take a breather, to rest again. I am full of wisdom, satiated with sustenance, and ready to go within."

Each of these seasonal energies can emerge in a single day. Every relationship and project, even our personal growth and evolution, have cycles, like all of creation. There have been countless days I've been up and writing first thing in the morning or sitting by a creek recording notes to transcribe the messages of Earth. Other days I absolutely can't look at the screen, or I just don't know what to say. I don't push winter away in those moments. Rather, I wait until the inspiration returns, reborn like spring. To bring an expression of who you are to life, you must honor the rise and fall of your motivation as the seasons move through you.

For example, in the summer of 2022—after starting off the year with several six-figure months—I tried the "scaling" and strategy you're "supposed to" do in online business, and it didn't work for me. It was a stark contrast from the success of doing things in my own, organic way. I was disappointed in the outcome but more so in myself for following a formula over my IntuWitchin. Even though I was faring wonderfully before, I decided to do what I had been *told* would work rather than continuing to be true to myself. I became dispirited; I needed a break. I didn't post on social media for months. My team e-mail and YouTube were flooded with questions: "Are you okay? When will you be back?"

It was hot and sunny outside, but I was in existential winter. I couldn't express myself outwardly; I just wanted to turn inward, ruminating. I didn't blame myself for being in the opposite season, "out of alignment" with Nature. My winter lasted six months! Come December, as the world outside my window was going into hibernation, I watched the Sinéad O'Connor documentary *Nothing Compares*, and the flames of inspiration reignited. I was fired up and spoke publicly for the first time about the programming inflicted upon us by the church, something I've studied relentlessly but never shared. It was so healing for others, my account grew 35K followers that month. From a snowy mountain cocoon, a sunny springtime butterfly was reborn.

Consider what season you are experiencing in your relationships, work, or inner realms. Have your creative juices been flowing? Or is taking a break, a metaphorical gestation period, what you need to bring forward your next idea or creation?

In a spring or summer phase, let yourself shine! Don't worry about anyone else's opinion. There will always be April showers and July thunderstorms, but no one *else's* seasons can rain on your parade. Give your creations all you've got to amplify their energy so that what comes forth carries you through quieter times.

OUR DRAGON GUARDIANS

Anybody who knows me knows I am a dragon queen. The ancient serpentine protectors of Earth present themselves in the mythical texts of every major society, mythology, and spiritual lineage worldwide. At a time when none of these civilizations visited one another—or perhaps even knew one another existed—it seems impossible that dragons are a figment of the entire global collective imagination. I believe they took great pride in helping build this beautiful planet. Why else would we call ley lines, the energetic meridians of Earth, dragon lines?

Dragons represent our most mystical powers, hence the church programming us to associate them with evil and worship those who slayed them. Dragons are meant to be *sleighed* (as in ridden), never slain! Their mention in so many Christian tales of important saints can be interpreted as proof that they once roamed the Earth.

So why are there no physical records of their existence? Animals that fly have very light, porous, hollow bones that are incredibly difficult to fossilize. But when you start to look for them, dragons express themselves through every facet of Nature. When I went to Loch Ness, home of the famous "monster" Nessie, the thunderclouds above me looked exactly like a giant storm dragon. Hundreds of people noticed it in my Instagram stories. One of the world's most famous water dragons showed Herself in the sky, clear as day, as I sat on her shores.

Dragons often reveal their faces in forests, too, making themselves visible in the shapes and patterns of trees' liquid-looking layers of bark. Perhaps you've seen them curled up with one another, pretending to be fallen logs or vines and roots. Make no mistake, *they are dragons.* If you see them, it's because they want you to. Often associated with the fire of their transfiguration powers, dragons return home to forests and alpine caves, always guarding the treasures of Earth. Where the jewels of the planet live, so do dragons. But they've hidden from us because we've broken their trust, idolizing their slayers. It's time to learn to ride our dragons, working *with* their fiery power!

Sitting and listening is a great start with dragon guardians. Their energy within us allows us to alchemize our pain into power and wounds into wisdom, mastering our magik for manifesting treasure in our own lives. They love sharing their messages. Try invoking them in channeled writing with the prompt "I call upon the dragons to write to me, through me, anything I am meant to receive in this moment." I'll do it now; let's see what they have to say. Some days, like now, you only get as far as "I call up . . ." before their prophecy streams through:

"People have been programmed to fear us and think we are vicious and evil. In the same way, you've been led to believe your own power, magik itself, and connection to the Earth is dangerous and untrustworthy. We are expressions of all these; power, magik, and the Earth—what is possible if you embody the creative force of the elements. There is a dragon teacher, guide, and friend for every human on Earth, if you seek us. We touch the

souls of those who have made the dragon movies adequately representing us and our codes. Our water magik is in Raya and the Last Dragon; *our light magik for invisibility is in* Pete's Dragon. *Learn about us not from those who speak ill but those who seek to show our truth. We are not dogs. Our intelligence is far beyond what humans can conceptualize; we are the cosmic wisdom of the Natural world. Look at how you treat the most beautiful gift created for you. A perfect planet with every unique ecosystem to satisfy any yearning or delight.*

We will speak to you in ways you have forgotten how to hear. Listen as much with your feelings as with your ears. Open your hearts, eyes, and minds, and remember we always have been and always will be here. You have only to call upon us.

A woman whose heart lets love fuel her power, her creations sourced from that magik, can be a portal for bringing dragons to life. We will come through you to reinhabit this plane if you allow us. We are honored to be the guardians of your womb. Once a dragon has been present within or around you, you will forever be safe, a true expression of eternal abundance."

Dragons are ready for us, and it's time for us to get ready for them and welcome them with an open heart. When you come upon a dragon, sit and speak to it. It will have a treasure for you, a gem of insight, or a jewel of transformational action to shift the trajectory of your existence. Give thanks for what it is sharing with you, and take that fiery action and be worthy of being treasured.

TREASURE *from the* WOMB *of* EARTH

Dragons often live in caves, some of my favorite places to spend time in; caves are wombs of the Earth. Crystals, jewels, gold, and precious riches are all found in caves, and we can mine the treasures of our psyche through them. It is in the body of the Mother Goddess that we find gems of wisdom, magik, and the potential to metamorphose.

I once visited a cave in New Zealand so deep, I had only hands on cavern walls to guide me in the pitch-black. I meandered back through twisting tunnels, tracking where I went left, knowing I would need to take a right on the way back. People have gotten lost and died in situations like this. But I felt called to go deeper into the darkness. When I emerged, it felt like being reborn. I saw my own inky depths with new eyes, and a greater trust in both my wisdom and my shadow. I left that sacred cave, returning to the States only days later initiated into a new iteration of my life. Within a few months of my return, I donned an iconic witch hat and forever changed the trajectory of my mission.

In myth and legend, the cave is the chalice, the womb. The word *hor* in Hebrew originally meant *cave* or *womb*—that's what a *whore* was! The womb-cave of Earth, the priestess, the Creator. This was never meant to be derogatory slang spewed at anyone; it's a holy place. Next time you find a cave, feel yourself having returned to the womb of your Mother, Mother Nature, and listen to what She coos to you.

How are you being asked to reparent yourself the way your parents never could? How is your healing, love, abundance, power, magik, and freedom? What does majesty feel like?

In sacred spaces, silence dials up the inner voice's volume, giving you more access to teachings that guide your every step.

OUR BODILY EARTH TEMPLE

The Earth element reminds us that care for our bodily temple's well-being is not only a solid foundation upon which to build but also clears the channel of our IntuWitchin.

When I first got into a partnership in 2019, I was the healthiest I'd ever been. But after a time, a few things felt off: I wasn't sleeping well, and my Scorpio sexuality had waned significantly. I figured the giant snoring bear was why I hadn't been getting good rest. But I was ignoring something deeper occurring in my body. It was also the spring of 2020, so the world, affected by COVID, wasn't exactly business as usual. I brushed off the abnormalities, presuming everything would balance out. What I didn't realize was that my IntuWitchin was using my body to get my attention.

Luckily, my partner encouraged me to get some basic blood work. It turns out my body wasn't producing testosterone! Weight lifting and supplements like Cordyceps and tongkat ali shifted things immensely. Beyond balancing my masculine and feminine energies, it was a reminder that if something isn't happening the way I'd like, I'm the one who must choose to actively shift it.

I stay connected with my motivation, sexuality, creativity, and overall sense of joy through intentional routines in Nature, ritual, movement, listening, and creation. Mother Earth echoes that we deserve to know and experience our inherent worth through our physical vessels. Making small, daily shifts in diet and exercise can have a huge impact on our sensitive tissues. Could it be any more obvious? If you want to follow your gut instincts, your gut better be good!

Hence nutrition is one of the most important components in caring for your body and the Earth. Let's zoom out for a minute. Millions of acres of rainforest are being cut down worldwide to plant palm trees for palm oil and grains like soy to feed livestock. This causes unfathomable damage to the "lungs of the Earth," drastically impacting our ability to breathe clean air, now and for the future. Her air represents our minds, polluted with all these painful programs convincing us not to listen to the wisdom of Her body or our own. This is only one example of how Her physical disease directly impacts us—and then we eat food grown in this energy.

Processed foods—meaning anything other than whole fruits, vegetables, and proteins consumed in the form they grow—can also create energetic and physical blockages in the body. Humans aren't designed to digest the molecular structure of margarine—which is closer to plastic than milk. Not to mention that manufacturing and processing extracts massive amounts of energy and resources from the Earth. Then packaging in single-use plastic, which we use for mere moments, remains on Earth for millennia. Unfortunately, it's getting harder to avoid processed foods, but we can always go back to basics in the produce section.

Supporting farmers' markets is your best option. You can also check out urban gardens or CSAs (community-supported agriculture), which trade time volunteering for veggies; it feels good to have your hands in the Earth. Even "organic" food can have unhealthy ingredients, so knowing where yours comes from is so important. Try your own canning! I love making pickles and dilly beans! It preserves much nutritional value and has fed families through many winters before grocery stores existed. If you buy canned goods, make sure they're salt- and BPA-free.

The equation is simple: When I eat more living foods, replacing processed snacks with green ones, I feel better. And when we take care of the people who take good care of the Earth, their food takes better care of us. Anyone who has eaten with me knows the food-blessing song I sing before each meal.

"Bless this food and the earth it came from.

Thank you, Mother, for sustaining us.

May we eat this meal together,

so we can live in Harmony.

Yummmm." (Sung like an om!)

Or perhaps get inspired by my friend Mike Posner, who takes three deep breaths before each meal. One for the food on his plate, giving gratitude to the sun, water, air, and Earth that grew it. One for all the people involved in making the meal: the farm workers and the people who cooked, served, and sold it. The final breath is for himself, his body, and how he wants to be nourished by the food.

ANCIENT ABUNDANCE

✳ ···································✳···································✳

I love the plane tickets money has bought me, the incredible castles I get to rent for my retreats, gas that gets me to the redwoods, and the laptop I'm writing this on for you. I have supported my students and clients, generating millions of dollars and massive abundance through my money magik and slaying scarcity rituals. I'm all for financial freedom allowing us to say yes to magikal experiences, growth, and fun. I wouldn't be here without it. However, when the energy behind our search for material wealth is out of alignment with Earth, there will always be that same energy of scarcity in how we *feel*.

That's why I manifest wealth through Earth magik. It's like the elemental Nature of reality teaming up to support your prosperity proliferating! This means rewriting the stories we have about money and reclaiming the truth that ecologically attentive people are the ones who should be wielding the resources of this planet, because ecological attentiveness is fundamental to living a magikal life.

Before we go any further, a note on the environmental crisis we're facing: The Law of Correspondence connects everything. Damage done to the Earth directly reflects in our reality with internal and financial scarcity, health challenges, and the overall mental illness, depression, and disconnection people experience. Her health unequivocally affects our own.

The Earth has been reduced from a living being to a *thing*—a resource to be drained for short-term personal gain, for use and abuse without repercussion. But the repercussions are the massive drain of our inner resources, such as our diminishing spiritual, emotional, physical, and mental health, escalating addiction, devastating drought, rampant wildfires, and much more.

We are so connected to Earth, that watching trees be cut down should evoke outrage. But we're oblivious to our own elemental nature and unaware of the impact atrocities performed on Nature—open-pit mining, the razing of forests, the pollution of rivers, lakes, and seas—have on us. Clueless that we're depleting true abundance, scarcity fuels our world. This is why many billionaires feel lonely, miserable, and unsatisfied.

The petroleum industry pollutes every element and was responsible for the discreditation of natural healing remedies, because modern medicine like antihistamines and cough syrup are made from oils and gas, or *petrochemicals*. Unbelievable but true. Money- and power-hungry tycoons driven by greed have infiltrated our minds so we fill our homes with *things* ordered insatiably online from Amazon—while the Amazonian jungle, the source of so much life, continues to burn unchecked. Disbelieving in the magik of Nature, we fill *our* bodies with pollutants, both chemical and emotional. We take and take, trying to *fill* an endless, gaping wound that wants desperately to be healed.

When we are reduced to mere *consumers*, divorced from our natural *creative* instincts, we have no care or concern for the impact of our species of ravaging the Earth. It is human nature to explore and nourish, but the what and how of our consumption have changed drastically over the past century. Plastic, the first substance completely void of a single natural molecule, was only invented in 1907. Now our urge for convenience and athletic gear has strewn microplastics though every element. Using something for a few hours or days that lingers unchanged on Earth for over 1,000 years is not what or who we want to be.

There is no throwing "away." All of our trash remains on this planet. Plastic cannot be absorbed back *into* the Earth because it is not *of* the Earth as all living things are. Prior to plastic, we only "threw away" biodegradable orange peels, apple cores, or animal bones, saving the hides for warmth. Now plastic sits on our planet, filling our rivers, oceans, beaches, and valleys.

The reason we feel guilty, upset, or ashamed of plastic use is because our IntuWitchin knows this is wrong and that we can do better. Though what our countries are permitted to produce and distribute is in the hands of Big Government, we have the power to choose what and how we consume. Activate and awaken to your personal environmental empowerment, vote with your dollars and actions, and be a real superhero for this planet. This is how we experience the conscious vibration of abundance permeating every area of our lives.

We *can* and *must* take this power back into our hands. If we keep ignoring these nonsensical yet habitual patterns, we'll be in trouble. Every choice you make impacts and communicates to the Universe. Yes, it's an issue of global leadership, and we must still do our best. Many countries will project their "limited" contribution to carbon emissions, not considering their vested financial interests in developing countries, wiping out thousands of miles of coral reefs or spilling oil off countless coastlines.

Every industry on Earth negatively affects the environment, endlessly plundering our planet's resources in the name of "prosperity," drilling into Her untouched depths for the same chemicals poisoning us. Polluting Her air and water corresponds directly with how humans have been poisoned by our pain mentally and emotionally. We're mined as consumers for our economic value without worry for our well-being long-term.

If governments implemented solution-based environmental policies, we would plant trees instead of annihilating forests, clean our air and water, and repair riparian zones; we would steward the Earth with tenderness the way our ancestors did. There is an abundance of alternative construction material available and enough steel in landfills from old cars and demolitions to rebuild every structure on Earth. But those holding the illusion of power are controlled by and only concerned with the almighty dollar, lost in the lie that money is the sole indication of prosperity.

We believe we play an insignificant, minor role as individuals. But each action we take ripples into the collective consciousness emanating and communicating what's most valuable and important to us. Intentionally doing what's best for the Earth makes a difference. We must never forget our seemingly microscopic efforts are reflected in the macrocosm. We each have the power to be leaders and role models.

If we remembered Earth is the source of our every blessing, every breath, we would revere Her like the loving Mother she is. Knowing we are loved encourages sharing love with others. Remembering we are a global family, we would care for her like someone we love. The first step is reestablishing the bond to our spiritual Mother, Earth, to reattune and align ourselves with the same energy that brought us into being, fighting for Her the way she deserves. This is the ancient abundance our modern world is longing to experience.

NATURE TALKS

The same way our body speaks to us through pain or disease, so too does the body of the Earth. There is always a multidimensional message.

When you notice trash on the beach or forest floor, take note: "What was I thinking about when I saw it?" "Do I ignore it? Pretend it's not mine?" It certainly isn't Hers; it's your responsibility to pick it up and dispose of it, the same way it is your responsibility to find ways to "clean up" your own inner landscape.

Weather speaks wonders to us. Air and water combine in clouds. How might our emotions be "clouding" our mind? What beliefs about our emotions block us from shining or taking action?

Whenever winds are blowing, consider your thoughts. Are the winds of change whipping in to shift your state of mind? If you're frustrated about something and wind knocks a pen off the table, or out of your journal, write yourself a new story.

Mud is where water meets Earth. When my partner first began diving deep into healing his trauma, he kept pulling the same oracle card, "stuck in the mud." He was refusing to release the emotions that had been stuck in his body since childhood, emotions that had been bogging him down and greatly affecting every area of his life.

Even plants have a unique frequency and either a toxic or tonic effect. A dandelion bursts through the concrete, mirroring your own capacity to overcome seemingly impossible odds! Or perhaps your body needs a liver or digestive detox, two of the main medicinal benefits of this magikal messenger (every part of which can be ingested for different intent).

SUSTAINABLE SOLUTIONS

Up in Sedona's gorgeous red rock canyon mountains where creeks are clear and swimmable year-round, storms bring rainbows almost every day. But the same way we can "look great" while experiencing aches, pains, and challenges below the surface, the beauty of Nature can mask what's really going on for our planet.

The truth is, we have been a parasitic bacteria for the last few hundred years, an infection in the muscles of Her soil, dehydrating Her, filling Her lungs with toxic smoke. The Earth has a great immune system, and as our contamination quota ramps up, if something doesn't change, She's going to start remedying Her issue. We've seen the force of Her tidal waves and hurricanes, earthquakes and wildfires. We must become the antidote for ourselves before she resorts to treatment. We must cry our tears, take deep breaths, move our bodies, and transform our harmful habits.

Living a magikal life means being conscious of your buying tendencies and overall environmental impact. Our species has lost sight of the Universal laws of balance and correspondence. Now we must uphold the truth that everything is connected, as our actions affect the planetary ecosystem as a whole.

Sustainability literally means the ability to maintain at a certain level. The way we're going is the opposite. What would it look like for you to live more sustainably? To enhance rather than subtract from the wellness of the planet and future generations? Yes, a big part of this is systemic change from the powers that be. But drops of water can change stone, even with small contributions—every dollar you spend is a little abundance spell showing appreciation for your values.

Here are some of my favorite tips for living a magikal sustainable life:

Get into Nature more often. Appreciate how important caring for Her is.

Be as plastic-free and waste-free as possible. Stop buying plastic bags and water bottles. Please! Get a reusable water bottle and refill it. Find alternatives to your packaging materials.

When in nature—hiking or in the country—pee outside. We shouldn't be polluting our water, but our soil loves that nitrogen.

Stop ordering from Amazon. Supporting artisanal vendors and small businesses gives the profits directly to their families and encourages ethical business practice. I love paying eco-friendly crafters and creative people fair wages for their offerings.

Buy from farmers' markets. Meet the people tending the land where your food comes from. Smell their apples and melons. The flavors have more vibrance and richness, and their soil is likely more nutritious. Ask them about their plants. They'll be excited to share.

Get your clothes, furniture, and other household items used whenever you can. Find pre-loved pieces online or at thrift stores. I buy almost everything vintage, only occasionally getting new things from small businesses, Etsy designers, or friends.

Be mindful of the fabrics you're wearing. Anything containing rayon, nylon, or polyester are just more plastics. I love finding secondhand cashmere, silk, and linens.

Compost, even if just in a box on your windowsill. Methane is produced by food rotting in landfills between plastics rather than being able to properly decompose in the ground. Some farmers' markets have compost drop-off points, and many towns have compost pickup services—often in exchange for fresh produce! Check out MakeSoil.org for more information.

Above all, remember that alignment with our IntuWitchin means healing the wounds hindering the craft of our wisdom and magik. Once we embody the Law of Correspondence, the more energy you dedicate to caring for the Earth, the more you are caring for yourself, your soul, and Source.

Practice — *Beach or Nature Clean*

Remember, garbage on Her body reflects garbage *in* yours! It is our collective responsibility to clean up our outer and inner environment. There is no "away" where you can throw anything.

Gathering friends for a beach or Nature clean is very fun and extremely rewarding. In Southern California, people go to beaches year-round, but any time is a great time to contribute to the health of the planet. You can even gamify the experience by having prizes, and whoever collects the most trash wins.

Get a big group together so you can cover a massive amount of ground. Agree on a rendezvous point and meeting time with your hauls. My friends and I once offered the winner a choice of two sessions of whatever our gifts were. First and second place got a comprehensive business and social media strategy session with me, then a lucid-dreaming lesson with another. Mutual benefit for all!

You can always include the ceremonial aspect: I like to lead a meditation at the beginning linking us to one another and

Mother Earth, letting Her know we are here to help serve and support Her, to listen.

Practice — *Cave-diving*

Caves—the womb and sacral chakra—are associated with water. They exist in the Earth, as the womb lives in our body. Reconnect to your own sensuality, sexuality, creativity, and emotional realm by visiting a cave. Return to the Mother's wisdom and knowledge. See how long you can stay. Can you listen? What do you hear? How do you feel?

How deeply can you extend your awareness to feel the cave as the womb? In what ways are you asking to be reborn? How must you surrender?

Let yourself be held by the Goddess, this sentient planetary deity. Without Her we are nothing. Let Her absorb you. What cycle of nature are you in? What is its significance to you? What is asking to be healed? Cleansed? Cleared? Reborn from within your womb cauldron?

If you don't have any caves nearby, try something that mimics the same feeling of darkness and silence. Go for a sensory-deprivation float tank, or play with your inner child by making a pillow fort. Or find the quietest place in your home, make enough space to comfortably lie down, and cover yourself with enough blankets to keep any light out. Or take a bath in the dark with the door closed. If you wish, bring crystals with you. When you have arrived in your makeshift cave, envision yourself in the womb cauldron of the Mother. You are safely held and enveloped by Her.

JOURNAL PROMPTS

How can you create a deeper devotion and connection to Mother Earth?

What habits are you being asked to look at or release that haven't been serving your body or Her body?

What does your body communicate to you right now or on a daily basis?

What does "healthy" look, mean, and feel like to you?

What does fulfillment and success look like for you professionally, financially, and romantically?

How is your stability and groundedness?

What part of your life is asking for appreciation?

The Wisdom
of Water

Our elemental journey flows from the caves of Earth into the primordial womb of all life, the waters. It is the oceanic profundity that lovingly challenges us to surrender into the unknown, trusting we'll be carried, lifted even, effortlessly, by the flow of life, the Mother in Nature.

Water is life, the full force of emotions coursing through us. Feeling feelings is considered "sensitive," but is not for the faint of heart. Rejecting or repressing them weakens our wisdom, an endless, vicious cycle only broken by choosing to tell a different tale about what emotions mean.

Emotions predate spoken communication and play out in the animal kingdom every day. When we are preverbal, feelings and emotions are our only access to communicating with the world around us, a physical and energetic language beyond words. We rely entirely on them both to interpret what we are experiencing and to ask for what we need. When we know how to listen, our feelings about a given situation show us what we need, believe, and desire. As we mature into social groups, we rely heavily on spoken communication.

Essentially, emotions present what's alive within our body, mind, and spirit. Feeling happy and joyful rewards your actions, encouraging continuation on the same path. You shine in the world around you, and the warmth of that energy is mirrored back into you.

If you're generally disappointed or frustrated in life, it is time to change course, seek fulfillment, and shift the stories that inform the mindset that's keeping you stuck where you are, believing this is all you are worthy of. Or it's a call to ignite the flames within you by doing something that perhaps you never thought you could do but have always wanted to try. If you are grieving, you are building strength, blazing a trail for others to be held in your arms when they are falling apart.

Knowing the depths of your own darkest shadows, sadness, rage, and grief is what makes the elation and ecstasy of excitement, love, and pleasure so thoroughly enjoyable. This is the beauty in the tides of life, our eternal ebb and flow, rising and falling like all sentient life since the beginning of time. This is the medicine from creatures of the deep: whales, dolphins, octopuses, sharks, and salmon, boldly going into the farthest reaches of our subconscious, singing their sacred songs, teaching us to be unafraid of deeper emotions we may not see clearly, always finding our way home. Anytime aquatic animals arise, they bring awareness to the water element in your life.

Because we grow within the waters of our mothers' wombs, built bit by bit from the blood of her uterine lining, water also represents our most deeply buried memories, transmitting the genetic codes of our ancestral lineage. Like how our fingerprints are painted by waves of amniotic fluid flowing in utero, water is the element most adaptable to form, and so it forms us. She yields to any vessel's shape as we contain our emotions.

Can we accept sadness filling us to the brim, releasing the floodgates of tears when it's time? Repressing rage does more harm than letting our inner volcano rise and erupt. Tainted water taints our emotions. We need it yet we mistreat it.

Emotions are literally energy plus motion. When emotions feel powerful and hard to understand, we have a tendency to attach to or identify as them. We hold on to happiness while rejecting sadness and doubt. But all emotions are designed to arise, deliver a message, and move on. Existential agony lies in abnegating whatever is flowing through.

We're taught to fear emotions, deny them their full expression. But tears are the only way bodies excrete the stress hormone cortisol; crying tears releases cortisol from your tissues. Water that doesn't move quickly turns stagnant, so I always encourage letting those tears fall, often! But men are told crying is "weak," and women are told that it's manipulative.

Suppressing tears, holding back any emotion, only creates more pain. We're showing the child inside of us that they are unworthy of experiencing their authenticity or being seen in vulnerability. We've been taught that damming up our inner rivers is a sign of strength and stability. But the lush riparian zones, wildlife populations and habitats beneath dams, entire ecosystems' flora and fauna are annihilated without flowing, hydrating waters, just as our bodies get destroyed by barricading emotions. In order to live a prolific life enchanted by exquisite magik, guided by our soul's voice and IntuWitchin, our waters must be free to flow.

Water's characteristics correspond to different displays of emotion: rains purify like tears, lakes teach calm stillness, rivers trust flow, oceans can be wildly aggressive or warmly welcoming. We are the waters of life: rivers, creeks, hurricanes, and rain. Water is the feminine soul song sung in streams.

Despite poisoning Mother Nature's veins, this essential element's spirit tells another story. Rain sings as it falls, ice as it hardens and forms, brooks babble over boulders, water makes art. She is creativity incarnate, taking the shape of anywhere she flows. When you learn to let your emotions live within you, you're a walking embodiment of Nature expressing the elemental world and life itself.

SACRED SPRINGS:
The POWER *of* PURE POTENTIAL
❋ ································· ❋ ····························· ❋

Humans and Earth contain around the same percentage of water—around 70 percent. Like our planet we, too, are tidal beings. Yet we are so ashamed of menstrual blood, which mirrors the moon's motion. Pollutants poison Earth's waters every day. In the same way, our relationship to our emotions has become contaminated by both toxic chemicals and cultural programming.

Alternative medicine doctor Masaru Emoto revealed the impact of our thoughts and intentions on water. He experimented by writing different words on containers of water that affected the crystalline cellular structures of the molecules. Words like love and joy created beautiful, symmetrical snowflake-like patterns. Exposure to words like hate and anger caused the impressions to become chaotic and disorganized, proving our emotional well-being and bodily health respond to our speech and feelings. We're impacted by our words, our spelling. We can choose to be crystalline structures of chaos or Divine beauty. If we betray and abandon our authentic selves, our body remembers. Is your self-talk and the language you receive from the world around you toxic? Or does it support your emotional structure?

Simultaneously, all over the world, drinking water has been corrupted by chemicals. Although we have "safe" drinking water in most of the United States, that doesn't mean it's good for us. We're told fluoridated tap water is good to drink for your teeth. But fluoride has been proven by the Harvard School of Public Health to be a neurotoxin particularly damaging to children's brain development. As such, it can be one of the greatest hindrances to IntuWitchin, as it adversely affects your pineal gland (the third-eye chakra responsible for melatonin production/ dreaming and visionary states). Water that travels through thousands of miles of plastic tubing, other people's toilets, gets pumped full of chlorine, and zapped of its original mineral content is so far from what truly nourishes and hydrates us.

Thus, the water we drink carries the vibration of "There is something wrong with you. Look at all the things we must do to 'fix' you, to make you 'safe.' You're not good enough as you are because you weren't worth protecting and caring for in the first place." Imagine its structure with that kind of (mis) treatment. It's the same story we've heard over and over. The element of reflection directly reflects to us our mistreatment of the Earth's blood, mirroring the lack of value we place on our emotions.

The holy waters were once sacred. Human waste once nourished the Earth; now it poisons the waters. In Western civilization, we shit in clean, fresh water that millions of people would kill to drink. A good "nature poo" feels so liberating, because it's the natural way—though, unfortunately, it isn't realistic for most people. Our modern relationship to the wellspring of planetary and personal well-being sends a clear message to water and emotion.

I know it may not be possible to drink pristine water straight from a spring most of the time, but try to pay more attention to your water's source. Spring water in a plastic bottle will contain microplastics. Glass bottles are preferable and are also much easier to recycle. The genius website FindASpring.com will show you places to gather water in the wild all over the United States.

Water reminds us everything is connected. Every natural body of water—mountain stream, canyon creek, and valley river—flows to the ocean, like all the veins in our bodies originate at our hearts. The adaptability and willingness of water to find its own path, easily overcome obstacles, fill cracks and crevices, carving the very crags of stones winding its way over and around, contains a powerful message.

Indigenous cultures who survived on salmon would wait by river mouths at the ocean to welcome the first fishes' arrival. They celebrated and honored the Piscean pilgrims' perseverance, surviving the return home to spawn in their native streams, waiting four full days for salmon to pass through their nets before harvesting one and sharing it as a tribe. Now we

mindlessly ravage creeks and our oceans, desecrating the populations of sacred ecosystems within them with no regard for the
fortitude of these beings.

Can we align with the fluidity of our emotions, surrender
our grip and attempts at control, and allow ourselves to be
moved by the currents of life? Never betraying our truth, but
responding to the situation at hand through our essence?

Water, like emotions, has many uses. It perfectly preserves
as it freezes: steam powers giant locomotives carrying hundreds of thousands of tons of freight; it can generate massive
amounts of electricity; and it can quench our thirst and cleanse
us. Our bodies know what to do with our inner waters, but
allowing their contamination only hurts us in the long-term.

Disrespecting and damaging water reflects in our bodies.
They're disregarded, and we've all seen what happens to children, adults, animals, and even houseplants who feel worthless,
like they don't matter: they wither away. Water—including the
water that literally makes us who we are—holds memory. Our
stewardship, tenderness, positive thoughts, and words impact
the state of our personal physical vessels and this incredible
planet holding us. Allowing our waters to flow, our tears and
rain to fall, signals to Mother Earth our intent to purify this
relationship. Without toxifying our vessels with judgment or
shame, we can cleanse our emotional realm and ultimately heal
our world. I always tell my students and clients, when we feel
the surge of our emotions rising to the surface inside, don't
choke them down, swallow, or suppress them. That is the ultimate IntuWitchin initiation with this element. They rise to
flow out of you. Keeping them in just hurts you and further per-
petuates the toxic cycle. We have to feel to heal.

TAKE *the* PLUNGE

＊┄┄┄┄┄┄┄┄┄┄┄┄＊┄┄┄┄┄┄┄┄┄┄┄＊

One of the fastest ways to connect with water is immersing yourself in it. Surrendering to be psychically transported back into our Mother's womb, intrinsically recalling our original, primordial nature. Because water is also what we use to clean ourselves, our minds can be instantly purified and reconnected to our essential ethos, clearing the path to our IntuWitchin so we may be energetically reborn.

You can feel held by the waters while surfing, soaking in a river, swimming in a lake or stream, floating in a pool or sensory-deprivation chamber, or steeping in a warm bath. Surfers talk about the state of oneness they experience united with the power of the ocean in the waves. With awareness, we can achieve this state anytime we are immersed in water.

Personally, I love jumping in creeks, no matter the season. They are generally quite cold, and I expand my lungs, inhaling more clarity and insight. Cold showers work, but they're less exhilarating. Speaking of showers, waterfalls are my favorite. Ritually standing beneath a purifying fountain, I let the cold deluge crack open my crown chakra, connecting me directly to the Divine. Mythologically, waterfalls are said to be portals to other realms and dimensions.

Waterways, thermal springs, and mountain spas have always been the domains of priestesses and Ladies of the Lakes. From the Grecian Mother Goddess Artemis to the Gaelic Sulis merged with Roman Minerva and Avalonian priestesses, every tradition has its water witches, servants of the Goddess who guarded the sacred springs. With this in mind, always approach waters with reverence. Physically lean into them, bathing your mind and thoughts in light. Wash your eyes and ears, clearing how you see and hear the world. Cleanse your vibration and speech with water in and over your throat. Coax tension from your shoulders, increasing your capacity to give love through your arms. Let any blockages from receiving love wash away from your heart. I often visualize a rainbow bursting forth from the light of my solar plexus as if I'm the waterfall, becoming the basin as it pools in my womb-space. Baptism is ancient pre-Christian water magik. Greeks, Egyptians, Celts, and more always engaged in ritual bathing, particularly before debate or dialogues of philosophical and spiritual context to ensure they were a perfect, clearly communicating channel of the Divine message. It signified washing away one's personality to be reborn from the womb, purified to the innocence of a child.

At the castle where I host my retreats in Scotland, spring water rises from the rocks below through the tap, making every shower a ceremonial healing activation. I close my eyes beneath the warm waterfall, where I can devour every drop. I gulp down the crystalline waters and sing affirmation mantras at the top of my lungs. I've never felt cleaner than when I emerge from that soul-satisfying saturation. With intention, every shower is a cleansing ritual—envision what you're washing away falling off your body and out of your energy field.

Try it for yourself. Tune in with your IntuWitchin getting clear on what you're releasing, even if just for the day. Visualize how that energy shows up in your body and where. Notice the color, texture, shape, and sensation of it. Then use your hands, or simply the water itself, to focus on cleansing it from your field. Activate the healing quality of water by turning beneath the spout three times—one turn to cleanse the old ways, one to bless your present moment, one to invite what's replacing this pattern for the future—as you speak the following affirmation out loud:

"I purify myself for X [healing, growth, creation]."

If you have time (and a tub), baths are even more relaxing. I love to add oils, herbs, crystals, and flowers to the water, be surrounded by candles, and meditate on what I'm releasing or manifesting. You can scrub the old ways away with salts or sensually stroke yourself with oil, giving your body exactly what it craves. Since water can be programmed, luxuriating in your desires is delicious. Once during a bathing ritual my partner came and read me a meditation from my favorite dragon magik book as I soaked. Now, *that* was an experience.

STAR WATER, MOON BLOOD

The womb is the most sacred vessel of our inner waters: the chalice, the cauldron inside. Mothers grow us in amniotic sacs, the womb waters literally incubating life. Hence water's association with sexuality and creativity. Regardless of our biological sex, using IntuWitchin to connect to the "womb-mind" powerfully activates our capacity for "birthing" new life. There are even theories that all life on Earth developed from the moon magnetizing ocean tides. Bivalves, some of the first sentient life, operate solely in response to the ebbing cycle of waters.

The generative creative portal through which new souls arrive earthside, the womb, or dantian, also brings dreams and visions to life. Connect to your inner cauldron as a nourishing home for IntuWitchin to powerfully help you manifest whatever you want—art, books, businesses, experiences. See them brewing within you, forming and growing until they're ready to be born.

Honor the waters and IntuWitchin by aligning your actions with your menstrual flow or understanding your partner's. If periods are "gross" to you, can you think of who may have first projected that programming onto you? Cultural aversion to the blood of life is very new.

The tidal currents of our moon time have been a natural and integral part of life for the entirety of human evolution. Long before we took daily baths, a woman with blood-strewn thighs was not only commonplace but beautiful and sacred. Moon blood being "disgusting" is yet another way women's natural magik has been suppressed. The patriarchy made the most sacred things we share as sisters into a shameful, dirty punishment, a "curse" inflicted upon us.

In alchemical texts, fairy-tale metaphor, and holy-grail legends, moon blood was considered precious, even supernaturally magikal. Often, historians who seek for truth beyond the allegory of Jesus, indicate that the original blood of Christ came from women. His blood we receive is eternal life, and moon blood really is the source of life. The Divine was always our Mother before the church. Christ means anointed one, or the anointed; moon blood is shed without violence. This holy sacrament was a blessing to consume, full of stem cells; it's the fountain of youth. Many ancient Tantric and Egyptian rituals involve drinking moon blood and gaining superpowers from it. Like Popeye's spinach, the liquid of life itself enhances psychic gifts and abilities. Rites of ancient Taoists blended it with semen to consecrate a union.

Once upon a time, women also bled together at the new moon. Before the advent of artificial lighting, fire and moonlight were all that illuminated the night. The darkest time cosmically heightened women's ability to see within. Over this period (literally) each moonth, women sat together in "red tents," engaging in communal ceremony, prayer, and music while receiving the wisdom of the Goddess in quiet introspection. Blood wasn't flushed down toilets. It was ritually returned to Her as women bled freely on the Earth. Now, doing everything we can to hide it, our waters never return to the ground. Seeing our blood and cyclical Nature as dirty highlights the inner Witch Hunter in society. The word *taboo* even to comes from menstruation.

But this is not the case in every culture. To this day, in Diné (Navajo) tradition, when a young woman gets her bleed, she's celebrated, waited on hand and foot. It's a big party with beautiful baked goods, women welcoming her, and men serving her. Every little girl deserves this entrance into womanhood! But these rituals have been lost in Western culture due to colonization.

Now women feel ashamed of moon blood, like there's something wrong with us (there's not). That story again. Imagine instead having fun with your mom, sisters, and aunties! With significantly less age disparity, three generations could bleed together in the same tent. Think about it: Does your cycle sync up with your friends or family members when you spend time together? That's a biological function so we could share this special time collectively. We would sing songs, talk to the Earth—no boys allowed. How differently would you feel about moon time with so much less stress and worry about pads, cramps, and the terrors of leaking in school?

Bottom line: our moon time is sacred. Reclaiming it is a vital part of living our most magikal lives. This time of the "moonth," we shed old ways and versions of ourselves, receiving direction from our IntuWitchin when we are most open and sensitive.

Personally, bleeding is my favorite time of the month. I honor my moon with sacred rituals, my IntuWitchin heightened during this phase. I don't work much the first three days, giving myself permission to do the most nourishing thing in each moment, whatever is pleasurable. I sleep a lot, take an edible, watch Disney movies, and connect with other sisters who are bleeding. Ask your body, your womb, or your partner, what would support her most?

Journaling at this time can also be an especially potent way to connect to your IntuWitchin. Reflecting on the past moonth, ask:

"Was I empowered? Weak?" "Where did I thrive? Fall?" "What have I learned?" "What is shedding with this blood?"

Our moon cycle is designed to help us emancipate every possibility or version of us that has not come to fruition, that was not meant to be. Anyone you've slept with and any potential child from your union disappears. Often after a massive healing or momentous event, you may find your womb shedding spontaneously. The day of my last Scotland retreat, I got my moon a full week early; the woman I had been was gone. Every time we bleed, the DNA we would pass on to the next generation is changed. Reflect on what's releasing each month as your blood flows.

Moon blood is *magik*! It helps your plants grow, is loaded with stem cells that make it speed up wound healing, and is amazing for face masks. I like to free bleed into the Earth, like we're meant to. I think about being a good ancestor to my lineage rather than a good descendent to the current status quo. This is how I want women to relate to their blood, differently than our mothers did. When I paint it on my face each moonth, I feel like the Warrior Goddess of my highest self. If you can feel this idea opening you to working with your waters in this way, you're likely wondering—and I get this question a lot—"How do I gather my blood?"

Dressed in black, honoring the magikal midnight darkness of the void, I listen to the sensations of my body as my cycle begins. I have accustomed myself to feeling for the moment when blood travels down from my cervix. That's generally the sharp, gasp-in pain, but you've got time before it leaves your body. I walk outside onto the Earth or into the bathroom, where I use a chalice, seashell, or other small, handheld vessel to collect blood as it falls from my yoni waterfall.

My 2017 dragon trip to Kauai initiated me into moon blood magik. The priestesses inhabiting that island were doing rituals with blood I'd never previously encountered. My dear sister Dakota welcomed us to her home one day, wearing no pants, with blood smeared across her thighs. She invited us into a gazebo turned temple with gorgeous statues and altars. Her cushions were covered with bloodstained sheets, and we sat down for tea like nothing unusual was happening.

In the moment I was shocked—and enlivened at how safe and comfortable she felt showing this "vulnerable" side of herself to us. My confusion quickly lifted into awe and reverence. They were drinking the blood, singing to it, and painting their faces with it for radiant glowing skin. It really works and is now one of my favorite rituals during moon time. Consider the beautiful metaphor of letting go of our capacity to give life, that which we release is also nourishing us as it goes.

You can make manifestation paintings with your blood. I drew castles for magikal education years before I ever created feminine transformation retreats in them. The power to bring life from your womb and the Divine supports you in bringing the visions of your heart to life. I generally only use blood from a really powerful cycle for a manifestation painting. If I've been happy that moonth, on it with my morning routine, harmonious with my partner, my blood is infused with strong, positive energy. I get a big piece of paper and focus on whatever I'm currently calling in. Mix the blood with varied amounts of water for thicker or more translucent colors in a sepia-spectrum palette. I also love to paint my partner. At six-five, he gives me full Viking warrior vibes. Very sexy.

Though edgy, try making a moon mask. Trust me, your skin will be mind-blowingly amazing after! You can add clay or oils, but the plasma itself is miraculous. Let day one shed first—gather your blood on days two to four. Put it on your face or on any wounds you might have, and let it dry. Just like any other mask, it tightens on your skin, and you can remove at your leisure. *Note: Make sure your blood smells clean before you do this. If it doesn't, there might be an imbalance, and you should consult your naturopath or doctor.*

I only use the blood for these rituals during months I feel overall represent and reflect the ways I want to show up in the world. If I have been too quickly frustrated, overly stressed, or depressed and unproductive, I want to shed those patterns along with the blood. On these moonths, I use the blood in my fire rituals instead, symbolically letting go of negative habits and energies.

Even without rubbing blood all over your face (I get it; it was an enormous hurdle for me at first!), simply giving yourself intentionally inward time can be such a healing and awakened gesture to your womb. Listen; let it navigate you into the primordial part of your being.

TIDES OF LIFE

Aligning with our inner waters' rhythm optimizes both generative energy and restful integration. Like the planet, our cycle has four seasons. The moon doesn't just illuminate shadows in her fullness. She brings the highest tides and drops our eggs when she's bright so we can make love bathed in her luminous silvery glow. Then, she draws down the blood from our bodies when the nights are darkest and tides are lowest.

Working with the rivers within to maximize creative potential means going with the flow of our bodies. Working with the metaphor of the seasons, we recharge in winter, get inspired in spring, act in summer, and prepare in autumn. The more in tune you are with the tides' cadence in you, the more clearly your IntuWitchin guides you to exactly where you need to be.

New moon/bleeding: Our inner winter, energy, and hormones are at their lowest. This is the dark moon time of the month when we would all sync up together, dancing around the sacred fire, before artificial and light pollution. We are losing iron, hence craving heavier, heartier food, and more of it, just like how we need a little extra layer in winter to stay warm.

Waxing moon/follicular phase: Our inner spring, the body starts preparing newly cleansed uterine lining by growing the follicles that produce and allow eggs to develop. We feel like getting out into the world again, our energy fresh and rejuvenated.

Full moon/ovulation: Our inner summer, when witchy things happen. Tides and emotions are high, close to the surface. Our wild sides come out to dance and play, flames ignited within. The fruits and seeds of our bodies are in bloom. We're our most fertile and, therefore, generally most turned on and craving sexual intimacy—as tends to be the case on hot, sweaty summer nights.

Waning moon/luteal phase: Our inner autumn. The womb lining thickens in preparation to support new life. If you're not pregnant, your hormones begin to drop, signaling the onset of winter for bleeding to occur again. We still have energy to make things happen, be out and about, but the body is preparing to slow down.

Dark moon: The day before the moon becomes new again, our uterine lining prepares to shed, just as we prepare in autumn's final days for the coming cold.

MORE MOON TIME ACTIVITIES

Spend time in Nature.

Pamper yourself.

Listen to your womb.

Bathe in fresh or wild water.

Lay your womb upon sun-warmed stones.

Rest.

Sing to Nature, the Goddess, Her aliveness in you, the elements, or waters specifically.

Womb or breast massage.

Thank the blood for shedding.

Dress candles or altars with blood to support your manifestations.

What sensual sensations do you crave to experience or receive more of? Are there certain parts of your body that fancy being tended to or worshipped, particular words you want to hear, flavors you want to taste, movement your body wants to express, things you want to say, textures you want to be caressed with?

Once you have discovered these things, create a sensual experience for yourself by gathering any items you desire or require to fulfill the inner yearnings of your body.

Choose a playlist of music that reflects the energy you covet—soft sounds if you wish to relax, energetic tones if you want to dance and move. Set your space with ambience that excites and entices you—light some candles and tidy up to clear the energy.

Begin with your hands on your body in stillness or gently touching the part asking for attention. Perhaps tenderly drag your fingernails down your throat or through your hair. Let the moment guide you. What does your body need? What senses are you called to scintillate? Further stimulate yourself by speaking words you've longed to hear from a lover's lips—it is so nourishing when they come from your own.

Take your time or push it to the edge of how much sensual delight you can tolerate. Maybe you just take 10 minutes. Remember, this practice is simply to revive your connection to your sensual nature. There's no pressure to orgasm or even experience sexual energy; this is just about pleasurable enjoyment of your body and five (or six) senses.

Be naked. If that's difficult for you, challenge yourself, and again—focus on the senses. If you'd like, have some sensual delights on hand. I like raspberries, whipped cream, sexy Tantric instrumental music, jojoba oil for my skin, scents of gardenia and jasmine, feathers, satin scarves, a fur flogger, and roses for caressing my body.

Practice — Healing Our Blood

Everybody, regardless of gender expression, has healing to do around how they have been made to feel about menstruation and moon time. The first step in healing is awareness. Use the following questions to understand where your past programming may be preventing you from connecting with the sacredness of this season in our cycle.

For those who bleed:

How have you been taught to treat moon time?
What was your mother's guidance around your blood?
How have partners responded to your bleeding?

For those who do not bleed:

How do you respond to moon blood?
What was your education on menstruation like?
How have you related to moon blood in relationships?
How might you be able to understand better?

During your or your partner's bleed, try putting into practice at least one of the invitations laid out in this chapter, even if that's just watering your plants with moon blood. The easiest way to acclimate yourself to honoring moon blood by creating reverent ritual is inventorying the past month and what ways are shedding. You can journal, share with another friend on their moon time, or tell your partner, whether they bleed or not.

Once you have acknowledged what is passing through this flowing water, consider what the most magikal method of honoring this release would be. Just bleeding onto the Earth rather than into a pad, tampon, or toilet is a ritual reconnection to our reverential ancestral origins. After I first shared about making a moon mask online, I got hundreds of photos of women who tried it for themselves and were astounded at how natural and beautiful it felt. Your body, your blood, your *choice.*

To start, try painting something small with your moon blood, whether on paper or your body. Draw whatever you feel called to. It may be a single line, a dot, or outlining your dream house. Whatever it is, place your conscious creation into the blood. This simple act works wonders for healing this sacred seasonal cycle within.

 JOURNAL PROMPTS

What does creative, sexual, and emotional fulfillment mean to me?

What do my heart and soul want to birth into the world?

Were you shamed for emotions, sexuality, or creativity as a child?

Where have you denied attention to emotion?

What are you being asked to cleanse, purify, or cry out and wash away?

What is water's message?

Chapter 8

The Colors
of the Wind

Spirare is Latin for *breath* or to *breathe life into.* It is the root of inspire, aspire, transpire, spirit, and the season of spring. We wed the wind, saying yes to the magikal potential in every breath, acknowledging our communication with the world around us through our spells.

Air is the relief in deep sighs of satisfaction, moans of love-making, panting from exertion, or gasping when laughter overcomes us—the multidimensional nature of breath. And breath is behind every word as we speak our intentions and existence into being.

Our lives are sustained by the plants exchanging this elemental energy with us. A warm desert breeze running through a canyon, a rush of cool wind whipping through trees on a dripping-hot summer day, sandstorms, and tornadoes—all are flavors of the wind. The textures and energetic expressions of air reflect different emanations of communication, thoughts, and imagination. We can speak softly, tenderly, or shout exasperatedly, whisper sweet nothings, or irrupt inconsiderately. Exclaiming our joy and accomplishment from the rooftops is very different than stewing in silence.

Though wind appears invisible, we feel it, hear it, and watch as it whips through the world around us, a reminder of the unseen forces animating life. Wind rustles the leaves, howling like crashing waves singing the same song as she flows over mountains. Whispering in your ear, playing with your hair, silent until it makes contact with leaves, the surface of water, or the edges of you. Same as thoughts, they float through our consciousness without much cognizance until they meet a preference, comparison, opinion, story, or judgment. Then they become loud.

Metaphysically, the air element represents mind, thoughts, words, songs, and the ways we express them. If we truly knew what a monumental role thoughts and words play in creating our reality, we would do anything to ensure they align with our aspirations for ourselves, one another, and the planet.

Our thoughts can convince us of horrible things or enkindle our imaginations, believing anything is possible. Some nourish and hold us, and others rip us apart, tearing us down. Some stories so deeply disempower us, we forget how to escape them and that we can choose to believe something different. This storm of thoughts, depression, suicidal ideation, unworthiness, or paralyzing fear of failure can sweep into our lives with the destructive force of a tornado. When you add water and emotion, tornadoes become hurricanes, flooding that leaves a wake of rot and mold in the foundation of our life, defiling our internal landscape and corroding our self-esteem.

IntuWitchin shows thoughts for what they are: programmed reactions and opinions, opportunities for opening our minds or amplifying desired beliefs, behaviors, and outcomes. We always have the authority to change our thoughts before we become too attached to them. Following the thread of how disempowering beliefs impact our lives, we can unearth the source of limiting programs, heal them, and release however we've been imprisoned by them. Now we are free.

Each practice in this chapter breathes life into the full embodiment of the magnitude of your radiance. We say "a breath of fresh air" to reference something new and innovative, arriving with the vibration of long-awaited relief. The winds of change speak when a gale wafts up around you or through the trees above.

"What was I thinking about?"

"Where has my mind been running off to?"

Placing your focus on the wind, release mental chatter to receive the message revealed by the breath of life. We must clear our minds to listen, but it is not a one-way street. Listening deeply to your surroundings, the gentle whisper of wind, and your breath, is one of the easiest ways to refresh your mind. It ignites us, bringing a sense of wonder and awe, breathing life into yourself to become a masterpiece.

The winged ones channel wind wisdom upon their sailing flight. Air animals portage prophetic insight, inviting us to rise above the suffering of the world to find ascended awareness closer to the breath of Creator in Father Sky. Owls soar silently through the night; ravens herald transformation through lifting the veil of our magikal intellect.

When I first noticed vultures consistently crossing my path, I avoided exploring their deeper meaning for the same reasons most of us disregard vultures. But IntuWitchin wouldn't be ignored. Finishing a profound meditation, I opened my eyes to a vulture soaring right above me and immediately looked them up. Not only are vultures the ultimate harbingers of peace, the only creature who kills nothing; alchemists of death and decay, they are also incredibly generous and community oriented. Flying up to 300 miles to alert another colony that they've found something good to eat, they invite them to share in the spoils, staying up cooing to one another in the trees at night. Good medicine.

BREATH OF LIFE

Many ancient cultures strengthened their mental and spiritual stamina, bringing presence and clarity through intentional breathing. Extremely helpful for anxiety, fear, and depression, when attention is elsewhere, breath guides our thoughts home to our body (Earth) and emotions (water). Like wind, breath is a tool for change, moving through challenging feelings and limiting beliefs in the landscape of our minds the way clouds and storms blow through the afternoon sky.

Transform your mind by maintaining breath awareness; instantly interrupting your worries and concerns. Breath work is a powerful mind-, body-, and soul-healing practice, helping us rewire and regulate our nervous systems for greater resilience.

In Yogic traditions, breath of fire (short, fast exhales through the nose followed by effortless inhales) and lion's breath (deep inhales through the nose and long, exaggerated exhales from the mouth, sticking out your tongue) activate and ignite energy. Connected breaths (long, deep inhales and exhales without pausing on either side) are remarkable for healing, melting the boundary between your conscious and unconscious mind to anchor new beliefs into your waking state. Alternate nostril breathing regulates the nervous system by slowing the heartbeat, lowering blood pressure, and decreasing stress responses. There are hundreds of other forms of breath work, from shamanic, Yogic, and Tantric lineages; try whatever modality calls to you.

For now, take 10 deep, long breaths. Exhale each big, full inhale with a sigh or sound. After just six deep breaths, the systems in your body relax. See how you feel. Only five minutes daily of intentional breathing majorly supports your resilience and mental health.

SOUL SONG
MUSIC *as* MEDICINE

✳ ·································· ✳ ·································· ✳

Perhaps my favorite air expression—while playing and connecting with others—is singing. There is so much medicine in resonating and harmonizing with other humans, we've been doing it since the dawn of time.

A song can hit the right spot in your soul and run on a loop for weeks! Singing can be exponentially impactful in reprogramming and rewriting your mental narratives. But it is also something to be wary of. If a song stuck in your head is repeating lyrics that amplify beliefs or behaviors you don't want to emulate, it could be requesting you dive into healing that wound. There's a reason brands advertise using catchy jingles that often won't leave you alone, embedding into your consciousness to influence your purchasing. I still know the quadratic formula from 10th grade algebra because we learned it to the "Jingle Bells'" melody. I've never used it since that class, but it's permanently etched in my mind. Why? Because music is magik.

Singing is celebratory, and it's also a sign of safety. We tend to sing when we are happy and joyful. If you were hiding, fearful, or staying silent, you certainly wouldn't be singing—you'd give yourself away for sure. Singing signals to the nervous system you are safe and rejoicing. With no Witch Hunter clawing at your back and dragging you down, your magikal vibes are high.

Another element of the suggestive strength of singing is that you are quite literally altering your own vibration. Whether we're opera sopranos or shower stars, our singing voices resonate differently with our hearts. Singing is a passage to transformation, shifting from normal waking consciousness where distractions and disempowering beliefs live.

Making song and music is a powerful tool for good—or evil. Whether consciously deployed this way or not, so much modern music is deeply disempowering. Lyrics that objectify women, encourage angry, violent, drug-dependent lifestyles, and promote hatred, greed, competition, and other negative societal syndromes are glorified through "popular" music. How can we possibly believe this isn't affecting our general well-being and both our personal and collective self-image?

When I first moved to LA in that toxic relationship, it was one of the unhappiest times of my life, and we exclusively listened to rap music. I never considered how negatively my gender was portrayed in the lyrics; I just loved to shake that ass.

Shortly after we broke up, I came across an article discussing how rap lowered self-esteem, increased violence, made people feel *more* aggressive and *less* fulfilled. Of course, encouraging negative comparisons to the celebrity rappers' yachts, fancy cars, and "fabulous" lives (the lifeblood of the capitalist machine) would make anyone living a "normal" life feel worthless. It struck a chord. A quick inventory of my inner world: I'd never felt comfortable in my body. I was dating someone who made me feel unsafe in almost every way, like I didn't deserve anything better. I convinced myself I needed a boob job to fit in in LA. I felt like a loser if I wasn't driving a luxury car and had a destructive shopping addiction, thinking one new thing or another would make me feel beautiful or worthy. I quit rap cold turkey that day. Thank the goddess some hip hop is returning to its original rebellious and awakening intent.

It was a very slow but steady climb out of the dark doldrums of depression. Shortly after, I learned to meditate, but I believe changing the subconscious programming of my music is what allowed me to be open enough for meditation's effects to truly take hold. The expanded mental space sustained my positive habits as new spiritual sustenance saturated my world.

It took many years for me to utilize music and singing as healing modalities, elevating my mindset completely to free my voice enough to receive the magik intentional music brings. As soon as I did, singing became one of the most deeply enjoyable and pure ways I transform my internal—and therefore external—reality. Beautiful Chorus is an amazing group with primarily single-line songs, like mantras you would use with a mala or rosary to chant prayers over and over—such is their music.

A group of my girlfriends living together always played Beautiful Chorus, usually with someone showering or cooking in the kitchen singing along. I was entranced the first time I allowed "I am everything I want to be, and I have everything I need" to wash over me.

Years later, leading sex magik at a retreat among the redwoods on my birthday *and* the Gemini new moon, we gathered for opening circle and the facilitator started playing that very same mantra. Tears cascaded down my cheeks, acknowledging my embodiment of this truth. I was everything I wanted to be, sitting there as an abundant, professional witch bringing healing magik to the place that birthed and *re*birthed me. Surrounded by sisters, singing, safe to be magikal, held by the bountiful beauty and peace of Nature, I had everything I needed.

When these are the words and vibrations you listen to and proclaim for yourself, you start believing their truth. Then you can choose to become the living expression of them.

But programming your mind about a life you are far from living that isn't even healthy for the person living it can be severely detrimental to your well-being. The thoughts we think and the stories we tell ourselves get lodged deeper in the subconscious the more we repeat them. The subconscious controls 95 percent of how we function in the world. If you have a song stuck in your head that degrades you, or anyone else, it's almost impossible to prevent absorbing that same opinion. Shifting the songs you listen to shifts your communication with yourself and your reality. Try it for just a week and you'll see!

Exclusively listening to and singing along with Beautiful Chorus for a month found me in full miracle-manifestation mode. I was welcomed into magikal retreat experiences to bring fun, good vibes to the space. I was given palatial homes to house-sit, escaping my apartment for ocean views and saltwater pools. I was with those same girlfriends in Eden, Utah, when a brand-new *Healing with the Fairies* oracle deck *appeared* in my suitcase—out of thin air (faeries are air and Earth elementals). I asked all the girls if they'd given me the deck or misplaced it—no one had any idea where it came from.

Faery legends often include mysterious disappearances or magi-kal gifts showing up. They were asking me to connect with them. I could hardly believe it. Music alone opened me to receiving all the treasure life had to offer, truly believing in order to see magik was all around.

A singing practice doesn't have to be formal or fancy. Simply chanting group *oms*, vibrating this sacred sound—considered in Yogic scripture to be the first of the Universe, where all sounds come from—even with just one other person gets you high on life quick. It's my partner's favorite way of connecting people at the beginning of an event, or anchoring the magik as comple-tion. It's otherworldly how we can alter our frequency with this one sweet sound. When high-vibrational music becomes part of your bhakti, or devotion, to yourself and your practice, magik happens naturally all around you.

You may have tried affirmations. Repeating positive state-ments to yourself *can* be beneficial in reprogramming our sub-conscious mind, but if you're not doing the deeper work, they'll never last long-term. Even if you are consistent, it takes hun-dreds, even thousands, of repetitions daily to convince your mind to release all those years of prior programming. That's why singing can be the ticket to really bringing them to life.

Music tuned to 432 Hz—a measurement of frequency—resonates with the vibrational tones of Earth's center (known as the Schumann resonances) and draws the human body into harmonization and natural healing, eliciting a slower pulse and heart rate, lowering blood pressure and stress-hormone lev-els. Naturally, the human brain relaxes when aligned with our planet's heartbeat. Music at 440 Hz or more not only eliminates the previously described harmonization with the planet, but its vibrational pattern also stimulates the brain inefficiently. High-frequency processing requires a greater amount of energy, acti-vating our systems but not like dopamine and serotonin do.

It's tough to tell the difference, but when I am working, I have YouTube soundtracks of "Forest Witch Bookshop 432 Hz" or "Enchanting Thunderstorm Elven Ambience 432 Hz" playing, and it feels wonderful.

My dear sister Reggie Riverbear (Riverbear Medicine on Spotify) says we only ever really need *one* song: the song of our heart that brings us back to center whenever we feel lost. She calls this our "best friend" song. It's always there for you, uplifting your spirit and reminding you what's true. It will travel the world, traversing your darkest days with you, and can always be relied upon.

Hers goes, "We call upon the fire, and we call upon the Earth, we call upon the water, and we call upon the winds of time, and we are so blessed, so blessed, so blessed. For we are limitless, limitless, limitless."

Kirtan, a Hindu genre of ancient Sanskrit mantras praising deities, is all about devotion through chanting. You sing your praise and give yourself and your breath to the Divine.

Whether your favorite is free-styling or feminine mantra, kirtan or Celtic medicine music, it's about whatever makes you feel best and most lifted. When you're intentional about what you're chanting (whether with your speaking voice or that next level/iteration of your expression), opening your heart, your connection to the Earth, yourself, and the Divine will change you, always for the better.

SPIRIT SPEAKS

Another way to activate our IntuWitchin is through voices and accents. Ritual theatrics, playing characters, or taking on the energetic expression of other versions of you can be profoundly healing. This is because speaking in a different accent can alter our state of consciousness and open new pathways in our brain. Our old childhood traumas and programming simply step out of the way because this is not the voice, or mode of communication, we received them in.

Giving a hidden part of you its say can feel awkward at first, but surrendering to this practice is so fun.

I was in the Rockies on a road trip with three girlfriends and one's new boyfriend, having a rough time. We'd driven 10 hours a day, three days in a row, and I was on my moon. I was uncomfortable, had cramps, was whiny and complaining—I was edging toward meltdown mode. To make things worse, after such a mission to get there, I wanted out as soon as we arrived. It was meant to be a gathering of peace, but the way Nature was disrespected all over the campsites irked me. We weren't bringing peace to Her; we were taking it away.

When you have a big personality (hi!) and you're not having fun, this energy can quickly leak into the group. I felt bad enough, and my internal experience was emanating outward. We were setting up camp in the pitch-blackness when, thank the Goddess, a character named Frank emerged from me. Frank was a guy from Kentucky who loved karaoke and was very expressive with his operatic singing voice. Now, my friends thought Frank was funny; they laughed at everything he said, lightening the mood considerably. But I thought Frank was hilarious. I was laughing uncontrollably at him. Keep in mind, Frank was coming out of me! "He" responded to everyone with the most ridiculous things, often singing his reply. It was so liberating to set my judgments aside and be silly like a child.

Embodying Frank was powerful medicine. Mia was frustrated and upset. I was judging myself for "making the wrong choice." But Frank was having the time of his life! My head was spinning with negative thoughts: Why am I here? I knew this was a mistake. But Frank was the part of me who doesn't question himself even in an unpleasant situation. He just embraces the experience and makes the most of it by singing and entertaining himself, if nothing else. I was feeling miserable and sorry for myself, and Frank saved me.

The resistance I felt to my situation was transmuted into glee and healing laughter. That was one of those moments where IntuWitchin just takes the reins and brings you along for a ride. I wouldn't have suggested playing improv in such a funky mood. It was the inner wisdom of my soul who said, "Move aside, missy. We're taking over here. Frank! Calling Frank to the front." Listening to your IntuWitchin lets it lead you to your liberation.

Have you ever played the role of somebody else and felt your personal fears and worries fall away? I always loved plays and musical theater as a kid because it was such a nourishing excuse to escape myself. Sometimes even dressing in an unusual way gives us a new sense of confidence or extra mojo. There is only one person I would ever, and have ever, fangirled about. I have plenty of celebrity friends in LA, but Khaleesi, from *Game of Thrones*, is my favorite fictional character of all time (of course the patriarchy turned her into the classic evil witch at the end, but let's not get into that). On my bestie's birthday one year, I wore a fully bejeweled baseball helmet with a foot-tall feathered mohawk and matching floor-length turquoise marabou-trimmed dressing gown, just for fun, to the grocery store—and bumped into Emilia Clarke. I thanked her: "That role gave me so much permission to just be myself."

She looked at my outrageous outfit, smiled sweetly, and said, "I think I can tell."

It was classic.

Have you ever experienced your friends talking you into doing something silly, ridiculous, or out of the ordinary, on a day you felt sad, that totally turned the tides of your emotions?

My third year at Burning Man, another voice emerged as a spiritual salve. It was a consummate metamorphosis in my life.

As I biked through the makeshift city that pops up for a week in the Nevada desert, I came across a phone booth labeled "Talk to God." I later learned you could find the other end of the line and become the voice of God when people picked up the phone. At the end of the week, I knelt to tie my shoe, and a glimmer of silver caught my eye. It was a rotary phone on the ground, underneath a tent. My heart skipped a beat. I walked over, asking the guy holding the receiver, "Is this the other end of the God phone?"

"It's all yours."

The moment I sat down, the phone rang. When I picked it up, a soft, ethereal British accent emerged. "Hello?" I purred.

The Australian guy on the other end responded, "Hey, God, how you going?"

"I am Divine, thank you. How can I support you?"

I didn't get up for six hours. Not to toot my own horn, but *beep beep*: I got to utilize my coaching skills and spiritual gifts that day in a way I'd never experienced before. Mia stepped out of the way and playing "God" made me into a vessel for channeling Spirit.

"Why did my father commit suicide?"

"Why have I lost my grandfather, the only person who was ever there for me?"

"Why did my partner leave me on our wedding day?"

"What's the point of all this?"

"Why do horrible things happen in the world? How can you let atrocities occur on Earth?"

"Why do you do awful things to good people?"

People asked me all kinds of questions Mia could never have answered, but God(dess) knew exactly how to respond. I relayed messages I couldn't possibly have known, as if their people spoke through me. The grandfather who'd passed showed me an image of a little boy fishing on a lake, his most cherished pastime. They each hung up in tears, sometimes of joy, others of sheer awe: they'd had a conversation with God. "That was the most powerful conversation I've ever had in my life," they told me.

To practice this in your life, gather those silly, weird, wild witchy friends who are down to play together and have fun with it! Let the moment ask for and determine what ridiculous voices emerge from you. Be a PerMissionary to be something and someone different than you've always been told you're supposed to be. Give the stage to parts you may never have met or parts of the collective consciousness you might disdain/distrust. Experiment! What you learn through IntuWitchin about yourself and the world will always surprise you!

After all, the way you talk to yourself largely determines how the world responds to you—so if we want to change our lives, we must change the communication spells we cast!

MAGIKAL THINKING

✳ ································· ✳ ······························· ✳

We can embody all the characters, listen to all the songs, and voice positive affirmations all day. But nothing transforms the mind like the magikal compounds of psychedelics and plant/spiritual medicine. I'm not going to say you must do ayahuasca to connect to your IntuWitchin—that might not be your path. As touched on, breath work alone can bring about altered states—our IntuWitchin is constantly communicating with us, with or without these compounds' assistance.

We feel called to different teachings and teachers, places, and practices, but if there's a stirring in your soul calling you to the Master Plants, I highly recommend you find a way to safely and respectfully respond to Spirit's suggestion. Microdosing with psilocybin is a great way to start out. This entails taking a subperceptible dose (meaning you can't actually feel the effects) and letting the mushroom medicine gently work its mind miracles. There are hundreds of studies on psilocybin's benefits of improved cognitive function, stress reduction, mood elevation, and an overall improvement in mental health and well-being. You can take these medicinal doses and get inspired for a work project, find creative solutions to challenges you've been facing, and feel a clearer, smoother sense of yourself.

Spiritual medicines, which have been used worldwide for millennia, are making a comeback in collective consciousness because of how much healing we need. We've never been sicker or more disconnected. The unanimous plant-journey takeaway is remembering our inherent interconnectedness. People who get called to these ceremonies, even under the impression it's the "cool" thing to do, end up getting exactly what they need and more. It's certainly not like getting high at a party, so even if that's your initial intention, you'll be shown the deeper reason you're there.

Plant support for magik and IntuWitchin is like using the express lane. You'll get there no matter which way you go, but plants expedite the process. Doing your research and being properly supported are imperative. When following this path, the integrity of your facilitator is crucial. Amazonian lineages have worked with ayahuasca and other plants for thousands of years. Someone who picked it up a few months ago in Miami generally doesn't have quite the same capacity for it. These plants are part of the culture, education, and medical systems of Indigenous civilizations, so having the utmost reverence is requisite. A shaman will often begin training in childhood and have such an intimate relationship with the Spirit realm that it's akin to having a normal conversation. That kind of person, or someone with direct permission from a wisdom keeper, is who you want guiding you.

I first sat with ayahuasca in 2014, knowing my spiritual journey had just scratched the surface. My first few experiences were mostly uncomfortable, practically unpleasant. I didn't have "visions" or "revelations," just violent purging most of the night. I thought She (ayahuasca's "feminine" spirit) wasn't for me, preferring my many other ways of hearing Earth's song, letting the tendrils of Her timeless wisdom infiltrate my subconscious through diligent devotion. She'd shown me the way on Her own. So I spent most of the next decade-ish doing practices that required no medicine beyond my breath, sound, and movement.

I returned when I felt the call again, eight years after my first ceremony, to sit with my sisters. I fell in love with Her for the first time. I was in a safe space emotionally to experience the full spectrum of myself. I knew everyone in the container intimately and felt seen, supported, and celebrated. I got to dance naked, generally forbidden in masculine circles. My sister Blu used her healing superpowers on me, and the medicine helped me work through my wounds as I faced off with my own inner masculine and Witch Hunter.

She has changed my life and the lives of countless friends. The clarity of purpose, enhancement of psychic gifts, raising of personal standards with friendship, boundaries, and self-care plant medicines inspire are some of the missing puzzle pieces on specific awakening journeys. Ultimately, the main reason for choosing any Master Plant teacher, like mushrooms, wachuma, or peyote, is to spiritually and physically heal blockages that hinder your capacity to align with IntuWitchin, your wisdom, the Divine, and Mother Earth. As always, tune in to your truth and guidance system to see if you are meant to use the plant power to support your healing and transformation.

When you feel compelled to engage, the most important thing is to know your *why*—your intention. What are you hoping to learn? Many people consume recreational and prescription drugs to numb or escape from existential pain. Perhaps they want to forget about a breakup, suppress emotions, or access courage they haven't summoned on their own.

But plant medicine and psychedelics are not for numbing. They are for *feeling everything* even more intensely—so it can be healed. They tend to thrust the very thing you're running from right in your face. That's their beauty and why they can be scary: it means confronting the deepest fears of your ego head-on! If you want to uproot unworthiness, rewriting stories about your inherent value, an intentional ayahuasca or psilocybin journey will show you its origin within your psyche to overcome it once and for all.

Support on this path is essential. That's the only complaint I have about many medicine carriers in the modern world. Integration is the main missing link. There's rarely anyone supporting you after the experience. In a tribal setting, you would never head home by yourself to a cramped apartment before trying to slip back into your "normal" life. You'd all sit together for some time afterward, if not indefinitely. I recommend finding a facilitator who does post-ceremony calls or another professional to guide you through implementing your epiphanies in your day-to-day. It's just as important as the ceremony itself. This could come from a coach or therapist, a dedicated teacher who supports your integration process, somatic healers, trauma specialists, and even a consistent psychedelic therapist. Check out the Psychedelic Coalition for Health. If this is available to you, I recommend it. You'll be safe and supported no matter what arises.

If you're not ready for this stretch, my partner's company created a digital therapeutic technodelic (a digital medicine of light therapy and biofeedback) called SoundSelf that simulates the same brain-wave states as psychedelics. You can get a dose before even taking medicine!

Regardless of your relationship to plant medicines, training yourself to live and breathe inspiration is how you make your mind a masterpiece. We've all experienced how chaotic and stressful life seems when the Witch Hunter wreaks havoc on our mental health. Distraction disconnects us from our truth and IntuWitchin, and our mind is a mess. Making your mind into a masterpiece is like becoming a masterful artist who understands spectacularly stunning creations. Yes, there is darkness and shadow, but the contrast plays brilliantly with light, bringing together a bigger picture we wonder at in awe. We can work with all of it, unafraid of facing it, with our IntuWitchin to guide the way.

Practice — *Mind over Matter*

As discussed, the beliefs we hold in our subconscious can profoundly impact our ability to hear and therefore act upon the invitations of our inner leadership. In this practice, take a deeper look at where your beliefs got programmed into you. Capitalist society benefits from perpetuating the negative beliefs we have about ourselves. When we think we are lacking, we *consume more*. It takes so much courage to uproot old stories and ancestral wounding that make us who we are and why. But breathing into where our inherited beliefs come from is how we propagate a new level of empowerment for the future.

To begin, write out a list of things you struggle with or things you would like to be different in your life. Think about your career, money, friends, family, partnerships/relationships, and list the beliefs you have about your challenges in each of these areas.

What do you find yourself saying over and over about them?

For example, do you say or believe things like "Men are pigs," "There are no good men out there," "Men can't be trusted," "Rich people are selfish," "Money is the root of all evil," "I hate my job," or "You have to work hard to be successful"?

Dig deep into what you find yourself saying and thinking about the thing(s) you want to change in your life.

Next, investigate where these beliefs come from. Who did you first hear those words from? A parent or teacher? Are they based on experience? Have you chosen men who aren't good to you and stayed with them, accepting worse treatment than you deserve? Perhaps you believe men can't be trusted because you watched your mom get disrespected over and over. She didn't know how to role-model anything better for you, and you formed beliefs about men and women from her behaviors. When we believe such things, the Universe often organizes itself to continue "proving us right."

To get familiar with the root of limiting beliefs, describe the experience and people involved in the situation where it comes from.

What do you know about their pain? Their life?

How did that situation make you feel?

When you look at this person's life, is it the kind you would like to emulate?

Do they operate in relationships, purpose, and financial well-being as you would like to?

If you got the belief that men can't be trusted from your mom, this might look something like: "I watched my mom date these alcoholic men over and over, and when they let her down, she would say 'See, honey? You just can't trust them!'"

What might this situation have been teaching or asking of you, even if you didn't see it then?

What behaviors do you have that are informed by this belief? Perhaps it's been labeling good men as "boring," keeping your guard up, and never letting anyone in. Maybe you cheat on your partner or with someone else's.

As you move through each belief, ask: "What action could I take to shift out of this?"

Now think about the kind of beliefs you would *like* to have instead.

"I deserve loving partnership."

"I am worthy of abundance."

"I am Divinely guided and destined to fulfill my dreams."

Where, if at all, have you seen these beliefs modeled?

Answer the same questions from above about this person/*situation.*

What might be a difference in behavior from the empowering belief instead?

You might not believe something will work or come to you, but if you act like you *do* believe it regardless, your energy affects and begins shifting the fabric of reality. You can prove any belief wrong to yourself by engaging in the *opposing* actions (i.e., overriding your conditioning), allowing reality to reflect its falsity back to you.

Your mission now is to go out and practice. Infuse the air element's mind with the fire of action! How would you act toward (wo)men, mission, and money if you believed you were worthy and deserving of everything you dream and desire with them?

This practice is a powerful way of seeding the awareness that our thoughts fuel our actions, but our actions can change our thoughts. Remember: *air fuels fire; mindset fuels action.*

Note: Keep in mind most of our beliefs are very firmly lodged in our psyche. You're not going to uproot the belief that you don't deserve wealth by buying yourself one fancy pair of shoes. Mind over matter is not a once-a-day kind of thing. It's all day, every day—even in your sleep. It can be supremely special to share your work through this process with a trusted friend or family member so you're not isolated. Make sure it's some-one supportive who can help hold you accountable with the way you speak about yourself and this issue, someone who can keep reflecting the high vision to you.

Practice — Music as Medicine

Building on the teachings above, take an inventory of the music you listen to. How do the lyrics make you feel? Empow-ered? Jealous? Motivated? Shut down? Are your playlists sup-portive of the kind of life you desire to create or the healing you want to experience?

Now create a new playlist making music your medicine. Be lyrically diligent, making sure each song aligns to what you're calling in. It doesn't have to be every single line specifically, but the energy needs to be there. When I was taking inventory of my listening tendencies, I made strict standards of listening only to this music. Every car ride, no exceptions, I was sing-ing along, programming my subconscious to believe my miracle mantras.

If you're calling in a partner, you don't want sad love songs about longing that make you want to cry. You want ones about what an incredible dream it is to be loved by them.

My self-love playlist has "Love Myself" by Hailee Steinfeld. She sings about not needing anyone else, because her self love is so fulfilling. I *do* need other people—I would wither away without my friends—but I *love* the confidence (trust, remember?) of knowing my own love is robust enough to fill any parts of me that feel alone.

I'm not the only one with Ariana Grande's "7 Rings" on my manifestation playlist. I'm not concerned with material possessions and new hair, but I love the sentiment of wanting something, like a book deal, media opportunity, or exactly the dress I'm searching for at a vintage store, and getting it. No matter what I dream or desire, it can be mine. I can apply my energy to saving and changing the world, living my magikal life, and bringing my fantasies to fruition.

Even if just for a week (a month is better), try listening exclusively to music that creates a high-vibration state or expresses empowerment you'd like to experience, positively programming you.

Practice — *Ritual Theater*

Experiment with giving a voice to the dormant characters within by practicing ritual theater with your friends. When I started hosting these sessions weekly at my house, they unleashed riotous laughter and such restorative joy!

The person who's up leaves the room with the "MC," sharing the name of their character and where their character is from before coming onstage. (By "stage" I mean in front of everyone in the living room.)

The MC introduces them, and from that moment on, it's full improv! You get to play whoever you want, however you want!

Ritual theater can be as seriously ceremonial or as silly as you want it to be. If you desire to take it deeper than playful improv, set a group intention at the beginning about which parts of you have been most silenced and suppressed or a way of being you've always fantasized about but have never understood. For instance, if you are shy, then playing a loud, extroverted announcer of some kind can be a hilarious excursion. If you have always been "the good girl," maybe you want to be a naughty little "slut" and do a striptease where no one will judge or shame you; they'll just cheer you on! Maybe you have a pretend conversation with your dad to tell him what he can do with his authoritarian rules.

We've had some absurd characters, running the gamut from Celestina, my Professor Trelawney-esque fortune teller, to a German spanking instructor, and an eccentric lady who created outrageously expensive art made of feces! I've had several experiences where I become my own inner Witch Hunter, and though it can be scary, it's so healing and cathartic to give voice to the parts of us generally imprisoned as dark and dirty little secrets. One of them ended up doing ayahuasca with the tribe he was trying to colonize and having an awakening—oh, Goddess, let it be so!

If just getting up there is a great start, don't force it too hard. But if that's the message you're getting, go for it. What most wants to be expressed from within and through you in the moment?

Not only do you allow yourself to be seen in a multidimensional way, fortifying the bond between you and your friends, but ritual theater also increases internal trust in yourself. It signals to your system and psyche, "I'm not afraid of this anymore. I'm expanding my comfort zone." Doing so in such a safe way builds confidence to broaden your belief in yourself in slightly more harrowing situations life may throw at you.

Chapter 9

Burn,
Baby, Burn

The completion of our elemental journey recalls the difference between intuition and IntuWitchin being action—the domain of fire. In closing, let's ignite the inner spark driving our most aligned actions.

The hypnotic dance and mystery of fire has mesmerized, enchanted, and entertained humanity since the moment we captured it. Sitting around warm, inviting flames was the original TV—telling stories and singing songs beneath the stars together. Fire thoroughly transformed the trajectory of our species by bringing light and power to our world. People who shine and walk boldly forward exemplify fire's rule of our drive, passion, motivation, and the capacity to transform. The fire of action is an imperative element, literally and figuratively, for IntuWitchin and living your most magikal life.

Everything on Earth receives light, life force, from our solar star, the sun. In our bodies, this is the electromagnetic energy making our hearts beat; why we describe functioning neurons as "firing." In magik-making, fire can be used to release or manifest, as the fiery practices in this chapter will show you.

Fire transforms through destruction and creation. When left unchecked, fire can lay waste to a landscape. But when it is harnessed and directed with laser focus, it is the fuel for our most powerfully aligned momentum. Firelight illuminates the path before us and the darkness within us. It helps us "see" the right next steps to take as we walk forward.

Hence fire's (and the golden yellow of its glow's) association with our solar plexus, our power center ruling drive, ambition, and motivation. The center of *our* fire, the solar plexus, is located in our gut, where we "digest" information and experience physical sensations of anxiety and revulsion (an intuitive no) or excited butterflies and compulsion (an intuitive yes), propelling us into action.

Fire reminds us to shine like the sparkling sun. But if we are reliant on finite sources of energy, our potential, too, is finite. We see this in the modern world, as we source our power from extraction of the Earth, external validation, material possessions, or societal status. The hustle culture behind superficial success has created the burnout epidemic you may have experienced yourself when you're overexerting, acting out of alignment with your IntuWitchin's inspiration, or feel like you're "running on empty." Remember, air fuels fire, the breath is our constant connection to presence; without the breath of life, our inner fire is extinguished.

This is why when we are burnt out, we feel frazzled, overwhelmed, and disconnected. We tell people who are worked up or frantic to "take a breath." When there's too much focus on action without refilling our tanks—breathing deeply, grounding into our bodies or connecting to the *why* behind the action—it is driven by fire's destructive aspect that desecrates mountainsides in moments. The landscape here being our physical (Earth), mental (air), or emotional (water) well-being.

IntuWitchin's voice will say, "Rest, care for yourself, and go to a ceremony with conscious community" when it is time to refuel. If we're too busy burning the candle at both ends, we might miss these nudges. The origin of the word *passion*, *passio* in Latin, is "suffering." That which we are deeply inspired and motivated by, we are willing to suffer for it. The fires of passion burn within, enlightening what matters most to us, but we must find the happy medium to bring our wishes into existence.

If we learn how to source our inner fire from the limitless solar, galactic, planetary, and spiritual energies, we too become limitless. This sustenance feeds our performance, asking us to shine our unique light our way. It guides us to take the kind of actions that truly "shine," make us feel alive, positively inspired, or even unstoppable.

How does your IntuWitchin yearn to express this aliveness within you? Are you shining, casting the spells you speak? In the way you show up? In how you serve the world and your family? Are you shining your light publicly or simply with your kin, your land? As a parent, as an activist? Behind the camera or the paintbrush? In what ways do you desire and feel compelled to express your light, your fire, your life force energy?

Finally, and most important, fire reminds us that our light also casts shadows and allows us to see the darkness within, which we must honor. Our greatness shows us our weaknesses—but we are not meant to shame or demonize these parts, just make the choice to shift them. When we embody the sun's boundless, joyful energy, using the fires of transformation to heal, transmute darkness, and enlighten our shadows, then we truly shine.

A single match creates enough light to illuminate the darkness within and without. To light a flame within ourselves and ignite the candles in countless others, you can use your brilliance to create joy, harnessing fire's high vibrational energy to return to refulgence, reminding us that acting on our IntuWitchin is the shining example we want to set for the world.

ELEMENTAL ENERGETIC ALCHEMY

Tantra is the backbone of my personal witchcraft and how I fuel the fire and stoke the flames in my life. The common misconception about Tantra is that it's all about sexual doctrine.

But Tantra is traditionally an exploration and cultivation of energy, igniting the brilliance within us in every moment.

An ancient Goddess-based (10 goddesses, actually—the powerful Mahavidyas) Yogic tradition, Tantra invites *all* of you to be ecstatically expressed and enlivened through embracing your energy, the splendor that lights you up spiritually, physically, and emotionally. Beyond sex itself, Tantra is a way to experience the enthusiasm and exhilaration of life making love through you and your every cell.

Tantra is elemental alchemy, breathing wind, moving Earth, sounding vibration, sweating, crying, or cumming, activating your fire and scintillating your spirit. It is the lifeblood of our inspired, aligned action.

I discovered Tantra through one of my dearest sisters Layla Martin, who told me I was innately a Tantrika simply by the way I experienced and enjoyed life. I'm one of those people who can find sheer orgasmic joy in popping seaweed bubbles between my toes, squinching through muddy puddles on a forest trail with my bare feet, or inhaling petrichor-saturated mountain air, the ecstasy of sensual sumptuousness.

A spiritual practice that invites the fullness of your being, emotions, expression, pain, and pleasure while exalting and encouraging you to touch these heights and depths within yourself? That's what I'm talking about! Not to mention I was already developing a deep embodiment practice on my journey; it just made sense.

Tantra solidified my desire to dive deeper, differentiating itself from other spiritual lineages by never saying, "I'm the only way." Whenever I hear that, I just think, *Well, then this is* not *the way for me.* There is *no* single way up any mountain. Birds fly, people walk, snakes slither, and mountain goats scale the cliffs; we all have different paths, none greater than others. Tantra relates to spiritual teachings by deepening your relationship to your own body, consciousness, and the world around you. I felt at home.

Then, of course, I learned Tantra is also a *dragon* system. Jade, black, white, and red dragons are all forms of Tantric wisdom and practices. I couldn't deny the synchronicities and the rarefied riches this lineage so clearly offered me.

The fire has all but gone out in most people these days. The beauty of Tantra reminds me to source from sunlight—moving my body, building pleasure, taking inspired action, and doing what makes me feel alive—not from the anesthetic "fake" light of my phone. When we spend all day focused on screens, we are squandering our attention, awareness, and creativity—our fire. My Tantric practice brings this energy to my actions and interactions in the material world, where there are always opportunities for ecstasy and magik.

Tantric philosophy asks us to be present and aware with how we direct our energetic fire by being intentional with our alchemical power of spiritual transformation. It ensures we become stewards of the fire, channeling it where it's needed most. This is the medicine of dragon energy. We must ground our transformation with integration in the body and in our Earthly life. We don't want to work *too* hard, or we'll burn out. We don't want to extinguish our light too early. Think about a stray spark that can catch fire and cause damage—or we can carry fire in a candle. Then it has a contained and specific direction that can be shared with countless others.

Tantra, and the dragons, ask us to get in touch with the elemental nature of our bodies and the world around us. A simple Tantric morning routine is an invitation to connect with your IntuWitchin, feel into your current energy levels, and respond to their requests. Do you feel amped up and want to activate your day even further, or could your nervous system use some soothing? Are you feeling sluggish and tired and want to tend to that energy or ramp it up to reawaken and reinvigorate yourself?

What does your body want right now? What emotions are present? What actions could you take in deepest service to yourself? How can you channel your energy today or burn away any blockages that might be dampening it?

A Tantric practice that really fuels the fire is "somatic shaking." As simple as it sounds, it just involves shaking your body and releasing any sounds, feeling, and expressing any emotions or speaking out anything that arises as you move. Not only does this create heat, but it can be incredibly supportive in shifting stuck energy that might have lodged itself in the unseen.

We can bring a Tantric approach to the boardroom by channeling our creative ideas with focused intention, maintaining connection to our greatest inspiration and the actions that make us feel excited to be alive—rather than just throwing anything at the wall to see what sticks.

I love a good Tantric workout, visualizing my muscles growing, talking to them, fueling those last few burnout sets with bursts of vivacity to push through even when I feel like stopping.

You can create immeasurable intimacy on a friend date by consensually bringing Tantric practices into the experience. This can involve creating a safe space for each other's intimate truths, doing synchronized breath work, playing with an energy loop where you send it up one person's spine and down the other, then switch. Or you could try eye-gazing for 5–12 minutes. Layla and I did this at a party once and stayed locked in for nearly an hour. Everyone who walked by stared at us, but our willingness to stay present and connected to each other despite all that was happening around us was one of the oceanic bonding moments in our friendship.

Each of these practices can clear the path that may have been barred by fear or programming, providing a more direct line to our IntuWitchin's invitations. Dragon energy is the medicine for mindfulness of your magik. Those stories that try to annihilate you, the voices that shame or ridicule you—you can fight ferociously against these falsehoods, standing up for who you know you are Divinely designed and destined to be. You can burn those beliefs to the ground with your fierce dragon flame and rise like the phoenix from the ashes.

The sheer intention to bring conscious awareness to animating your body is the fundamental pillar of working with

Tantra to restore the fire in your life. Call upon the dragons any-time you need a little fire lit under your ass. They have watched entire empires rise only to crumble and fall again and again. They want spiritual leaders to succeed, for us to remember the genuine fortune that is our connection to Nature, to hear their voices and the song of the Earth as we invigorate our inner wis-dom, supernatural power, and marvelous magik.

This is how we become the embodiment of our own inner dragon, the most magikal version of ourselves, an elemental amalgamation of the strengths and gifts of Earth, water, air, fire, and Spirit. Without action, it all means nothing. We have these five (or six) senses for a reason. We are meant to experience the world through taste, touch, scent, sight, and sound. Dragon energy, Tantra, and IntuWitchin are the mightiest vanguards for carrying us forward to a reconnection with the sensory and sensual elemental world, to the restoration of harmony within ourselves and with each other, safe in our own essential Nature.

SACRED RAGE

Rage has incited much change throughout history. We've dis-cussed the witch hunts and how rage inside those early Chris-tian priests led to a worldwide genocide. So how can rage be sacred? Because the fury felt by those who survived but stayed silent flows through us all. The pain and anguish of losing our direct connection to God and our loved ones at the hands of vio-lent "leaders" lives inside our very DNA. Take the rampant drug abuse, violence, and mental health crises among Indigenous com-munities, particularly the First Nations people of North Amer-ica. These conditions are intrinsically linked to the inhumane and abhorrent treatment of their cultures and civilizations by colonizers, exemplifying rage with no safe outlet or permission, being turned against the self.

Perhaps you have been enraged at the shocking barbarity endured by the women of Iran. At the time of writing, the Iranian regime is ruthlessly murdering girls as young as seven for standing up and shouting, "Women, life, freedom." Should they simply accept their fate without standing up for themselves? Should the world sit idly by while they are persecuted? No. Their anger, all the emotions they've been told never to feel, and our responsibility to support them in solidarity are cause for *sacred rage*: rage that deserves to be expressed, healed, and alchemized into motivation to change the world.

If excitement and inspiration is fire in its fullest yes, rage is the flame of our fiercest no. A result of suppressed anger, sadness, or pain, rage is commonly the result of a crossed boundary, where the truth, or no, was restricted or in response to a lack of safety. Rage can be our way of preventing and protecting ourselves from being harmed. It is the repercussion of repressed emotions; anything you were told you shouldn't or couldn't feel throughout your entire life still lives within your body.

Women particularly have had their anger silenced and villainized. If she gets upset, she's marked as "crazy," "aggressive," "a bitch" who needs to be "put in her place," whereas men who get angry are considered powerful, justified, assertive. Anger is a "signal emotion," meaning it's an indication of distress or affront. In the animal kingdom, anger is a clear "Back off" or "Don't mess with me and my cubs." But if women get angry due to insult, violence, or nonconsensual interaction of any kind, *they* are the ones who are penalized.

Rage gets demonized where it's most warranted, especially for women and people of color, because it is often the precursor of change. Rage is suppressed to prevent us from revolting against the oppressors because that fire inside us leads to inspired action. Great things can be accomplished when anger reaches the point of eruption. And if we united, inspired to destroy these villains, no weapon would stand a chance.

We've all felt the moment anger starts rising; the texture of the very emotion is fiery and can destroy relationships or be turned upon ourselves. But if we learn to wield it to our benefit, bringing that Tantric awareness and acceptance to it, we can use our rage to make miracles. Women's outrage has made massive strides in civil rights, LGBTQIA+ rights, and in many waves of feminist movements. This is the face of fire-forged transformation. But we must be willing to act upon IntuWitchin's voice inside us saying, "This isn't right. I *have* to do something."

Did you know hospitals burn placentas after women give birth, as if they're toxic waste? Every other mammal eats this precious nourishment to replenish their iron. There are Indigenous communities who believe that destroying placentas, the vessels of creation, is directly related to the prevalence of wildfires and desecration of forests. If you've ever seen a placenta, they look like the tree of life. It's just further disrespect of Mother Earth, fueling her inner fires. She expresses this exasperation in Her quakes and erupting volcanoes. Whether active or dormant, this ferocity of her fire invites us to look at how our anger might be causing destruction—while simultaneously seeing what we can learn from the dust settling and lava cooling.

Eventually, that liquid fire will harden, and millions of years from now it will become a lush, mossy rainforest with shoots and flowers. Even that once-devastating eruption is part of the cycles of creation and can bring new life. This shows us how important it is to express ourselves, never letting emotions get restrained for too long.

Is there anything in your life that might be asking for volcano medicine? Anger that's gone unexpressed, lurking beneath the surface, with pressure building? If you wait, will the eruption cause destruction? How can you be a steward of that fire, your inner lava (a combination of our liquid emotions and pumping passion)?

Channeling sacred rage into an intentional practice is a cathartic experience and is always a favorite ritual at my retreats. Many women have never given themselves full permission to feel the entirety of their rage, and the results of doing so are astounding. Simply allowing old, stored emotions a safe place to release can burn away anything that may have been impeding your progress. The side effect being a much clearer channel for calling in and creating more of what feels like a full *fuck yes.*

I got a powerful reminder of this when facilitating my first castle retreat in the Scottish Lowlands. The castle brought in a falconer who worked with gorgeous birds of prey to fulfill the Hogwarts fantasies of our participants. We spent the session with these magikal creatures wide-eyed, like the owls perched on our arms. Owls represent wisdom, taking in a 360-degree view and seeing crystal clearly in the darkness. Hawks hold the bigger picture, higher vision, and perspective, and an eagle, queen of the winged ones, the highest flying and clearest seeing of all, the closest to Creator, aided our communion with Spirit.

But the majestic female eagle was the only bird the falconer never spoke the name of or let fly through the air. He kept her tied to his hand. She tried taking off, only to be torn back from her flight as he swung her upside down by her feet, onto his arm again. Tears stream down my face as I write this. It was agonizing to watch. He yelled at all the birds, calling them "idiots." We were in awe of their beauty and pained to see them treated this way. This man had obviously gotten into the industry because he loved the sacred wild creatures, but that love had gotten lost. He said people were mostly ambivalent about him and the animals. We were not most people. As the day progressed, a volcano of rage began bubbling up from below.

I felt helpless, like there was nothing I could do to ease the eagle's torment. Yet she called me closer, in awe and wonder at her brilliantly yellow giant dragon feet, scaled and taloned. I was filled with veneration for her, and with a beat of her massive wings, she molted a precious feather for me: a treasure and a gift, all she had to give, as if she was setting a part of herself free—I was overcome with gratitude. I had been calling in an eagle's feather, one of the highest honors from the Natural world, to connect with that sacred spirit for years. I could never have imagined meeting the angel it came from and *Her* giving it to me. In American First Nations tradition, receiving an eagle feather (by a person let alone the majesty Herself) is the utmost honor of respect and gratitude, only carried by the truest of the tribe and often awarded to warriors for great valor and bravery, a sign of their deserved reverence. I felt Her acknowledgment of my mission. Her feather remains one of my life's most cherished, precious blessings. It tears my heart out to this day that I didn't rip her from his grasp then and there to set her free.

Instead, as he was leaving, I simply asked, "What's the eagle's name?"

"It's a stupid name," he replied. "Artemis."

Chills shot through my spine and my eyes glistened. Artemis: the Goddess of the wild, waters, and woodlands, caretaker of creatures, children, and all we birth into the world.

She was being treated the same way as the feminine, the Goddess, women all over the world—tied down, caged, kept from doing what the Divine designed us to do: to soar, to fly.

The spirit of Artemis kept me up all that night, enraged. I got a cosmic bitch slap in my mind, receiving Her wrath like never before.

"How dare you let him talk to me, to us . . . to treat us this way and not say *anything*?! You just stood there! *Silent*, acquiescing to him and his toxicity, his patriarchal pain projections. *You* are the leader here. *You* are the teacher; you did *nothing*. You failed me. I am so disappointed. . . ."

I could see Her, feel Her panting and pacing like an angry queen before the fireplace in my room.

She was devastated; I'd broken Her heart. I hadn't stood up for Her, when my whole life is about guiding others to do so for themselves. I've always felt Her loving encouragement. This was the first time I'd experienced Her being utterly let down by me.

The next morning, Her fire coursing through me, I fumed down the stone steps of the castle. We weren't going to make our morning walk. I showed my students (to the great dismay of the more sensitive attendees) the full force of my rage and indignation toward that man. My example was screaming at the top of my lungs, "How dare you!" I have never shown the depth of my emotions in public like that. It was a moment I'll never forget (and likely neither will my students). Too many times women have been tied by the feet, kept in proverbial prisons, had their wings clipped, or been forced into some man's idea of what was right for them without regard for their feelings or purpose. We couldn't save Artemis that day, but we didn't have to stay silent and suck up our sadness at witnessing her plight.

"Change of plans, ladies. It's time for a rage ritual." There has been no better occasion for introducing a group to the sacred rite that I have exercised in my personal practice for years.

"Everyone go out and gather as many sticks as you can find, as big as you can swing. With each branch, think about every word you've held back, every person who has ever crossed your boundaries, shut you up or down, hurt, shamed, dismissed, disrespected, or punished you, and we're going to let them have it."

I'd facilitated rage rituals before—but this was the largest group and the only time the full force of my own fire was flaming fiercely inside me as I led others.

We cleared the driveway behind the castle, stacked tall piles of mossy branches on the edge of the beech forest, and began. As for the details, you are invited to try this practice for yourself at the end of the chapter or come join me on a retreat.

Learning to master and channel my sacred rage is an ongoing process that's brought me to the edges of my own power and capacity. Even I still become engulfed in the flames, drowning in the empathic experience of just how much suffering we inflict upon each other and the planet.

My father always modeled rage. He had a quick fuse and would blow up on a dime, lashing out with vicious words, his dagger tongue something I also inherited. I emulated his behaviors for far longer than I care to admit, emitting low-grade wrath at the injustice of the world since childhood. Reflecting his conduct back at him was a surefire way to exacerbate the situation, so my anger stayed mostly hidden inside, a storm unleashed only upon myself.

Sacred rage is not projecting your pain onto another or inflicting violence. Working with it means allowing yourself to feel the full force of fire inside you. Fire unchecked burns the people around you, and it hurts. They're going to feel singed by you. Just like when our waters are overflowing, we can flood our inner landscape, washing people away in our depression or misery. All our emotions have the most impact on the people around us if we can't maturely and responsibly regulate and hold them.

Rage is often the protector or predecessor of sadness, so we'll scream when what we really want to do is cry. And sometimes because we feel sadness is a more "acceptable" emotion, we'll cry when what we really want to do is scream.

We get angry at the hurt that's been caused to us or another, and we get angry with authority. With all the human rights violations happening in the world, your rage is holy, Divine, and important. Too many millions of people have had their outrage suppressed, and it is ready to be released. When you learn how to channel your sacred rage, you can be part of this purge.

Perhaps you feel rage at your own disenchantment and disappointment with life: Rage for how many of us choose to stay in a slumber rather than work on solutions for the problems we face. Rage for the children being sold into slavery. For racism, for inequality. Rage for what's being done to our planet. There's plenty to rage about. If your life is beautiful, and everything is working out, rage for all those less fortunate than you.

I'm so grateful to support people who never touched that fire inside themselves so they can learn how to work with it. When I lead sacred rage rituals, it can be hard for people to let it all out because of the generations before them who would have been killed for doing so. We hear the shameful stories in our heads telling us we're crazy or worrying what someone will think. Well, I encourage you to rage right back at that voice too. Tell the Witch Hunter what you think of their attempt to keep you small, and show them they'll never be able to extinguish your fire again.

SACRED SEX

The way rage is our protective force, sex is our receptive force. We open our bodies and hearts to another, receiving pleasure though touch and connection, whether we are the ones doing the penetrating or not. We are naked in every sense, allowing ourselves to be truly seen, if we can let down the shields and armor. Though sex is actually an alchemy of all the elements—our bodies and sweet waters uniting with another's as we breathe—we honor the fire by making sex sacred through the energy and attention we bring to it.

I'm sure we can all attest to feeling more Divine and connected to our IntuWitchin after a nice, juicy orgasm, but far too often we limit our climatic energy to the physical realm. When we are actively engaged in our sexual connection, spiritually, emotionally, and energetically, we can use sex for healing wounds and limiting beliefs, manifesting dreams and desires into reality, and creating soul-satiating safety and intimacy with ourselves or another.

Sex is the cultivation of creative energy, the animating force behind all life—the most potent and generative in the Universe. As the bees, butterflies, and hummingbirds stick their long, languid tongues into the fruiting flowers to pollinate and spread the seeds, life is making love to us all the time. Unfortunately, sex has been demonized, dragged through the mud, and devalued by porn, patriarchy, and religious programming. But how can that which brings each of us here be shameful and dirty?

Birth is often considered the ultimate expression of feminine power. A close second is the way pleasure writhes and courses through Her during orgasm. But before birth must come sex. A motivating force behind many wars, epic novels, song, myth, and legend, our sexual pleasure is a sacrament within all of us, and it's time to give it the reverential honor it's due.

Sacred sex is simply creating an intentional lovemaking experience beyond casual pumping with the goal of getting off. If you choose, it can be an opportunity for proliferating more love between you and your partner, deep healing through sexual release, or embodying new archetypes and ways of being you want to actualize in your life. Meanwhile, sex magik (which I'll share the specifics of) is a practice for intentional manifestation. After all, our sexuality is the physical embodiment of creativity—how we "birth" what we want into the world, whether children or any other creative babies we magikally bring into existence.

Sex magik can be a solo pleasure practice or with a partner, but it can be easier to get the hang of it on your own at first. If we don't know what our body likes, or how to bring ourselves to orgasm, it can be difficult to reach those states of pleasure with another or guide them to what feels best for you—let alone feel safe enough to do so. Learning how to connect to your personal flavor of sexual energy, what the most sensational parts of your body are and what they desire, is so important and is foundational for sacred sex with a partner.

When it comes to IntuWitchin (and sisterhood), cultivating trust within ourselves supports us in trusting others, and trust is essential for sacred sex. I trust you to hold all parts of me, good, bad, and ugly. I trust you not to judge me, my body, my fantasies, or my fetishes. Think about this: When you have sex with someone, what are you entrusting them with? When you open yourself to another, not just physically but spiritually and energetically, you have to trust them implicitly in order to be fully surrendered to the moment. A lack of trust is what leads to disappointment and hurt feelings.

Having as much sex as you want with whomever you want is how some people celebrate life, freedom, and fun. When it comes to having casual sacred sex, the imperative is understanding why. What's the driving force behind your motivation or desire? If we are motivated by validation or confirmation that we are good/hot/strong/sexy enough from an external source, casual sex might not be the healthiest activity. But I know plenty of empowered women who simply enjoy experiencing all the different flavors of their own sexuality brought forth by multiple lovers and their sacred sluttiness. They like touching that cosmic power inside themselves, regardless of how or by whom they're being held.

In my case, I am just about the opposite. I refuse to have sex with anyone less than the kind of king I dreamed of who can hold and handle all of me. Rather than get to know my sexuality in relationship with as many other partners as I could, after one too many poor judgments with men who let me down, I decided I was going celibate. What I thought would be a few months turned into almost three years without so much as a kiss. There were moments of loneliness, fear I would never find someone, and too many friends who said I should just "try the dating apps" or "give him a chance" (i.e., settle for less than what I truly desired).

Not a chance. I dedicated and devoted myself to deep personal pleasure practices using solo sex magik to call in my current partner, as well as this book, and everything I have in my life now. Goddess, it was worth it! During this time, I saw massive growth personally, financially, and professionally before my king even appeared!

Let's get into the details of sex magik. This practice uses the fires of your sexual energy and pleasure for personal transfiguration and manifestation, sending your wishes up into the Universe at orgasm or peak pleasure. There are many different methods, but this is the essence of how to practice according to my Tantric path.

For this or any version of sacred sex or sex magik, you can be as extravagant or unembellished with your setup and ambience as you'd like. What feels sexy and inspiring? Do you like candles burning? Are there colors, fabrics, scents in the air, tools, or toys that turn you on most? What music do you like to listen to? I personally can't have anything with lyrics because I'll find myself singing along and would rather be fully present. Do you like to shower or bathe before or after? When I'm preparing with my partner, we love to spend time without our phones beforehand, either dancing/moving or just connecting so we're disentangled from the distractions of the day when we come together.

Both sex magik and sacred sex are opportunities to engage all five senses more wholly than ever before. Expand your energetic body with sunlight, breath, movement, or embodiment to prepare for filling up with fire. This is fuel for healing and manifestation, as it amplifies your power to project into the multiverse. Again, the process is the same with or without a partner. Here are the steps.

To begin, set your intention and really *feel* into it.

Want a fulfilling, purposeful job you love? Envision what's around you as you work. How's the view? Hear people thanking you or presenting you an award for your service. What does fulfillment feel like? What are you wearing to this job? What does the air smell like? What do you eat for lunch? Imagine talking to your employees or co-workers. Visualize yourself creating something you love, signing a contract, or getting that first big check. Taste the champagne you toast with to celebrate.

Perhaps you want to call in a new home. How do you feel when you walk into your space? What do you experience? What does safety and relaxation mean for you? Is your nervous system settled in a place you love? What are the colors inside or outside? What does it smell like? Is fresh bread baking or are blackberries ripening in the sun? Who's with you? Do you hear birds, laughter, or the river right outside your door?

Or are you calling in a partner? What would look different in your life with them? Where would you travel together? Can you imagine the home you'd share? How do you feel in their arms? What do they whisper in your ear? How do you love to spend time? How does your body open to them? Imagine them gazing into your eyes, kissing your favorite spots, and showering you with exactly the kind of affection you've always dreamed of.

We call this your "five-senses reality." What would you experience with all five senses if you had this goal or dream? Get clear on all aspects so you can hold this vision when you orgasm at the crown chakra. What would you touch physically and feel emotionally? If this had already come to fruition, what would you see, hear, smell, and taste? Go even deeper with your sixth sense: What do you *know* as this version of yourself, and who are you in this vision? What emotions arise from this manifestation coming true? When you establish the reality you are calling in so clearly that you can see, hear, smell, touch, taste, and *feel* it, you are perfectly set up for orgasmic manifestation.

Now it's time to drop fully into your body. You can touch yourself or connect with your partner in any way, at any point, using feathers, flowers, fabrics, a crystal dildo, or your own 10-digit mastery. Try to avoid vibrators, as they really desensitize your body and can rush your physiology faster than it wants to go naturally.

Start turning yourself on and then spend at least three to five minutes breathing into each chakra as you cultivate pleasure, thinking about the color, element, and what that energy brings out in you. Let your desire swirl up from your root with a primal, wild, animalistic Earthiness. Hold it in your watery womb-space, the sacral chakra, your creative cauldron portal. As it rises into your solar plexus, acknowledge the action required, feel the fire shining in you. Breathe gratitude into your heart chakra, inhaling deep love and appreciation into your vision and exhaling open to receive.

Release sound at the throat chakra. What is the vibrational expression of what you are manifesting? Notice how sounding enhances and juicifies your orgasm! Let the clarity of vision burst into your third eye. What are the thoughts, stories, and beliefs you are claiming in your life? How are you ready to see yourself and the world?

As your pleasure begins to peak, allow the connection between you and the Divine to blossom. Open your crown, releasing your fantasy into the heavens as your reality. Feel the luminous halo of your orgasm launching your sensual revery out into the Universe. Experience your vision cascading like a waterfall over your body in a holy fountain of ecstatic bliss. Speak it out loud on your own or with your partner. Shout it from the rooftops as you're cumming! Whether volume increases effectiveness or not, it certainly feels like it.

If unsupportive or distracting thoughts come in during the practice, go back to your breath and the sensations in your body. Be patient with yourself—it's okay if these thoughts come through. Just move forward again, and allow Spirit to ignite within you. Your pleasure is an emanation of the Goddess's infinite life force energy.

If working as a couple, ideally your partner is aware of what's going on and what you're calling in, whether together or independently. Again, the solid, immersive imagination of already having it is the key. If you want to get really witchy, go deeper by creating a sigil, a magikal symbol, representing your vision. Paint it on yourself or your partner and focus on it at orgasm.

The most common question I get around sacred sex with partners is how to bring intention and ritual to the act. Many of us, and most commonly men, have never conceptualized sex as being about anything more than just getting off. If your partner doesn't seem receptive at first, you can engage in the energetic practice on your own, with and without them. Usually, they'll notice a pleasantly surprising difference in your power and presence energetically and sexually rather quickly and want to jump on board.

A great practice to get the truth, love, and intimacy flowing is called Fears, Desires, and Loves. Start with sharing what you feel afraid of with one another. This can be around deepening your sexual relationship or with life as a whole. Next do the same with desires, current or general. Then you tell each other what you love about each other. Seeing where your partner feels fear and what they want and sharing more of the things they love about you in the moment opens hearts and minds in minutes. If they are against trying this practice, it's an opportunity to ask them why or to do some inquiry of your own. Why have you called in a partner like this? Are your own stories of unworthiness blocking you from leaving and being with someone better aligned for you?

Being vulnerable, asking sincere questions, connecting your hearts, and engaging in a long make-out session before you begin can help set the tone while also being incredibly nourishing and soothing to the nervous system. For women especially, our capacity for orgasm is dependent on our stress levels; we must get out of our minds and into our bodies to experience sexual ecstasy, which is much harder when we are filled with anxieties of the working day. Regardless of your partner's willingness, your sexual experience is largely up to you, so you can create sex magik within your own imagination and have a blast!

The process of engaging in sex magik is the same whether you're on your own or with a partner. I have some friends who do their sex witchery internally without even telling their lover. It's all about their internal energy and relationship to the experience regardless of whether their partner is interested or not.

The best time to try sex magik is *any*time! Like everything in this book, I'm offering you an invitation to connect with your body, energy, and your life in a more conscious, intentional way. There are no strict rules and regulations; if there were, they'd be made to be broken. New moons, as discussed in Divine Timing, are great for planting seeds. If there's one coming up and you'd like to bring sex magik into your ritual, go for it!

The only no-no is if you're feeling really low or sad, having a hard day, or have been arguing with your lover. Always follow your IntuWitchin, of course, but that's generally not the state to be in for manifestation and amplification. However, sex itself can be incredibly healing and nurturing during those moments. My partner will make love to me when I'm sad, letting me just sob my eyes out, and I always feel so much better afterward, not only because sex generates endorphins and all our happy hormones but also because I get to be held in a safe space to express my emotions, which is healing all on its own.

Humans have flourished by the flickering fireside since it captivated our consciousness and we in turn caught its flame. Icy-cold bones turned toasty and warm, dark nights illuminated beyond the light of the moon, flavors of food transformed into delectable degustation. Fire changed our lives and can light up your life too, should you choose to let it transform you.

Below are some of my favorite practices to harness the enchanting gifts of fire within yourself and your life. Remember, *every* action you take on your journey is an opportunity to either snuff out or fuel the fire inside of you. No one can force you to do anything here; you are the only one who can get out of your own way and find the modalities that will help you heal your wounds and the people who inspire you to keep rising higher. This is the true medicine of your IntuWitchin's guidance toward actions that will lead you to your most magikal life.

Practice — *Stoke the Flame*

Simply getting hot and sweaty is a way to stoke the fire within, and you can do this however feels best for you. I recommend a shaking session with a little dance mixed in, making sounds, stomping, and taking big heating and energizing breaths.

As you set the intention to ignite your inner fire, bring your IntuWitchin to where there is any resistance and ask yourself: "Where do I hold back or stop myself from taking action?" "Where am I refusing to face the flames?"

You can journal your response, speak it out loud, or just contemplate the answer inside. Then put on some music and start shaking. I like to let different parts of my body lead the movement while taking deep breaths with long sighs to get the fire flowing. Though it sounds simple, shaking can be a very triggering practice because of the movement of energy occurring. It can be uncomfortable just to notice how resistant we are to giving our bodies permission to move, thinking we look "silly" or "stupid," so we push back against what can be genuinely transformative and healing. Let the invitation of the fire be to keep going through it no matter what stories come up during the process.

Make sure you have privacy and safety wherever you are; the greatest change comes from not giving a fuck about what anyone thinks. Try to make as much sound as you can just releasing whatever arises, moving your body however it wants. Let different parts of your body guide you at different times, and get *loud*.

Practice — *Write and Burn Fire Ritual*

Write and Burn rituals are a straightforward yet powerful practice that symbolize letting go of any beliefs or behaviors that have been hindering your inspired actions.

Get a journal and set up your space however feels best for you. I encourage you to use any journal prompts or questions from the previous chapters that revealed old habits you want to let die so you can be reborn, like the phoenix rising from the ashes. Here are a few more to help you tap directly into your relationship with the fire element:

"How do I overexert myself, burn the candle at both ends, or act from a place of scarcity or unworthiness?"

"Where and why do I shy away from taking action?"

"Where have I burned myself or others in the past?"

"What is the fire here to teach me?"

"Where am I too fiery, and where could I use a little ignition?"

Jot down all the behaviors you are ready to let go of, along with anything else you're releasing from your life. I like to write everything out once just to get all my thoughts on the page, and then if I want to empower what is replacing these old ways, I'll go back and restate the transformation of those patterns as if they have already happened.

For example, if you are motivated by unworthiness and keep hustling just to prove you are good enough, to yourself or others, your original burn might read like this:

"I am sick of being burned out! I'm fucking exhausted from working so hard. I hate this job! I am done with it and all the patriarchal programming that says I am anything other than enough just as I am! I am never going to work for someone else's dream again. If you don't like me, that's your problem, not mine. I love myself. I am a badass witch!"

Restated, it might read:

"I am free from old habits of hustling. I command my mind, body, and spirit to receive these new truths. I love my life and my work. I feel empowered and energized by my liberation from the lies and limiting beliefs that hard work equals success. I am Divinely worthy. I surround myself with people who see me for who I am and celebrate me for who I am becoming."

I like to read the restated versions out loud at least three times before burning both in the fire. If you aren't able to build a fire, a match and a bowl will do the trick.

After you've completed this ritual, you can bury the ashes, signifying the return of these patterns back to the Earth to alchemize them into seeds for your future growth.

Practice — **Sacred Rage Ritual**

Create a safe space to do your own sacred rage ritual. I prefer to practice outside, deep in Nature, where I can gather lots of sticks while I get myself worked up. You want long enough branches to hit the ground with, and you will need more than you think! Make sure they're already dead and dried; don't take anything from living trees. Let every stick you gather represent something you are blessing with your sacred rage. I choose a place where I'm not killing anything, like a gravel path or barren patch of Earth, and begin my practice.

It's great to set an intention first, but if you're already fired up, it's okay to just let yourself feel and heal. Begin with about five minutes of long belly breaths. You can use the sound *ha* or anything that emerges as you exhale, bringing your hands down to your thighs or elbows to your ribs with arms bent. I also like to speak out any words or conversations that are spinning in my head, things I wish I could say. If you've kept quiet about something all your life, this is a great time to let it out. Get started by yelling, "I feel . . ." angry, frustrated, disappointed, confused, etc.

When the blood (emotions) are flowing, start grabbing your sticks and begin hitting the ground with them as hard as you can. My teacher Ally Bogard, who first gave this assignment to me, recommends "at least twenty minutes or until you can't lift your arms." Keep your breath deep and long through this process. When tears well up inside, let them come out! This is the moment to release anything and everything that arises. Now you can rage back at all the moments you held your tongue or kept quiet because of other people's limitations. That's not your responsibility anymore, especially at this moment.

Once you feel complete, take some quiet time to sit with yourself. Lie on the Earth, meditate, get in a nearby creek, or simply be in silence.

Reflect and journal on your experience or say it aloud with a friend, if you did it together, when you're done.

What did it feel like to let your anger out?

How have the fires of transformation burned something away within you?

What was it?

What action do you feel inspired to take now that you've cleared this new space within yourself?

How can you keep these fires ignited in a safe way?

What version of you still needs to be burned in the ashes?

Let any aspect of your experience emerge and notice how your life is a result of what you learned in this ritual. Then you can begin to take even small steps and actions toward transformation.

As previously mentioned, I have made some miraculous magik using candles. My personal process is simple and involves nothing more than a hefty dose of IntuWitchin combined with ingredients I already have in my cupboards. There is, however, an intricate science to this practice to dive as deeply into as you desire.

Before beginning your spell, you can set up an altar space or just use your kitchen counter. You can bring offerings like flowers, photos, statues, or build a crystal grid. Let your Intu-Witchin guide you. The most important thing is having a fire-safe base for your candle, like a stone slab or lazy Susan, and a quiet space where you won't be disturbed while you sit with your candle until it goes out.

You can invoke any angels or spiritual support, the astro-logical archetype you're aligning with, like Venus for abundance or Jupiter for opportunity, and use the specific corresponding herbs, numbers, shapes, colors, crystals, and days of the week to bring that energy into your ritual. I personally just let my IntuWitchin guide my hands as I look through the kitchen cabi-nets (of course, when I look up the significance of the herbs I use, they are exactly aligned with my intentions!).

Choose your candle. The spell candles sold in many local spiritual shops typically burn for about two hours, less if they're heavily doused in herbs. Perhaps use color magik in your selec-tion. The first time I did this ritual, I used a red candle—not typically associated with abundance, necessarily, but we've already discussed how much significance red has for me.

Gather your oil and herbs. I make a tiny puddle of oil (you don't need much) and a separate pile of my chosen herb(s) to roll my candle in beside it.

If you want to carve any words or magikal symbols onto your candle, that's the first step in preparing it. I like to use my fingernail just to show the dream/desire my level of involvement, but you can also use a crystal point. I wouldn't recommend using a knife, because that's not the energy you want to bring to manifestations.

Anoint and dress your candle by rubbing the oil from base to wick, bottom to top *only*, going *toward* you, like you're drawing this energy into your life. As the wick is facing you, I usually hold it around my heart or solar plexus, but again, there are levels to this.

Once your candle is anointed, rub it in the herbs again going toward you, rolling the candle back on the plate/cutting board in the direction of your body.

If you don't have a candle holder, you can simply melt the bottom of the candle to stick it to your fire-safe base, and you're ready to go. You can set a circle, call in the directions, hold certain crystals to affirm different mantras, take a bath with your candle, sit in meditation, dance, sing, do yin yoga, play music, or make art that expresses your desire during this time. What would be the most aligned action to take? Then just wait for the magik to happen.

The number one rule of candle magik is *never* extinguish your candle; that's like extinguishing your dream. You must let it burn all the way until it naturally finishes, symbolizing the completion of the spell and reception of your wish. There's also something beautiful about giving that much uninterrupted devotional time to your desire.

Not every candle magik spell has quite the same results as the time I manifested $12,000! If your desire does not come true within six months, try the spell again and do a deep inventory of what beliefs or behaviors might have blocked it from coming to you. What would you do differently now? Show the Universe what you've learned.

Conclusion

Learning to read and speak the language of the Universe has been my greatest gift, and it's a lifelong exploration. After traveling through the Earth of our bodies, water of our blood, wind of our breath, and fire of our power, we come to the completion of this cycle with the fifth sacred element: Spirit.

Spirit is the amalgamation of every path we've traversed throughout this journey; it's what links us as species and souls. It's the central unifying aliveness behind every gaze, every leaf, and eye of the storm. You are *Spirit made manifest.* Your Intu-Witchin's cosmic component is entirely unique to you; it's the light you follow to the spiritual practices and disciplines that resonate and invigorate you. It's the voice of God(dess) in your heart. It's the only Truth you'll ever need, because once you do, you are shown the way.

Your relationship to Spirit is so personal. Everything I've shared with you is just in hopes that you will strengthen this bond, revel in how perfectly illustrated Spirit is in Nature, and remember it looks back at you from every face and facet of yourself.

I'll leave you with these key points:

- *Magik is real.* It can—and will—support you in eradicating physical, mental, and spiritual blockages; healing your wounds; and strengthening your super*natural* gifts and power.

- *Everything is information.* Pay attention. It's in the type of tree on your block, the bird that just flew past you, and even the color of your neighbor's car. You can decipher and decode so much by taking in the scene of your circumstances and seeking significance.

- *Take action.* The difference between hearing and listening, intuition and IntuWitchin, is what you *do* about it. Even if you try to brush this all off, there will be undeniable moments it takes your breath away, so give your inner wisdom the benefit of the doubt, follow its directions.

- *The elements are you!* You are made of the same matter (remember the origin) as the Universe, as our Mother, Earth. Treat her with reverence, like a reflection of you, and your life will blossom like Her fruits and flowers.

These truths alone can completely change the trajectory of your existence. You do not have to escape into fairytales or fantasy or rely on fiction and imagination to feel the thrill of magik awakening within and all around you!

The end of this book marks the beginning of a new chapter in your life. I hope you find yourself lifting your face up to falling rain, letting it cleanse and caress you as it kisses your skin. I hope you lay your body upon the sacred ground and feel the power of our planet pulsing through you. I hope you gaze in wonder at the world, breath taken away, or breathed into you. That the fires within you are ignited and even when they feel extinguished you will remember how to stoke your own flame.

The world is awakening on a mass scale. It might not seem like it yet, but the fact that I can even write these words, that you can walk into any bookshop and purchase spiritual books freely without fear of retribution, is progress compared to where we've come from. That is the spiritual renaissance giving the truth space to be heard, felt, received. The remembrance of our Divine Nature and connection is occurring slowly but surely throughout the human organism. The outdated systems *will* crumble and those who know how to stand in sovereignty will lead us toward the New Earth.

Let us be leaders, teachers, stewards, and devotees of Earth, Wind, Water, and Fire. Let us feel entirely safe to be all of who we truly are, to heal from our trauma and wounding and rise like the phoenix from our own ashes, inspiring others to do the same.

There was a moment during the writing process where I almost threw in the towel. I am so much more comfortable speaking, and it doesn't come naturally to communicate in this way. I was spending 15 hours a day, six or seven days a week, going back and forth with editing. In that time, I lost hold of the life I loved so much, the life that taught me IntuWitchin and made my dreams come true. I looked up to the Goddess one day, just ready to give up, and said, "Why am I doing this if it's so hard and I'm so much better at all my other things?" She responded by reminding me of what now feels like the greatest gift of writing this book.

IntuWitchin is just the entryway. I have an entire eco-system of courses, meditations and manifestation, rituals, retreats, and transformational coaching opportunities for you to immerse yourself in. This is a collection of the Spirit's wisdom within me, the manifestation of my gifts, creations born from my power and quest through personal alchemy. I genuinely want you to live your most magikal life—that's what I'm here to help you do! And it's so much more fun together.

It has been my deepest honor and pleasure to introduce you to your IntuWitchin. I am so grateful to you for coming on this journey with me, for caring about the planet and Her wisdom, which rewards us so richly when we reconnect. I cherish the privilege to have created something for people who I know will hear, listen, and take action in their lives with the information received.

I hope I have inspired you to step fully onto this path. Committing consistently to even *one* of the practices I have shared will leave a lasting imprint on your life. If you try them all, your outer world will quickly come to reflect your inner transformation, and you will unlock the secret dimension of those sacred inner realms. Seeing signs, symbols, and synchronicities becomes a game you get to play with the Universal cosmic forces. Witnessing deeper meaning in the world's expression to us, the way wisdom weaves through it all, we become exponentially more empowered, and not so easily swayed by society's silly illusions.

IntuWitchin is here so you remember who you are, reclaim your innate Divine power, and consciously, collaboratively co-create your most magikal life with the Universal forces of Nature.

This really is *just* the beginning.

All my love and Magik,

Acknowledgments

Thank you for opening this book, for trusting and allowing me to lead you deeper into yourself and your magik. Without you, I'd be a wild little witch in the woods all by myself.

Reverent gratitude to Mother Earth—thank you for choosing me to speak on your behalf and help my fellow humans remember our connection to you. To my own Mama, who is endlessly tolerant of my wildness—despite being us total opposites—and fell back in love with the forest by my side. Thanks for all the days I wrote in your living room so I could be in the Redwoods, all the meals you cooked, dishes you did, and time taking care of the kitties. You are always a safe, soothing shelter no matter the storm.

To my soul family, who believed in me when I was seemingly delusional but singularly focused on creating this magikal life. Those who held and housed me as I navigated my confusion and utter despair at trying to shrink to fit into life in a muggle world.

To Josh, Rachel, Layla, Andrew, Venus, Zahara, Liz, Johann, Moun, Brittan, Ryan, Chris Pan, Liana, Dean, Yari, Julia Grace, Charlene, Ashley, Jade, Alice, Katie, Jules and Blake, the OG in NYC Rusty, Lauren Brand for leading me home to my Witchy Shit, and many more.

Bear: The first man I've ever truly trusted. You are a new blueprint and imprint for me with the masculine. The grounding force for my tornado and peace for my chaos. Thank you for taking a weekend to read the entire book. For feeding me when I wrote all day. For holding me when I was falling apart. Your patience is saintly. Thank you for waiting while I learned to open my heart and let our love grow and blossom.

To the greatest amplifying cheerleaders for my career: Sahara, you gave me a platform and shared my wisdom before anyone else appreciated it. Thank you for lighting the fire within me.

Sah, you are so infinitely generous; your mother's spirit alive inside you. You are the reason this book exists, and I hope someday I'll be able to return the favor.

My two favorite writers of all time: Jess Winterstern and Laura Lombardi, thank you for sitting beside me to create and always inspiring me.

To all my sisters and Sycamore, who brought so much magik to this process, deepening into love as I rose and rode the waves. Blu and Nadia, Anye, Reggie, Jolie, Alyssa, Lily, Kendal, Dr. Liz: thanks for all the laughs and epic adventures, how you call me home to myself, and encourage me to keep flying higher.

To my teachers. Mostly trees and stones, but also people I knew I wanted to learn from and dive deeper with. They have undeniably transformed me. Ally Bogard, Dennis Andres, Special Blackburn, Govind Das, Merrill Ward, Theresa Bullard, and my dear friend Dakota Chanel, who is a living embodiment of priestesshood and walks her talk in such sacred integrity. I have never met another online creator I feel so confident learning from.

To Lisa Horgan, my friend, client, and most magnificent first employee. None of this would have been possible without your endless, undying support. You built this with me, just us. I can't imagine a kinder, more compassionate, patient, loving person to have embarked upon the business journey with. You changed my life and the lives of thousands of others. You change the world in your own way. I love you eternally.

My amazing A-Team who kept my business running smoothly and successfully while I was deep in the writing vortex for 8+ months. You've created so much safety and security for me, especially during the first time we all met IRL in an Irish castle—GOALS. Thanks for the medicine and mission of magik, which has become so precious and sacred to you, and helping me make it our reality.

My incredible agent, Coleen, who worked tirelessly to get me an unheard-of deal for a first-timer. She said it was impossible to get a publishing contract signed, sealed, and delivered within 10 days of submitting—I was leaving for Antarctica, and wanted it complete before I left.

"Trust me, Coleen, I'm a witch." The day before I set sail, it was done. Thank you for taking the leap with me.

To Hay House and my editor, Anna, who made it all happen and facilitated my sharing this message with the world.

I'd like to thank Northtown Books for the endless provision of fuel to stoke the fires of my wild imagination. If it were not for your shelves full of fantastically adventurous and magikal girls, I might not have known that I too could become one.

Robin Wall Kimmerer for writing *Braiding Sweetgrass*, and to Martha Beck for *Diana, Herself*. To Leonard Schlain—your dedication to the Goddess is something I hope all men will reawaken within themselves. Thank you for paving the way.

To Sinead O'Connor, you left this Earthly plane a week before I completed my final draft. I hope you feel the power of the fire you ignited in me. I will continue to blaze the trail you began. You were *not* mentally ill; you were *right*. You were eloquent, brave, truthful, and legendary. Thank you for healing me, thank you for teaching me, thank you for helping me.

About the Author

Mia Magik is a PerMissionary for your most magikal life. She grew up in the ancient old growth redwood forests of Northern California, a wild hippie child. Her conscious entre- preneurial parents raised her with the values of allocating resources to philanthropy, the environment, education, and adventure over material possessions. It is a lifestyle of sustai- nability that has become a pillar of her platform.

She has studied a plethora of alternative healing modalities and ancient wisdom traditions for the last 15 years, bringing their teachings to the world in her own non-denominational, interactive way. A fervent proponent of our individual rela- tionship to God and the Divine, Mia's work acts as a lighthouse for those seeking to find their way home to themselves.

Prior to the founding of her school for Magikal Artistry, which has had thousands of students worldwide, she was a conscious coach for entrepreneurs, professional athletes, and industry leaders in technology, film, and television. She focused on supporting their full expression, spiritual healing, and well- being and helped them access their inner wisdom and guidance system: their IntuWitchin.

Mia teaches live-in retreats at castles across the globe, gui- ding people to actualize their greatest personal power, libe- rate limitless sexual energy, and experience their true, Divine Nature. She can be found at **www.miamagik.com**.

HAY HOUSE TITLES OF RELATED INTEREST

YOU CAN HEAL YOUR LIFE, the movie,
starring Louise Hay & Friends
(available as an online streaming video)
www.hayhouse.com/louise-movie

THE SHIFT, the movie,
starring Dr. Wayne W. Dyer
(available as an online streaming video)
www.hayhouse.com/the-shift-movie

WITCHERY: Embrace the Witch Within, **by Juliet Diaz**

WITCH: Unleashed. Untamed. Unapologetic., **by Lisa Lister**

*SPELLS FOR LIVING WELL: A Witch's Guide for
Manifesting Change, Well-being, and Wonder,*
by Phyllis Curott

THE WITCHES' WISDOM TAROT:
A 78-Card Deck and Guidebook, **by Phyllis Curott**

**All of the above are available at your local bookstore,
or may be ordered by contacting Hay House (see next page).**

We hope you enjoyed this Hay House book. If you'd like to receive our online catalog featuring additional information on Hay House books and products, or if you'd like to find out more about the Hay Foundation, please contact:

Hay House, Inc., P.O. Box 5100, Carlsbad, CA 92018-5100
(760) 431-7695 or (800) 654-5126
(760) 431-6948 (fax) or (800) 650-5115 (fax)
www.hayhouse.com® • www.hayfoundation.org

———

Published in Australia by: Hay House Australia Pty. Ltd.,
18/36 Ralph St., Alexandria NSW 2015
Phone: 612-9669-4299 • *Fax:* 612-9669-4144
www.hayhouse.com.au

Published in the United Kingdom by: Hay House UK, Ltd.,
The Sixth Floor, Watson House, 54 Baker Street, London W1U 7BU
Phone: +44 (0)20 3927 7290 • *Fax:* +44 (0)20 3927 7291
www.hayhouse.co.uk

Published in India by: Hay House Publishers India,
Muskaan Complex, Plot No. 3, B-2, Vasant Kunj, New Delhi 110 070
Phone: 91-11-4176-1620 • *Fax:* 91-11-4176-1630
www.hayhouse.co.in

———

Access New Knowledge.
Anytime. Anywhere.

Learn and evolve at your own pace
with the world's leading experts.

www.hayhouseU.com